T0299729

FEMALE ECONOMIC STRATEGIES IN THE MODERN WORLD

Perspectives in Economic and Social History

Series Editors: Robert E. Wright
                   Andrew August

Titles in this Series

FORTHCOMING TITLES

FEMALE ECONOMIC STRATEGIES IN THE MODERN WORLD

EDITED BY

Beatrice Moring

LONDON AND NEW YORK

First published 2012 by Pickering & Chatto (Publishers) Limited

Published 2016 by Routledge
2 Park Square, Milton Park, Abingdon, Oxon OX14 4RN
711 Third Avenue, New York, NY 10017, USA

Routledge is an imprint of the Taylor & Francis Group, an informa business

BRITISH LIBRARY CATALOGUING IN PUBLICATION DATA

Female economic strategies in the modern world. – (Perspectives in economic
and social history)
1. Women – History – Modern period, 1600– 2. Women – Economic conditions.
I. Series II. Moring, Beatrice.
305.4'0903-dc23

ISBN-13: 978-1-84893-350-7 (hbk)

Typeset by Pickering & Chatto (Publishers) Limited

CONTENTS

LIST OF CONTRIBUTORS

Richard Wall (1944–2011), Senior Research Fellow University of Essex, Department of History, UK.

Anne-Lise Head, Professor, University of Geneva, Switzerland.

Maria Dolores Valverde Lamfus, Professor, Universite' de Pays Basque, Spain.

Susannah Ottaway, Associate Professor of History, Carleton University, Minnesota, USA.

Verónica Villarespe Reyes, Professor, Universidad Nacional Autonoma de Mexico, Mexico.

Ana Patricia Sosa Ferreira, Lecturer, Universidad Nacional Autonoma de Mexico, Mexico.

Marie-Pierre Arrizabalaga, Professor and Maître de conference, Université de Cergy-Pontoise, France.

Margareth Lanzinger, Senior Lecturer of History, University of Vienna, Austria.

Beatrice Moring, Research Associate, University of Cambridge, Cambridge Group for the History of Population, UK and Associate Professor in Social and Economic History, University of Helsinki, Finland.

LIST OF TABLES

INTRODUCTION

Beatrice Moring

Women and the Family, Work or Poverty and Isolation

In 2006 Lynn Abrams raised the question whether despite of decades of research into the history of women the historical narrative still remains predominantly male. The image of women as the victims of male society can easily be added as an extra chapter while the actors in politics, economy, social development, organizations etc. are men. At home they have dependant, passive wives controlled in marriage and marginalized in widow or spinsterhood.[1] Assigning women the role to produce new generations primarily, and measuring their success in ability to marry and remarry and lack of success in failing to do so has also been criticized by Todd and Pelling.[2] These views echo those of Hufton in 1984 when in her article 'Women without men', she queried why women have been viewed primarily as wives and household members, not individuals, in family history research.[3] While twenty years separate these statements the tendencies to discuss women as being in need of the protection of a man and assumed to desire marriage and remarriage seems to have persisted.[4] The fact that papers produced in the last decade can include statements that 'old women' (as a group) lacked chances on the marriage market because they were 'infertile' and 'sexually unattractive', with 'tendencies of physical and mental illness',[5] raise the question to what extent studies of women penetrate not only mainstream but even the family history and demography field.

The approach to women has also been affected by some of the traditional tools of family history, where family has been understood to equal the conjugal couple. A widow with children lived in an 'incomplete family', adult siblings lived in a 'no family' system and persons living with servants or companions were 'solitary'.[6] Such a perspective ignored the wider views of the family concept extending both horizontally and vertically and the notion of kin as family.[7]

Understanding the husband and wife dyad as the only real family unit was of course not new to the 1970s. Already in the nineteenth century statisticians had created a phenomenon 'the normal family', a unit of husband wife and two or more children under the age of 10, 15 or 18 depending on time and place. The normal family regularly appear in surveys of budgets focusing on the household economy of 'the working man'. Such households, as a rule containing young children and babies served their purpose in boosting male breadwinner ideologies. Bowley, however raised the issue, whether the normal family was normal, as in his studies of early twentieth-century household economy he found that actually only a minority of families fitted the criteria.[8]

While it is understandable that domestic ideology could obscure reality in the past our own approach should be more critical. Snell and Millar have demonstrated that while the reasons were different, the so-called incomplete families were as common in the past as they are today. The female household head was not an anomaly but a normal part of life.[9] The other issue that needs to be highlighted is that while poverty and female headship often has been associated, this was not always the case. Even among the propertied classes female headship was not an unusual phenomenon. What did distinguish these families, however, was the frequent presence of horizontal extensions, i.e. adult siblings, aunts, nephews and nieces etc.[10] We find examples of the female clustering discussed by Hufton and Hahn rather than the domestic ideal of the 'normal family'.[11] Such co-residence units negate the concept of female isolation and inability to cope when deprived of a male household head postulated by Fuchs. They also demonstrate the presence of female agency questioned by, for example, Chabot.[12] In the eighteenth century widows continued their husbands' businesses and could hold positions related to the state and local community or private enterprise.[13]

While working class widows suffered hardship in widowhood more often, this was linked to the dual problem of lack of capital, a problem for working class people in general, and being marginalized on the labour market because of the male breadwinner ideology.[14] This situation did not, however, necessarily result in loneliness and isolation. Sokoll has demonstrated frequent co-habitation of the poor, Thane systems of kinship assistance in the past and the present and Wall, Rose and Robin have found frequent examples of a combination of support systems and family collaboration including poor relief as only one part.[15]

One of the reasons for the assumptions that working class widows and unmarried mothers were living of poor relief is the defective registration of female work. Women were often registered by marital status, rather than by profession like men. While the under-registration of productive activity was particularly bad in the case of married women, many women were affected by the definition of work in the censuses. Only full time waged activity outside the home fell within the specification. As women often were engaged in multiple part time activities like, washing and cleaning, seasonal agricultural work etc. they were not working according to this definition.[16] Horrell and Humphries have also pointed out that the bad income levels of women affected views of their capacity to run a family.

The income levels and the nature of work could be affected by availability of work on the local level and by the domestic ideology, which encouraged 'secret' work of casual nature.[17] Anderson however demonstrated already in 1984 that widows in mid nineteenth-century Britain combined work with assistance.[18]

As we can see, the question of women in the past is far from unproblematic. The aim of this volume is to analyse the framework in which women have been operating and to what extent we can detect strategies and how women did cope when living without husbands either as spinsters, with or without children, and as widows or abandoned wives. What we want to examine is to what extent women relied on their own work, inherited or other family resources or on assistance from public or private bodies. To what extent were they able to act and to what extent their efforts were curtailed by legislation, economy or a gender segregated labour market.

Approaches and Themes

The themes of this volume are focused on female options and strategies for economic survival. While including women from sixteenth-century England to present day Mexico, from rural Switzerland to urban Finland, it touches on recurring problems and unexpected parallels but it also reveals similarities in solutions.

Lola Valverde, Richard Wall and Beatrice Moring approach individual families in their analyses of the relative importance of work, family collaboration and poor relief for women in the past. Wall uses a longitudinal approach of English society working on listings of inhabitants, poor relief records, micro simulation and family budgets to study the economic strategies of widows in England over time. Valverde and Moring focus on late nineteenth- and early twentieth-century urban communities, Valverde on the economic strategies of poor women in two urban communities in northern Spain using the so called censuses of the poor. Moring uses Finnish censuses, family budgets and economic surveys to address the question whether it was possible for working class women to support themselves and their families as widows or single. She assesses female earnings in comparison to male earnings, strategies for survival and family collaboration.

Central themes in the contributions of Susannah Ottaway, Anne-Lise Head-König, Veronica Villarespe Reyes and Ana Sosa Ferreira are poor relief policies, female response to these and the efforts to build strategies for survival in eighteenth-century England, nineteenth- and twentieth-century Switzerland and contemporary Mexico.

Susannah Ottaway analyses residence systems of poor women in listings of inhabitants from two communities, one in the early and another in the late eighteenth-century England. Through residence patterns she aims to reveal networks of female collaboration and assistance. Anne-Lise Head-König studies social policies in rural and urban Switzerland until the introduction of old age pensions and family allowances. With the aid of censuses, poor relief records and legal documents she demonstrates the implications of these policies for the lives of poor women and their children.

Veronica Villarespe Reyes and Ana Sosa Ferreira work on statistical surveys of poverty, education, work and time use. They present information to launch a critique of the efficacy of the so called *Progresa Oportunidades* programme as a means of improving the socio economic situation of poor women in late twentieth-century Mexico.

Margareth Lanzinger and Marie Pierre Arrizabalaga on the other hand analyse female position and activity in relation to family property in eighteenth-century Austria and nineteenth- and twentieth-century southern France. Marie Pierre Arrizabalaga works on family genealogies in the French Pyrenees, inheritance and property transfer documents, wills, inventories, marriage contracts and interviews. The objective has been to map the economic situation, the migration and employment history, the marriages and ultimate social destinies of all the family members. Her aim within this volume is to determine the existence of female strategies and the use that were made of them by the daughters of landholding families, particularly as depicted in migration, work and marriage. Margareth Lanzinger has studied the economic position of widows in two judicial districts in Austria. Her data comes primarily from marriage contracts, wills and other documents related to property division and transmission. She sets out to evaluate the relative economic security for women and particularly widows, created with the help of contracts within systems of joint marital property in relation to separated property.

Female Work, Earnings and the Family

In their contributions Valverde and Moring highlight the problems raised by Higgs of defective registration of female employment in census records. Spanish censuses in general registered female work badly. Men were identified through profession even when they were unemployed, the majority of women however, lacked occupational information. While Finnish censuses registered female work more efficiently than the Spanish ones the situation was still problematic, particularly in relation to married women. In both cases the reason was that casual work like washing, ironing or cleaning was not regarded as 'proper' work. Other female sources of income like keeping lodgers or boarders or renting out rooms were also not regarded as an occupation. Through an analysis of the information about earnings and residence in the census of the poor Valverde is able to reach a conclusion about female income strategies. Moring extracts information about female work and income from budgets. Both Valverde and Moring underline the importance of lodgers as part of the female economy.

Villarespe Reyes and Sosa Ferreira, Valverde and Moring demonstrate in line with Humphries, that because of carrying the burden of household duties, married women or mothers with children could often only operate within the informal sector. As a result their income could be very low and the casual nature of the work made it fall into the unregistered category. Moring however demonstrates that it was possible for women to reach the income levels of unskilled men. Villarespe Reyes, Sosa Ferreira and Valverde underline the effect of the unequal labour market and the inequalities in education on the ability of women to attain satisfactory earnings.

The vicious circle of poor women having to force their children into unskilled low paid work, thereby interrupting their education, discussed by Humphries, is also illuminated by Valverde, Villarespe Reyes and Sosa Ferreira. The latter reveal that even in contemporary Mexico discrimination in the labour market means that girls need more than basic education to reach the wage levels of boys and fosters disinclination to keep girls in school even when assistance is provided.

Poverty, Poor Relief and Gender

The image of old women, particularly widows, living of and depending on poor relief has been repeated ad nauseam even though disputed in previous research.[19] Wall, Valverde and Moring discuss the proportions of female poor in relation to men. Valverde found that about half of the families registered as poor, were headed by women and that the rate seemed to be slightly higher in manufacturing than in service dominated areas. While many of the poor women were widows, married female heads and single women also belonged to this group. In some cases the husband was absent because of spending his time in a hospital or charitable institution. Wall highlights the fact that while widows were a large group among poor relief recipients, being a widow did not necessarily mean that you were poor and on poor relief. Moring raises the issue of the need to observe demography when analysing poor relief recipients. Because of female longevity and a higher proportion of old women in society, similar proportions of men and women among the assisted actually means a higher proportion of men needing help in old age.

Goodman and Honeyman have demonstrated how domestic ideologies had a detrimental effect on the ability of women to effectively contribute to the family economy in the past[20]. In the contributions of Villarespe Reyes, Sosa Ferreira and Head König the ideological element in assistance policies of the twentieth century are discussed. The internalizing of domestic ideologies resulted in an inclination to reward 'good mothers' withdrawing from the labour market and devoting themselves to their children. The demands for good mothering skills have also made it possible to choose those deserving assistance. Such views disregard the fact that combining bourgeois domestic virtues with bringing up a family is not always economically feasible. Particularly in the Mexican case the policy has proved to be problematic, the mothers stay at home to receive assistance but the daughters still don't receive better education and improve their position. Wall and Head König also reveal that in the twentieth century, motherhood was seen as increasingly important as a lever to assistance. 'Mothers' were to be supported in their homes and have higher priority than other female groups.

The presentations of Ottaway and Head König bring to light certain similarities in two superficially totally divergent poor relief systems. The Swiss policies through the nineteenth century were focused on the need for widows to work and support themselves or for adult family members to assist their kin, while the English system recognized the need for society to contribute. However, the boarding out of the old and incapacitated and the young with the lowest bidder in Switzerland was not totally dissimilar to the placing of the infirm on relief together or with families and individuals in eighteenth-century England. Widows were expected to generate earnings in both cases and the threat of the workhouse in the one case certainly meant loosing the authority of the children as did the removal of the children for boarding with strangers in the other case. Even the issue of returning people 'home' to their parish of origin and splitting up families was far from unheard of in an English context, as have been demonstrated by Levine.[21] In both scenarios people with land and capital were better placed for caring for themselves or others in old age, with the result that the proletarian women were most likely to find themselves on the mercy of the authorities. Consequently situations arose when all options would be explored before relief was applied for. On the other hand individuals can also be found who used the poor house as a temporary measure.

Head König concludes that while the poor relief system experienced some progress it is not until a national social policy system of old age and widows pensions was introduced that the material problems of widows from poor families could be solved. Reyes goes even further and points to the need of greater equality in the labour market to make women able to support their families instead of relying on support that ends up being used for living expenses instead of education.

Loneliness Contra Family Co-operation and Female Clustering

The historical basis for the image of the poor and lonely old woman has been disputed by Sokoll, Hufton and Hahn. These have shown female co-habitation and co-operation among family and kin but also among distant relations and non related women in the past.[22] Ottaway sets out to determine whether the female clustering studied by Hufton can be detected in eighteenth-century English localities. Moring, Villarespe Reyes, Sosa Ferreira and Valverde demonstrate the prevalence of mothers living with daughters, married or unmarried, but also female clustering among relatives and strangers through the lodging system. Ottaway ponders potential pressures by the authorities to promote such clustering, Moring and Valverde, however see such systems as voluntary action in response to economic problems. Valverde and Ottaway underline the virtual absence of the combination of loneliness with poverty. Ottaway however, detects an inclination among wealthy women to live in households with servants or companions and the poor wanting to stay out of workhouses or use them as temporary solutions

Wall, Horrell and Humphries have in the past raised the issue that families with mothers and children were not only supported by the mother but once the children reached working age, the joining of incomes became possible. Horrell and Humphries have in fact like Roberts demonstrated that at some stage in the family life cycle the mother tended to withdraw from the labour market in Britain. In their contributions to this volume Wall, Ottaway, Villarespe Reyes, Sosa Ferreira, Valverde and Moring all discuss the cohabitation of women with children of different ages. While Ottaway assumes economic dependency in some examples of women in the households of adult offspring, Wall, Valverde and Moring demonstrate the size of the economic contribution by children in specific families. Wall demonstrates that widows could receive extensive support from their families but usually they were not relying on a single source of income but supported themselves by earnings, assistance from children and poor relief. This combination of sources continued over centuries.

Villarespe Reyes and Sosa Ferreira incorporate the issue of income by children into a general scenario of the subsistence of female headed households. In none of these cases is the importance of a combination of family incomes questioned. Valverde underlines that the collaboration with relatives and children is of major importance to women who have problems in finding or keeping permanent employment. The family income could in such situations be augmented through begging by children and elderly or infirm family members.

Standard of Living and Strategies for Spending

It has been assumed that the lower income levels of women and the differences in expenditure between male and female headed households can be taken as an indication of female inability to care for their families. In their contributions Wall and Moring discuss expenditure patterns and highlight evidence that contradict earlier assumptions. While widows had a more problematic economic position they manipulated their spending and by eliminating certain costly items favoured by men they provided their families with adequate nutrition at a lower cost.

Wall shows that the income and expenditure patterns of poor widows reveal that their standard of living was close to labourers with young families. By the start of the twentieth century the budgets reveal that widows were able to provide a more nutritious diet from depleted resources than families with a male head.

Moring shows that with a combination of income strategies and through adjusted spending the family of a widow could have a similar standard of living as families of unskilled men.

Women and family property

One of the issues that have been raised in connection with studies of women from propertied families is the claim that such women lacked agency, all the power lay in the hands of men.[23] Arrizabalaga and Lanzinger in their respective ways query such conclusions. Both the contributions demonstrate that women could inherit landholdings and other property and participate in the process. They also reveal that women made choices, assessed their options and secured their property.

In the French Basque country birth order had higher priority than gender and in Austria direct descent awarded women inheritance rights. Holding on to the property through marriage and in widowhood could make it necessary to embark upon the production of extensive contracts both before and during the marriage. In the rural areas described, family property and its transmission was of major importance, particularly as the land was generally not divided on its journey between generations.

Where the property was of a different nature, as in urban areas, contracts could protect a dowry or secure assets for the time of widowhood. The activity of women in drawing up contracts and setting up wills all demonstrate the ease with which these women approached property and the authority with which they handled it.

Lanzinger analyses the ways in which husbands and wives secured property brought into the marriage, bought or inherited or accumulated. Through retirement contracts, stipulations of the right to retain houses or income for life effectively blocked claims from kin or children eager for inheritance and property division. Such contracts were of particular importance for second wives and children after the death of the father. Head Konig also points out that in the parts of Switzerland where retirement contracts were in use landholding women were relieved from the economic problems faced by the landless discussed in her contribution.

Arrizabalaga demonstrates how a need for contractual activity arose for the heir and the older generation after the introduction of laws about equal inheritance. She also highlights the fact that in a region with gender neutral inheritance practices the possibility of heirship for women resulted in training for a number of economic tasks and promoting a high degree of self-determination. Even when heirship was not an option individual choice was present. Women married locally or migrated and their patterns did not follow those of their brothers either geographically or socially. In regional towns they found occupations suitable to their skills. Their activity on the marriage market also indicates independence. Where candidates of suitable social standing not be found they stayed celibate. An examination of their property at the end of life, however, shows that in most cases this was not a road that led to destitution. Another piece of evidence supporting the theory of Pelling and Froide that spinsterhood can be not only an unwanted destiny but a choice and a strategy.[24]

Conclusion

We have demonstrated that women have lived not only as family members but heads of household. While in many cases society did not promote female independence and the situation was rife with problems it did not mean that women were not capable of creating strategies for survival. Even the very poor could do so. While such strategies varied depending on time and place the notion of the poor lonely woman should by now be discarded. Women collaborated with children, siblings and other kin. Where family members could not be found friends and lodgers could be the partners in collaboration. Women born into families with property did not let it slip through their fingers but actively pursued economic advantages. While marriage was important it was not seen as the only option. In many instances women had to contend with adversity like difficult relief systems or unfair treatment in the labour market. Using multiple strategies, however, work, family co-operation, housing strategies and available support systems they managed to survive and support children or other family members.

Collaboration was the key word and it was not only in situations of destitution that we find family co-operation.

1 WIDOWS, FAMILY AND POOR RELIEF IN ENGLAND FROM THE SIXTEENTH TO THE TWENTIETH CENTURY

Richard Wall

Introduction

In 1789 Mary Chilcott from Aff Piddle in the county of Dorset, a widow with four children, the eldest of whom was nineteen, was spending six shillings and six pence a week on bread and flour.[1] This represented 89 per cent of all her expenditure on food and 69 per cent of all her expenditure. Apart from bread and flour the only other food purchases were 4 pence on bacon, 6 pence on tea, sugar, butter and cream and I penny on yeast.

Just over a century later in York, another household consisting of a widow aged sixty-three and a daughter aged twenty spent 22 per cent of their income on meat and 16 per cent on bread. For these two women we also know what they ate at every meal in the first week of March in 1901. For example, on Monday 5 March 1901, their breakfast consisted of bread, butter and coffee, dinner (taken in the middle of the day) of meat, potatoes, bread and tea and a tea (evening meal) of bread, butter and tea. Indeed, breakfast was always limited to bread and butter and either tea or coffee, except on Saturday. Nor did tea vary greatly, involving usually just bread, butter and tea. Dripping was added on Wednesday and Thursday and on Friday the bread was toasted. Supper was only eaten on Saturday and Sunday. Five of the seven dinners included meat as did one of the suppers. However, monotonous this diet (no vegetables other than potatoes and onions) and no fruit were purchased during the week), the variety of food was greater than the widow in Aff Piddle had available at the end of the eighteenth century. Mother and daughter in this York household were also eating meat much more frequently than almost all the widows who headed households in the working-class district of St George in the East in East London in 1845. Only 4 per cent of such households ate meat more than five times a week. Nearly half had meat just once a week.[2]

Detailed evidence on the diet of a somewhat more prosperous widow can be found in the study by M. F. Davies of households in Corsley, Wiltshire.[3] This 'aged' widow of a small farmer in Corsley, Wiltshire, was supported by her children and according to Davies she experienced neither primary nor secondary poverty in that her income was not only sufficient for her needs but provided an adequate surplus. Analysis of the budget suggests bread was only 8 per cent of the total (given and bought) while meat was 61 per cent.[4] Her meals on Monday 14 January 1906 were for breakfast at 9am, bread, butter and tea, for dinner (taken at 1pm), fried bacon and potatoes, tea at 4pm, buttered toast and tea), and supper at 8:30pm, bread and cheese and a glass of beer. During the fortnight that a record of her meals was kept, bacon featured in half of the breakfasts, bacon, ham and pork in thirteen of the fourteen dinners and cheese or meat and a glass of beer at all fourteen suppers.

Such detailed budgets provide fascinating details on the standard of living of particular widows but with so few budgets available for study the evidence that they provide has to be used cautiously. It would, for example, be unwise to rely on this evidence alone to infer how the standard of living of widows may have varied either from place to place or over time. Davies was certainly of the opinion that the living standards of the poor had improved significantly in the later nineteenth century. Cottagers, she remarked, would around 1880, have bought one ounce of tea or coffee and one pound of sugar to last them the whole week. Fifteen years later the same families would purchase every week a quarter pound of tea and three pounds of sugar.[5] From other information provided by Davies, it appears that the diet of the poor in Corsley was more nourishing than the diet of the poor in York in that in Corsley garden produce provided a large proportion of the food with even the poorest households consuming onions, greens and other vegetables in addition to potatoes. Green vegetables featured in the meals of the two widow headed households in Corsley whose purchases of food are recorded but were rarely part of the meals of the two widow headed households in Rowntree's study of York.[6]

As well as recording the expenditure patterns of widow-headed households, information is required concerning their sources of income. The households of the three widows whose economic circumstances were detailed above were supported in different ways. Only one, the household of the widow in Aff Piddle, received any support from the Poor Law and the majority of the income of even this household (70 per cent) was derived from the earnings of the widow's children. The widow's household in York was entirely supported by what the widow and her adult, but delicate, daughter were able to earn. In the four-week period covered by the budget, the widow was the principal earner providing 60 per cent of the income.[7] The third widow, from Corsley, lived alone but was entirely supported by relatives. A daughter paid her rent and sent bacon, butter, potatoes and wood if her own supply did not last out. Other children assisted occasionally. A niece, living near, provided care.

To help determine the extent of the poverty experienced by these and other widows, comparisons can be made with the income and expenditure patterns of other households that social investigators such as Rowntree and M. F. Davies classed as poor such as the households of labourers. It is more difficult given the scarcity of detailed budgets for female headed households to discover whether the expenditure patterns of these widows are representative of those of other widows at that time although some comparisons are possible with the budgets of a few other female headed households at the end of the eighteenth century and for Corsley in the early twentieth century.[8] Information about the sources of income of widow headed households in different periods can also be obtained by analysing the various surveys of the poor that detail both their earnings and the payments of out relief authorized by the Overseers of the Poor.[9] Even in the absence of information on the earnings of specific individuals, some inferences are possible about the relative contribution of earnings and poor relief to the household budgets of both widows and male headed households by comparing average wage levels of men and women in a given area with the amounts paid out by the Overseers in the form of out relief.[10]

Widows Receiving Out Relief

There are many gradations of poverty. Steven King when examining the incidence of poverty in four English parishes in the later eighteenth and early nineteenth centuries, listed in addition to persons receiving out relief from the Overseers of the Poor, persons in receipt of charity, paying a low rent, those whose goods had been sequestered, were late in paying poor and other rates, or excused payment of taxes.[11] In both periods, persons receiving out relief constituted less than a fifth of all those identified as poor and just over 10 per cent of the total population.[12]

Calculations on similar lines can be made for widows. For example, analysis of the census of Cardington, Bedfordshire, that was taken in 1782 suggests that 82 per cent of all the widows in the parish could be classed as poor as their late husbands had been either labourers or craftsmen. However, only 55 per cent of these widows were receiving poor relief when the census was taken. In the Dorset parish of Corfe Castle which comprised both a small market town and rural districts, a higher proportion of poor widows in Corfe Castle than in Cardington were receiving out relief (71 per cent).[13] However, fewer widows were identified as poor in Corfe Castle than Cardington in that only 55 per cent were recorded in that they were either wage earners or in receipt of poor relief. Two conclusions are clear: first not all widows were poor, and secondly, of those widows who were considered poor by their contemporaries, a considerable minority did not receive out relief.[14]

As King has noted,[15] there are a number of reasons why it is often difficult to calculate precisely both the number of persons who were poor and those dependent on out relief. Major problems are that dependants of persons receiving poor relief might not be included in the lists of recipients and that, given the rarity of local censuses, it is often necessary to estimate the total population of a parish.[16] Counts of the number of widows in poverty in Cardington and Corfe Castle avoid these particular problems as the total population is known, as is the number of widows in or out of poverty, as indeed is the number of their dependants. The problems that remain are that the population of poor widows is not defined in exactly the same way (although it appears to be broadly compatible) and the Overseers of the Poor may have differed in their assessment of the degree of poverty that merited the granting of out relief. Nevertheless it is clear by referring back to King's estimates of the proportion of the total population in poverty or receiving out relief, that higher proportions of widows than of the overall population were poor and that higher proportions of those who were poor were awarded out relief.

Further details on the proportions of poor widows who received assistance from the poor Law in the form of out relief are set out in Table 1.1. The populations included in addition to Cardington and Corfe Castle are Causton in Norfolk and Ardleigh in Essex for which information is available on the numbers of poor and those receiving out relief in 1601 and 1796 respectively.[17]

Two particular issues are considered: first, a comparison of the proportions of poor widows and poor men awarded out relief, and, secondly, examination of the variation by age in the proportions receiving relief. In all four communities, out relief was granted to more than half of the widows deemed to be poor but awarded to 10 per cent or less of poor men in Cardington, Corfe Castle and Ardleigh. Only in Causton in 1601 were appreciable numbers of poor men assisted by the Poor Law through out relief.

Table 1.1: **Widows and men in receipt of outdoor poor relief as a percentage of the population at risk of poverty in four English parishes.**[1]

Marital Status	Age	Causton Norfolk 1601	Cardington Bedfordshire 1782	Corfe Castle Dorset 1790	Ardleigh Essex 1796
Widows	<45		70	67	75
	45–64		40	78	83
	≥65		67	67	60
	All Ages	66	55	71	76
	N	32	31	24	21
All Men	<45		8	2	1
	45–64		6	7	0
	≥65		38	40	10
	All Ages	48	10	7	1
	N	56	131	238	146

[1] Population at risk of poverty has been defined as follows:
Causton: Persons identified in the 1601 list as poor, others 'not so poor' and 'not able to give'. The ages of those deemed 'not so poor' and 'not able to give anything' are not specified.Cardington: Craftsmen, labourers and their widows. Corfe Castle: Wage earners and persons receiving poor relief. Ardleigh: Craftsmen, labourers and their widows, plus farmers recorded as poor or smallholders.
Sources: Calculated from Wales (1984); Baker (1973); photocopy of Census of Corfe Castle in Library of Cambridge Group; Erith (1978).

Examination in the variation in the proportions of poor widows at various ages in receipt of support, reveals that old widows (those over sixty-five) were no more likely to be receiving out relief than were widows who had not yet reached the age of forty-five. In Corfe Castle and Ardleigh, the highest proportions of poor widows on relief were recorded for middle-aged widows (aged forty-five to sixty-four). This is something of a surprise as one might have expected widows at this age to have at least some children of working age and still resident at home and contributing to the household economy, thus making it easier for the Poor Law authorities to withdraw or not grant out relief. Only in Cardington in 1782 was the proportion of middle aged widows on out relief lower than for older and younger widows. A significant factor in Cardington may be that girls as young as six could find work as lace makers and when older as spinners of jersey and linen while residing with their parents.[18] At all ages and in all populations, higher proportions of poor widows than poor men were assisted by the Poor Law although the proportions of men assisted did rise significantly for men over the age of sixty-five implying that men were assisted by the Poor Law when old age and ill health reduced their ability to earn.

Variations with age in the proportion of widows receiving out relief can also be explored from another perspective by comparing the ages of widows appearing on lists of recipients of out relief with the estimates of the age distribution of widows in England produced by demographic micro-simulation. As a number of the lists of recipients of out relief do record both the age and marital status of the beneficiaries, this enables many more communities to be studied than is possible when analysing local censuses. The micro-simulation suggests that just over 10 per cent of widows would be under the age of forty, and between forty and fifty per cent between the ages of forty and fifty-nine or over the age of sixty. In the second half of the eighteenth century, the proportions of widows who had passed the age of sixty were a little higher and the proportions in middle age a little lower than in the first half of the seventeenth century (see the final two rows of Table 1.2).[19] Much higher proportions of widows on out relief lists were over sixty than in the national population. The most plausible explanation for the difference is that it indicates increasing proportions of widows falling into poverty in their old age and needing and receiving assistance from the Poor Law. The role of other factors, however, should also be considered such as variations in the age structure of different populations and different decisions by Overseers of the Poor as to whom they considered worthy of assistance and where that assistance should be provided,[20] whether to the poor in their own homes (out relief) or by removing the poor to a workhouse or poorhouse. The vast majority of the lists analysed in Table 1.2 do not include any poor widows resident in institutions and policies by the Poor law authorities to differentially place older widows (or indeed younger widows)[21] in poorhouses or workhouses would lower the proportions of widows in those age groups on out relief lists and increase the proportions in other age groups. Different attitudes to the award of out relief and/or relatively few elderly inhabitants might also explain why there are some communities such as Norwich and Ipswich in the late sixteenth century and Cardington, Bedfordshire, in the late eighteenth century, where the proportion of widows receiving out relief who were over the age of sixty were below the proportion of widows in the national population over the age of sixty.[22]

Table 1.2: Age distribution of widows in receipt of outdoor poor relief in certain parishes in England 1570–1796, and in simulation of numbers of widows in national population.

Parish/Town	County	Date	<40	40–59	≥60	Age Unspecified	N (= 100%)
Norwich[1]	Norfolk	1570	20	44	35	0	183
Ipswich	Suffolk	1597	12	53	35	0	17
Cawston	Norfolk	1601	0	24	76	0	32
Salisbury	Wiltshire	1637	0	13	87	0	54
Cardington	Bedfordshire	1782	35	41	24	0	17
Corfe Castle	Dorset	1796	0	35	65	0	17
Ardleigh	Essex	1796	19	31	50	0	16
Winslow	Buckingham	c. 1796	0	42	58	0	19
10 parishes[2]	Cumberland	c. 1796	5	23	67	5	60
Chesterfield	Derbyshire	c.1796	0	15	77	8	13
Derby	Derbyshire	c. 1796	7	33	60	0	30
Wirksworth	Derbyshire	c. 1796	10	22	65	3	31
Wolverhampton	Staffordshire	c. 1796	0	5	83	12	43
Halifax	Yorkshire	c. 1796	26	39	34	0	38
England[3]	Simulation	1600–1649	13	44	43	0	
England[3]	Simulation	1750–1799	12	41	47	0	

[1] All widows listed as poor. [2] Parishes of Carlisle, Cumrew, Cumwhitton, Harrington, Hesket, Kirkoswald, Sedbergham, Warwick. [3] CAMSIM micro-simulation: Calculations by authors from simulations by Jim Oeppen, Max Planck Institute for Demographic Research, Rostock. Sources: Calculated from Pound (1971); Webb (1966); Wales (1984); Slack (1975); Baker (1973); photocopy of Census of Corfe Castle in Library of Cambridge Group; Erith (1978); Eden (1797). Age distribution for simulated population from demographic micro-simulation programme CAMSIM, developed by Jim Oeppen when at the Cambridge Group.

The proportions of middle aged widows (those aged forty–fifty-nine) and young widows (aged under forty) in the national population generally exceeded the proportions of middle aged and young widows on relief lists. This may indicate greater reluctance on the part of the Overseers of the Poor to assist younger widows and/or the fact that they might have been less in need of assistance than were older widows, earning more, and in the case of the middle aged, tapping some of the earnings of their adolescent children.

Table 1.3: Age distribution of widows in receipt of outdoor poor relief in Ipswich, Suffolk, in 5 Scottish towns in 1907 and in York in 1901 and age distribution of widows in the national population in 1901.

Town	Category	Aged <45	45–64	≥65	N
Ipswich	Wage Earners	61	20	0	51
Glasgow	All Outdoor	26	43	30	23
Govan	'Typical Cases' from Outdoor Roll	48	20	32	69
	All Outdoor	23	36	41	22
Greenock	Families with Female Wage Earners	53	25	23	53
Kilmarnock	All Outdoor	55	21	24	42
Paisley	50 Consecutive Outdoor Applications	33	33	28	18
York 1901	Primary Poverty[1]	33[2]	37[2]	30	389
Census 1901	England and Wales	15	45	40	

Notes[1] Family income insufficient to obtain the minimum necessary to maintain physical efficiency, Rowntree (1913): 117.[2] Age groups <50 and 50–64.
Sources: Royal Commission on the Poor Laws and Relief of Distress (1909); Rowntree (1913); Census of England and Wales 1901.

A similar exercise can be carried out for the first decade of the twentieth century by comparing the age distribution of widows on out relief lists with the age distribution of widows as reported in the 1901 census (see Table 1.3). The situation appears very different from that in the sixteenth, seventeenth and late eighteenth centuries with higher proportions of younger widows (defined in this case as under forty-five) and fewer older widows (over sixty-five) on relief lists than in the national population. In the case of Ipswich and Greenock the proportions of younger widows are inflated as the sources listed only those widows who were wage earners. However, the other lists which registered 'typical', consecutive or all widows on relief lists can be considered representative recipients of out relief and also indicate higher proportions of younger widows and lower proportions of older widows on out relief lists than their share in the national population. Analysis of the households of widows in primary poverty in York in 1901 also reveals the same pattern.[23] It seems likely that in the early twentieth century higher proportions of older widows than in earlier centuries were being refused out relief and removed to workhouses.

Sources of Income of Poorer Widows

Even though the death of their husbands did not plunge all widows into poverty and receipt of out relief,[24] the high percentage of recipients of outdoor poor relief who can be identified as widows implies that widows constituted a disproportionately large proportion of the poorest people in society. In addition to widows, the Poor Law had to support other disadvantaged persons including illegitimate children, orphans, some step-children, families deserted by the father, the dependents of soldiers and men serving in the militia, married men whose earnings were insufficient for the maintenance of their families, and the long term sick and disabled. Nevertheless women specified as widows constituted 32 per cent of those assisted in the extensive set of lists of the recipients of outdoor relief at the end of the eighteenth century which Eden included in his *The State of the Poor.*[25] Widows formed a larger proportion of all recipients in the smallest settlements (41 per cent)[26] and their presence was least marked in some of the largest towns covered by Eden, notably in Wolverhampton (Staffordshire) in 1794 when widows were just 20 per cent of all recipients, and in Halifax (Yorkshire) where widows were 25 per cent of recipients.[27]

Information about the income of widows is much harder to obtain. At the start of the twentieth century, however, it is clear that widows formed a larger proportion of the very poor than they did of those sections of society immediately above them. For example, in Rowntree's study of York in 1899, widows were 25 per cent of the poor whose household income was less than 18 shillings but only 19 per cent of households whose income lay between 18 and 21 shillings and just 4 per cent of those with an income in excess of 30 shillings (see Table 1.4, calculated from Rowntree 1913). The proportion of widows of those considered by Rowntree to be in primary poverty, that is with insufficient income to maintain the physical efficiency of themselves and their dependants, was very close to their proportion of the poor with lowest earnings. The study by Maud F Davies of the Wiltshire village of Corsley in 1906–7 provides a point of comparison. In Corsley the proportion of widows in primary poverty was lower than it was in York at 21 per cent but as in York, widows formed a lower proportion of those who were in somewhat better circumstances, measured in the case of Corsley in terms of those in secondary rather than primary poverty. Secondary poverty signified sufficient income to sustain physical efficiency had their earnings been used more effectively (see Table 1.4, calculated from Davies 1909).

Table 1.4: Percentage of widows in different sections of the wage-earning population of York in 1899 and Corsley, Wiltshire, in 1907.

Population	Weekly Family Income (shillings)[1]	% Widows	N[2]
York	< 18	25	51
	18–21	19	52
	21–30	15	46
	≥ 30	4	45
	Primary Poverty[3]	26	1465
Corsley	Primary Poverty[3]	21	58
	Secondary Poverty[3]	16	81

Notes[1] Rowntree placed lager families (those with more than four children) one income class lower and families with one child one class higher. Rowntree (1913): 58.
[2] Cases identified by Rowntree as typical although Rowntree also reports widows constituted 45 per cent of all families whose income was < 18 shillings, Rowntree (1913): 73.[3] Family income insufficient to obtain the minimum necessary to maintain physical efficiency, Rowntree (1913): 117. 4 Family income sufficient to maintain physical efficiency but devoted to other purposes, useful or otherwise, Rowntree (1913): 118
Sources: Calculated from Rowntree (1913); Davies (1909).

Some surveys of the poor undertaken by the Poor Law authorities also provide information on the income of widows at various times between the late sixteenth and early twentieth centuries. These surveys have been analysed in Table 1.5 to indicate the proportion of the household income provided by the widow herself, by her children and by the Poor Law for one particular group of widows, those who had wage earning children and received assistance from the Poor Law in the form of out-door poor relief. All the populations were urban and the number of widow headed households too few to determine whether there was any trend over time in more or less support from children or the Poor Law. However, the general position is clear. In the first place, assistance from the Poor Law was only a supplementary (although no doubt very necessary) source of income, for those widows with wage earning children in their households. Secondly, support from the Poor Law was provided even though the widow and her children were employed. Thirdly, the children of the widows contributed by far the largest proportion of the income earned from employment in three of the four populations, indicating the importance of the availability of support from other members of their families for the widows' standard of living. On the other hand, it would be unwise to assume that the children handed all of their earnings to their mothers to support the household. Evidence on this point will be discussed later.

Table 1.5: Share of income of families consisting of widows and wage-earning children contributed by the widow, her children and by poor relief in Ipswich, Salisbury and Corfe Castle.

Contribution to Earnings	Ipswich 1597	Salisbury 1637	Corfe Castle 1790	Ipswich 1906
Widow %	35	52	11	27
Children %	65	48	89	73
Family earnings (pence)[1]	18.2	29.3	87.3	212
Family Earnings + Poor Relief (pence)[1]	20.2	35.1	111.3	289
Poor Relief as % Income	9.9[2]	16.5	21.6[3]	26.7[4]
N	9	6	9	21

Notes[1] Values specify earnings and income including poor relief divided by number of families (mean earnings). Median earnings were similar.[2] Only 3 of the 9 families received poor relief. For these 3 families poor relief provided 39% of their income.
[3] Assuming an average contribution from the Poor Law of 24 pence in line with the scale of relief in other Dorset parishes at the time, see Wall 1994:319.[4] Includes estimated cash value of flour based on price of flour in budgets of families in receipt of out relief in 1906 in parish of Linton in adjoining county of Cambridgeshire.
Sources: Calculated from Slack (1975); Webb (1966); photocopied census of Corfe Castle and Royal Commission on the Poor Laws and Relief of Distress (1909).

A significantly higher proportion of the income of those widows who lived alone, as could be expected, was provided by the Poor Law. For widows with some earnings, receiving poor relief and living on their own in Ipswich in 1597, the Poor Law was providing 48 per cent of their income. In Salisbury in 1635, such widows obtained 49 per cent of their income from the Poor Law and in Corfe Castle in 1790, between 50 and 60 per cent.[28] Some of the widows in the surveys were over the age of 75 but were still recorded as able to earn.[29]

Information about the income of widow headed households can also be derived from analyses of the household budgets from the late eighteenth century assembled by David Davies and Frederic Morton Eden.[30] These budgets with many others have been already been extensively analysed in a series of articles by Jane Humphries and Sara Horrell.[31] The budgets of widow headed households from Eden and Davies are examined again in the present study to compare first the proportion of the household's income contributed respectively by the widow, resident children and the Poor Law. Secondly, as Davies and Eden also included some budgets of households of married women who had been deserted by their husbands, it is also possible to compare the economic situation of widows and deserted wives. The third objective was to measure the income available to support a widow or other female headed household relative to that of a household headed by a married man employed as a labourer in the same community. Comparisons can also be made between the proportions of expenditure that widow and labourer headed households allocated respectively to the purchase of bread, flour and yeast, and meat.

In order to compare the standard of living of widow and labourer headed households, it was essential to take account of the different size and composition of their households. Examination of the widow headed households documented by Davies and Eden revealed that these were large households with between six and eight members. The majority of English households were considerably smaller (averaging 4.75 persons per household) and households headed by women smaller still).[32] The most appropriate comparison for the widow headed households recorded by Davies and Eden is therefore with similarly large households of labourers although comparisons will also be made with households of labourers with fewer members in order to assess the impact of household size on living standards. Another aspect of the larger households of both labourers and widows with important impact on their economic viability is that they would be likely to contain not only more dependent children than most households but also more secondary earners as older children entered the labour market. The contribution that household heads made to household income would be proportionately lower in these households than it would be in most households.

To take account of differences in the consumption burden of households, household income was then divided according to the number of consumers but taking into account that children and women would consume less than adult males. Other historians have also assumed that there were major inequalities in the ways in which the resources of the household were distributed but there is no consensus about the degree and type of inequalities. The assumption made here are that male household heads consumed 50 per cent more than females over the age of 15, other males over 15 a quarter more, children aged 10–14, 75 percent, and children aged 1–9, 50 per cent, of that of an adult female.[33] Whether the resources of households in the late eighteenth century were allocated in the ways suggested is not known but the estimates are not far removed from the assumptions Davies made to calculate consumption of bread or flour by the households of five labourers and one deserted wife in St Austell Cornwall *circa* 1790. Consumption was estimated by assuming that a man would eat 50 per cent more bread than a woman but placed the bread consumption of the 'average' child at 75 per cent of that of a woman.[34]

We can begin by considering through Table 1.6 the relative contribution of widows, their children and the Poor Law that is suggested in these budgets. Widows never contributed as much as half the earnings in these households, which is in line with the evidence provided by the surveys of the poor as set out in Table 1.5. However, there was considerable variation. In a couple of households, the widow contributed almost nothing; in another household as much as 43 per cent of the earnings of the household.[35] There was also considerable variation in the proportion of household income provided by the Poor Law, ranging from total support in the case of the widow's household in Llanarmon in Denbighshire to a fifth of household income for the widow from Seend in Wiltshire. Support from the Poor Law for these households was considerably greater than indicated for the households in the surveys of the poor but still in most cases only served to supplement the earnings of household members. What the budgets also suggest is that earnings of households where the wife had been deserted by her husband were a little lower than in the households of widows, that the proportion of household earnings provided by the deserted wife exceeded that of the widow, and that the Poor Law provided a larger proportion of the income of the households of the deserted wives than it did of those of the widows.[36] The meagre earnings of the households of these deserted wives taken in conjunction with the more extensive support provided by the Poor Law would suggest that these women were in even more straightened circumstances than were the widows whose budgets were studied but whether this was generally the case is another matter. For both widows and deserted wives, the chief determinant of the earnings of the household was whether they had sons who had reached working age.[37] The household with the least income was that of the unmarried woman from Cumwhitton in Cumberland. With no children to help support the household and no contribution from the Poor Law only her meagre earnings and savings were available to maintain the household.[38]

Table 1.6: Income of eleven female headed households contributed by female head, children and poor relief according to family budgets collected by Davies and Eden at the end of the eighteenth century.

Location	County	Marital status	Earnings (pence)	Contributed by Woman (%)	Contributed by Children (%)	Earnings + Poor Relief	Contributed by Poor Relief (%)
Aff Piddle	Dorset	Widow	71	1	99	101	30
Sherborne	Dorset	Widow	57	43	58	87	34
Tanfield	Durham	Widow	84	7	93	120	30
Monks Sherborne and Basing	Hampshire	Widow	60	30	70	108	44
Seend	Wiltshire	Widow	114	14	86	174	20
Llanarmon/ Llandegla	Denbigh	Widow	0	0	0	48	100
Barkham	Berkshire	Deserted	48	25	75	108	55
St Austell	Cornwall	Deserted	66	9	91	114	42
Newent	Gloucester	Deserted	84	61	39	96	8
Glynde	Sussex	Deserted	12	100	0	60	80
Cumwhitton	Cumb.	Unmarried	17	100	-	19	0

Sources: Eden (1797) for budgets from Cumwhitton (1796) , Glynde (1793) and Seend (1796); remainder from Davies (1795) from period 1787–9.

Comparisons of the income of the households of widows and deserted wives with those of the income of labourers' households, both large and small, are set out in Table 1.7a, b and c. The income available to the members of female headed households, measured in terms of consumption units, which calculate the number of consumers according to age and sex, was 24 pence when the household was headed by a widow and in households headed by a deserted wife just over 22 pence.[39] The amounts are not dissimilar from the income of consumption units in the households of labourers and suggest a similar standard of living.[40] The explanation lies with the criteria Davies and Eden appear to have used when selecting particular households. Those households with a female head contained wage earning children while most of whose children in the households of labourers were too young to work (see last two columns of Table 1.7a,b and c).

Table 1.7a, b.c: Income per consumption unit for 11 female headed households and for labourers from same populations with large and small households according to family budgets collected by Davies and Eden at the end of the eighteenth century

Table 1.7a Female headed households.

Location	Marital Status	Househld Size	Consumption Units	Weekly Income (pence)	Income per consumption Unit	Age of Eldest Child	Weekly Earnings Of Children (pence)
Aff Piddle	Widow	5	4.0[2]	106	26.5	19	75
Sherborne	Widow	7	4.25	87	20.5	12	33
Tanfield	Widow	7	5.0	120	24.0	16	72
Monks Sherborne and Basing	Widow	7	4.5	108	24.0	14	42
Seend	Widow	7	5.0[3]	174	34.8	16	92
Llanarmon/ Llandegla	Widow	7	3.75	48	12.8	10	0
Barkham	Deserted	7	5.0	108	21.6	16	36
St Austell	Deserted	7	5.0	114	22.8	16	60
Newent	Deserted	7	4.5[4]	96	21.3	10–14	30
Glynde	Deserted	3	2.0	60	30.0	<10	0
Cumwhitton	Single[1]	1	1.0	18.8	18.8	-	-

Notes[1] Marital status not specified by Eden but inferred as unmarried from Eden's summary of her family background. [2] Assumes that in addition to the 19 year old child specified by Davies, that of the other three children, one was aged 10–14 and that the remaining two were under 10. One child assumed to be over 10.

[3] The eldest two sons have been excluded as it appears that they did not live with their mother. [4] Assumes that the two eldest children were aged 10–14 and the others under 10. Sources: Calculated from Davies (1795); Eden (1797). Consumption unit defined as in Wall 1994: males heading families = 1.5 consumption units, other males 1.25, females over 15 = 1, children aged 10–14 = 0.75 and children 1–9 = 0.5. Children whose age was not specified were counted as equivalent to 0.5 consumption units.

Table 1.7b: Labourer with large household.

Location	Household Size	Consumption Units	Weekly Income (pence)	Income per consumption Unit	Age of Eldest Child	Weekly Earnings of Children (pence)
Aff Piddle	8	5.25	112	21.3	11	15
Sherborne	6	4.5	96	21.3	9	0
Tanfield	7	5.0	90	18.0	8	0
Monks Sherborne and Basing	7	4.5	120	26.7	9	0
Seend[1]	7	5.25	168	35.2	10–14	24[4]
Llanarmon/ Llandegla	8	5.75	93	16.2	13	9
Barkham	7	4.5	112	22.7	8	0
St Austell	7	4.5	84	18.7	8	6
Newent[2]	7	5.0[3]	73	14.6	<10	0
Glynde	7	4.75	168	35.4	10	12

Notes[1] Eden does not record household size or number and ages of children. Budget estimated assuming household contained five children with the eldest aged 10–14. [2] Davies

(1795) states same income for all male headed households in Newent regardless of household size and numbers of children and does not report any earnings for the children.[3] On the assumption that all children were under 10.[4] Estimated based on arbitrary division of combined earnings of wife and oldest child reported by Eden (1797): 796 and assuming wife able to work full-time and earn 30 pence weekly as assumed by Eden for a healthy woman without young children.

Sources: Calculated from Davies (1795); Eden (1797). Consumption unit defined as in Wall 1994: males heading families = 1.5 consumption units, other males 1.25, females over 15 = 1, children aged 10–14 = 0.75 and children 1–9 = 0.5. Children whose age was not specified were counted as equivalent to 0.5 consumption units.

Table 1.7c: Labourer with small household.

Location	Household Size	Consumption Units	Weekly Income (pence)	Income per consumption Unit	Age of Eldest Child	Weekly Earning of Children (pence)
Aff Piddle	5	3.5	84	24.0	6	0
Sherborne[1]	4	3.5	90	25.7	5	0
Tanfield[2]	5	3.5	90	25.7	6	0
Monks Sherborne and Basing	4	3.5	120	34.3	6	0
Seend[3]	4	3.75	168	44.8	10–14	24[5]
Llanarmon/ Llandegla	6	4.0	78	19.5	8	0
Barkham	4	3.5	102	29.1	7	0
St Austell	4	3.5	84	24.0	7	0
Newent[4]	4	3.5	73	20.9	<10	0
Glynde	3	3.0	102	34.0	6	0
Cumwhitton	6	4.0	83	23.2	5	0

Notes[1] Household 6 in Davies (1795).[2] Hous3hold 5 in Davies (1795).[3] Eden does not record household size or number and ages of children. Budget estimated assuming household contained two children under 10.[4] Davies (1795) states same income for all male headed households in Newent regardless of household size and numbers of children and does not report any earnings for the children.

[5] Estimated based on arbitrary division of combined earnings of wife and oldest child reported by Eden (1797): 796 and assuming wife able to work full-time and earn 30 pence weekly as assumed by Eden for a healthy woman without young children.

Sources: Calculated from Davies (1795); Eden (1797). Consumption unit defined as in Wall 1994: males heading families = 1.5 consumption units, other males 1.25, females over 15 = 1, children aged 10–14 = 0.75 and children 1–9 = 0.5. Children whose age was not specified were counted as equivalent to 0.5 consumption units.

Although on average female headed households, representing a later stage in the development of the household would be more likely to contain older children, some should contain only young children just as there ought to be older children present in some of the labourers' households. Neither Davies nor Eden therefore collected a representative sample of labourer or female headed households.

Nevertheless the information in these budgets is still valuable as it demonstrates that that the standard of living of widows and deserted wives who had wage earning children living with them was roughly equivalent to that of labourers with young families.[41] It can also be inferred that the standard of living of older women would fall below that of these labourers when the children of widows and deserted wives left to establish their own households or should there be no surviving children. Furthermore, the standard of living of labourers with older children resident with them would even have exceeded that of female headed households containing children of working age.

Another source of income that needs consideration is the significance of self-provisioning; that is the estimated value to the household of the produce of the garden, any waste or common land. Horrell and Humphries estimated this at 5.3 per cent of the household income of female headed households between 1787 and 1815.[42] Again according to Horrell and Humphries, this was a lower contribution than that achieved from self provisioning in male headed households. One reason for this may be that widows and other women heading households found it more difficult to afford the initial outlay required for example to purchase a pig. One of the widows studied by Davies was also without a garden.[43]

Support from Outside the Household

A number of cases of children supporting elderly widowed or disabled parents, even when they did not live with them, have been documented for English populations. One elderly man in Corfe Castle in 1790 was, for example, at least in part supported by his children who lived elsewhere.[44] On the other hand, Eden documented from Seend, Wiltshire, in 1796 much more limited assistance to a widow by a son aged eighteen, living independently, who was only giving his mother sixpence a week as payment for her washing and mending his clothes. The rest of his earnings of ten shillings a week as a bricklayer were devoted to his own maintenance. From the information given by Eden, sixpence constituted 5 per cent of his earnings and just over 3 per cent of the income of his widowed mother who had several wage earning children residing with her and was in receipt of poor relief.[45]

Examination of some family budgets from Corsley, Wiltshire in 1906–7 reveals the variety of arrangements that might be made. Analysis of the housekeeping budget of the elderly widow, to whom reference was made in the introduction, indicated that her daughter provided 61 per cent of the food budget in the first week of observation and 81 per cent in the second.[46] Three children helped to support another widow in Corsley, Two married sons each contributed two shillings per week and a married daughter made a home for her mother, taking three shillings and sixpence (88 per cent of the four shillings) to meet the cost of her keep. In the summer the mother undertook some housework while her daughter was working in the garden and in return the daughter gave her a share of the profits from the sale of garden produce as pocket money, amounting in all to 12–13 shillings.[47] The experience of this family thus demonstrates not only cooperation between siblings in the provision of care to an elderly parent but also the way in which an elderly widow could still make a contribution to the family economy and see that work rewarded by a transfer of cash from daughter to mother.

In general, however, married children with families of their own could only provide limited support to their parents. In 1906 in Market Drayton, Shropshire, married sons were typically paying six pence or one shilling to the Poor Law Guardians as partial compensation for the amount of outdoor relief the Guardians were providing to their widowed parent.[48] These amounts represented between 3 and 7 per cent of their earnings and between 17 per cent and half of what had been granted in poor relief. Many married children with households of their own did not provide any financial support to their parents. Analysis of the information that was provided on some 'typical cases' selected by the Royal Commission from the list of outdoor poor in Govan, Glasgow, again in 1906 shows that only about half of the married children provided any assistance to a widowed mother.[49] The evidence collected by Booth on the economic circumstances of the elderly in rural areas of England in 1892 also indicated that support from family members (identified simply as relatives), when available, was usually combined with other sources of income. The amount of assistance was not specified but the sources of support were given. Only 5 per cent of the elderly were maintained solely by relatives while almost a quarter supported themselves from their own earnings and close to a further quarter from their savings and property.[50] A quarter of all rural elderly were reported as receiving some assistance from relatives. This compares with almost half of the elderly who relied on their earnings to supply a portion of their income, the third that used savings and property and the fifth who received some assistance from the Poor Law. Looking specifically at those receiving support from their relatives, a third were also assisted by the Poor Law, almost a third by charity, a fifth from earnings and 14 per cent from property.

Family budgets also indicate that on occasion some support might be provided by siblings who resided elsewhere, more distant relatives and even neighbours.[51] However such support (usually provided in kind rather than as cash) was usually limited and taking into account the number of potential donors, whether neighbours or relatives, was not often available.[52] Employers (or former employers) and local landowners might also provide some assistance. This could involve the provision of food while at work, allowing their labourers to buy grain at below the market price and permitting the gathering of firewood. The value of such assistance, given the many forms it might take, is difficult to estimate but was almost certainly less than the pensions some employers were paying to elderly former employees or their widows in the Thingoe Poor Law Union in Suffolk in 1906. These pensions of two shillings a week, paid by agents employed to manage the estates of the landowners, represented 80 per cent of the amounts granted as out relief by the Poor Law Guardians. Payments of out relief were, however, apparently not curtailed nor were the pensions even recorded in the records of the Poor Law because these agents, many of whom also served as Poor Law Guardians, thus ensured higher incomes for their pensioners at very little cost to the landowner.[53]

Expenditure Patterns of Widows and Labourers

Davies and Eden gave details not only of the income of the poor households which they investigated but also their expenditure. Two categories of expenditure have been selected for analysis: the proportion of their total expenditure that went on the purchase of bread, flour and yeast, and the proportion spent on meat. In each case expenditure by the households headed by a widow can be compared both with the expenditure of households headed by a woman whose husband had deserted her and the expenditure of households that were headed by a male labourer (see Table 1.8).

Table 1.8: Percentage of food expenditure on bread, flour and meat by 11 female headed households and for labourers from same populations according to family budgets collected by Davies and Eden, 18th century

Location	Female headed Household[1] Bread/ Flour/ Yeast	Female headed Household[1] Meat	Labourer with large Household[2] Bread/ Flour/ Yeast	Labourer with large Household[2] Meat	Labourer with small Household[3] Bread/Flour/ Yeast	Labourer with small Household[3] Meat
Aff Piddle	89	4	70	0[4]	69	10
Sherborne	82	0	71	14	66	12
Tanfield	49	10	49	10	42	12
Monks Sherborne and Basing	73	12	73	12	57	14
Seend	71	0	-	-	79[6]	-
Llanarmon/ Llandegla	65	0[5]	64	0[5]	64	0[5]
Barkham	71	17	80	9	71	16
St Austell	78	11	79	10	73	15
Newent	75	4	74	4	74	5
Glynde	67	13	62	17	64	18
Cumwhitton	60	3	-	-	60	7

[1] Widows in Aff Piddle, Sherborne. Tanfield, Monks Sherborne and Basing, Seend and Llanarmon; Deserted wives in Barkham, St Austell, Newent and Glynde; unmarried woman in Cumwhitton. Household size = 7 except Aff Piddle = 5, Glynde = 3 and Cumwhitton where woman lived alone. [2] Household size = 7 except Aff Piddle and Llanarmon = 8 and Sherborne = 6. [3] Household size = 4 except Llanarmon and Cumwhitton = 6, Aff Piddle and Tanfield = 5 and Glynde = 3. [4] Purchase price of pig (14 shillings) raised for meat is excluded. [5] None of these budgets specify any expenditure on meat. [6] Percentage of total expenditure including some non food items.
Sources: Calculated from Davies (1795); Eden (1797).

However, in presenting these comparisons it should be noted that the details of expenditure were not necessarily a record of what these households actually spent but estimates of their expenditure provided by a clergyman or landowner resident within or with interests in the various communities. In a few cases the use of estimates is made explicit. For example the account for St Austell, Cornwall, states that expenditure on bread by the poor had been calculated using the assumption that a labourer would consume daily three pence worth of bread, his wife two pence and a child one and a half pence. A different and more detailed set of estimates was suggested for Newent, Gloucestershire whereby a labourer would consume weekly 15 pence worth of bread, a woman breast-feeding 12 pence, other women 9 pence and lads depending on their age between 6 and 15 pence.[54]

In some other cases it is highly likely that the expenditure of households in other communities has been estimated as some households of the same size apparently devoted exactly the same proportion of income to the purchase of both bread and meat.[55] Indeed it may be that the only reliable set of budgets in the whole collection are those produced by Davies himself for Barkham, Berkshire, and those from Aff Piddle, Dorset, where households of the same size were reported as allocating different proportions of their expenditure to bread and meat. On the other hand, some of the actual expenditure seems to have been included even in the budgets which explicitly incorporated estimates as it was also stated that information on the households in Newent had been derived partly from information given by the labourers and partly from the accounts of local shopkeepers.[56] In addition, even when expenditure has been estimated, it is significant for the comparison below of expenditure by widows and labourers that it is the size of the household and not whether its head was male or female that determined the proportion estimated as spent on bread and meat even though to construct some of these budgets the assumption had been made that the value of the bread consumed by a woman would be just 60 per cent of that of a man.[57]

It would, nevertheless, be unwise to argue that the information on expenditure patterns of the poor given by Davies and Eden are anything more than approximations to what labourers, widows or deserted wives actually expended just as there is uncertainty about their exact income due to the receipt of some payments in kind, irregular earnings and occasional assistance from more wealthy members of the community. However, as these are the only budgets of the poor taken before 1800, it is with these one must work despite their limitations. Considering first, then, the budgets of widows and deserted wives, on average 72 per cent of the expenditure of widow headed households was used to purchase bread and just 2 per cent for the purchase of meat. The households headed by a deserted wife on average spent 73 per cent on bread and 12 per cent on meat.[58] The lower expenditure on meat would imply a poorer diet in widow headed households. Comparison of the expenditure by all female headed households with that of labourers with large households reveals similar proportions of expenditure on bread but with labourers spending more on meat. Labourers who had smaller households were in an even better position, spending less on bread and even more on meat. Analysis of the expenditure patterns of female headed households thus suggests their diets were more defective than those of labourers in the same community. What is particularly interesting is that the comparison of expenditure patterns implies a greater degree of deprivation in female headed households, and in particular in households headed by a widow, than was indicated by the comparison of incomes (above Table 1.7). The reasons for the discrepancy are unclear. One possibility is that the way income and expenditure were calculated involved too much inaccuracy but another possibility is that widow headed households found it more difficult to purchase meat lacking contacts or the necessary credit.

A similar comparison of the budgets of widows and labourers can be carried out for the end of the nineteenth century using the information collected by Seebohm Rowntree (1913). These budgets were compiled with greater care and were more informative in that they included calculations of the quality of the diets measured in terms of their protein content and energy value. Table 1.9 summarizes the information available for the households of the only two widows who were studied, three labourers, one with a large household and two with a much smaller ones (measured in terms of consumption units as calculated by Rowntree), as well as the average for all 14 male headed households.[59]

Table 1.9: Nutritional value of diet of two families of widows and families of labourers in York 1899 whose income per week was < 26 shillings.

	Soldier's Widow	Office Cleaner Widow	Labourer Budget 4	Labourer Budget 1c	Labourer Budget 13	Average 14 Labourers[6]
Consumption units[1]	2.86	1.57	2.86	4.86	2.14	-
Weekly Income (pence)	180	141	180	239	280	236
Protein as % standard[2]	78	75	50	66	73	71
Fat as % standard[3]	83	84	72	75	73	83
Food Expenditure as % Income	52	46	52	61	44.5	51
Bread Expenditure as % food	15	20	20	24	8	20.5[5]
Meat and Fish Expenditure as % Food	20	29	31	22	46	32.5[5]
Food expenditure per consumption unit[4] (pence)	34.4	42.0	44.2	29.4	61.4	44.1[5]

Notes[1] Defined by Rowntree (1913): 270 as dietary needs of family members depending on age and sex. With a man engaged in 'moderate' muscular work and needing daily 125 grams of protein and 3500 calories, a woman = 0.8, boy 14–16 = 0.8, girl 14–16 = 0.7, child 10–13 = 0.6, child 6–9 = 0.5, child 2–5 = 0.4, child under 2 = 0.3.[2] Standard 125 grams per man per day.[3] Standard 3500 calories per man per day.[4] As defined by Rowntree (1902): 270.[5] Median.[6] Includes one carter and one polisher.
Sources: Rowntree (1913): 278–9 for rows 1–5, rows 6–8 calculated from information provided by Rowntree (1913), pp. 310–37.

The weekly earnings of the two households which were headed by a widow were less than those of most of the male headed households whom Rowntree placed in the same class. Yet the level of deprivation was often no greater in the households of widows than in the households of male labourers and in many respects was actually less. The households of widows, for example, spent a lower proportion of their income on food; the energy value of their diets was close to the average for male headed households and the protein content was higher. On the other hand, the two widows spent less of their food budget on meat and fish than did labourers and, taking account of the size and composition of their households, less on food.[60] None of the diets, labourers or widows, could be classed as good as all failed to provide the necessary protein and energy. However, the standard of living of the households of the two widows were somewhat higher than might have been expected in view of their low earnings, lower expenditure on food and less expenditure on meat and fish. It could simply be that these two widows were particularly adept at managing their meagre budgets but another factor that might be significant is that they did not have the expectations of a husband to consider when provisioning their households.

The budgets of the households of the two widows can also be compared with those of individual labourers. There seems to have been a high level of deprivation in the household of the labourer with five children. Rowntree calculated 4.86 consumption units in this household as against only 2.86 and 1.57 for the two widows and the household of the labourer was spending more of its income on food, a higher percentage of its food budget on the purchase of bread and the protein and energy value of the food was lower. The amount spent on food per consumption unit in this household was also less than in the households of the two widows. The situation was different for labourers with smaller households in that their expenditure on food per consumption unit exceeded that of the widows. In particular they spent higher proportions of their food budgets on meat and fish and one of them much less on bread. The protein and energy value of their diets, however, still did not equal those provided by the widows.

Rowntree also recorded the content of each meal taken by members of these households during a given week.[61] During the week meat and fish were present in a quarter of the meals in the households of widows as against 44 per cent of the meals in the male headed households. A comparison is possible with households of the poor in Corsley, Wiltshire, in 1906 and 1907 that were studied by M F Davies.[62] Some of these households were classed by Davies as suffering primary poverty; others as above the secondary poverty line.[63] The percentage of meals taken which contained meat or fish rose as the burden of poverty eased although not dramatically: 45 per cent of meals with meat or fish for male headed households in primary poverty and 51 per cent for those escaping even secondary poverty.[64] Although the three widows in Davies's study were also above the poverty line, there was meat or fish in only 41 per cent of the meals they consumed. However, the difference between the diets of the widows and male headed households with the same level of poverty was less marked than in York. For three of the male headed households, Davies also noted the diets of different member. This information reveals that married women were no more likely than were widows in Corsley to have meals containing meat or fish. The implication is that any deficiency in the diets in widow headed households was not primarily a consequence of poverty occasioned by widowhood but represented a continuation of eating habits acquired during their marriages when they had favoured their husbands in the allocation of food.[65]

Conclusion

A considerable body of evidence has been presented above on the living standards of widows between the sixteenth and early twentieth century whom their contemporaries regarded as poor. The large numbers of widows who appear out relief lists and the higher proportions of widows in poverty than was true for the population in general suggest that widowhood did plunge many women into poverty. Yet close examination of the income and expenditure patterns of the households of widows indicates that their standard of living was roughly equivalent to that of labourers raising young families in the same community. Indeed when evidence is available on the protein and energy value of diets at the start of the twentieth century, it becomes apparent that the value of the diets in widow headed households exceeded those even of labourers who had fewer children to support, considerably higher earnings and spent more of the food budget on meat and fish. By spending less on meat and fish than did married women who had to provide the food that their husbands considered essential, widows seem to have been able to provide a more nutritious diet from depleted resources.

It has also been possible to show the extensive financial support widows could receive from members of their families, particularly from their unmarried children of working age who lived with them. Of course not all widows were in this position and in old age and for those without children the support of the community through the Poor Law was much more important. The usual situation, however, was one where widows, even elderly widows, were not dependent on a single source of income but supported themselves from what they themselves could earn, any savings they might have, assistance from children and other family members, whether these lived with them or elsewhere, and contributions in cash and kind from the Poor Law and charity. What is more difficult to determine, given the fragmentary nature of much of the evidence, is the extent to which the share of support derived from a widow's earnings, family members and the community changed over the centuries. What is clear is that widows were still able to rely on a variety of sources of income despite Poor Law reorganisations in 1834 and again in the 1870s, and changes in the nineteenth century in employment and migration patterns. At the beginning of the twentieth century the standard of living of widows was significantly better than it had been at the end of the eighteenth century but so too had that of the rest of the population. However there is no evidence of marked changes over time in the relative standard of living of widows as measured against that of labourers in the same locality.

2 SURVIVAL STRATEGIES OF POOR WOMEN IN TWO LOCALITIES IN GUIPUZCOA (NORTHERN SPAIN) IN THE NINETEENTH AND TWENTIETH CENTURIES

Lola Valverde Lamfus

The nineteenth century saw new manifestations of poverty among the proletarian population in the industrialized countries of Europe. This new expression of poverty had different characteristics from those of the eighteenth-century agrarian societies, and was therefore subject to different solutions. The primary, underlying ties of solidarity which knitted communities together and provided protection for both families and individuals in a critical situation were broken by migratory movements and the process of urbanization. Poverty and destitution were to present their crudest aspect and submit the working classes to serious risks while, systems of mutual aid and, later, systems of compulsory assistance were slowly being set up by the states.

The event of industrialization had profoundly transformed society. The former farm workers, mutated into general labourers, populated the run-down neighbourhoods at the extreme of working and living conditions. Once mutual support systems had broken down and new difficulties had to be faced in order to survive, the poverty of these people became the object of interest for new studies in sociology and anthropology. Social reformers of both sexes deduced from their analyses that there existed a type of plague which was destroying the working classes and which they called 'pauperism'. Some of these reformers (in particular, females), quickly verified that it was the women who fell into poverty more easily and more often than the men and, therefore, tried to find an explanation for this phenomenon.[1]

Although it has been mentioned that the characteristics of poverty under the Old Régime were different from those of the industrial era, it must be pointed out that, in the course of time and with different methods of production, there were always more women than men among the poor. A fact which lead to a search for the causes of poverty among the feminine gender viewing the issue from the perspective of: the passage of time and the methods of production. The most impoverished groups were not only to be found among the women: but also among the children and the aged.[2] In the case of children poverty hit regardless of sex, while over the life course women were poorer than men and proportionally also their lack of protection for survival. This is easy to understand if a number of factors are taken into account, the majority of which are related to the world of work. The women who had access to remunerated jobs always received a lower salary than the men and, in general, the salaries did not reach a level of subsistence for one person, let alone for a family. In reality, women were not expected to be able to subsist on their work alone – which would have granted them a measure of autonomy, a prerogative of the male – it was, therefore, logical that a woman's salary should be considered as subsidiary; it should function as a humble contribution, the economic responsibility of the family pertaining exclusively to the man.

However, the patriarchal shadow while constantly present had its limitations. There were times in life when the protection of a father or husband or even an elder son was absent. In the nineteenth century, young, single, orphaned and poor women appeared who, nevertheless, had access to a certain education and who made a living as teachers, governesses and ladies-in-waiting. This figure, which appears so often in the literature of the time,[3] was more frequently found in Anglo-Saxon and Protestant countries where women were educated better and earlier than in Catholic, Mediterranean countries. Those women who could only fall back on their capacity for manual work and who had no formal education would find themselves near the poverty line or fall below it, as will be shown.

Censuses of the Poor

In Spain, the Public Welfare Law of 1855 decreed free medical and pharmaceutical assistance for poor families in towns of over 5,000 inhabitants. Every year, a census was published with a list of heads of families who were allowed to take advantage of this aid, having offered proof of their extreme situation of poverty and having undergone the pertinent inspection.[4] In San Sebastian, in order to be included in the census, it was necessary to earn less than a peseta a day per family member. However, a maximum income of 4 pesetas per day was set, disregarding the fact that a family of six or seven would by necessity have a higher consumption level than that of a family with four members or less. In Tolosa (the town to be analysed together with San Sebastian), the same clauses existed.

San Sebastian was, and is, the capital city of the province of Guipuzcoa. In 1900, it had just over 40,000 inhabitants, a figure which doubled in summer when it became the Royal Residence. It was a cosmopolitan tourist resort, a synonym of luxury and wealth, only slightly industrialized and with a work force dedicated to the service sector, while Tolosa, in the heart of the province, was intensely industrialized and, in 1900, had just over 8,000 inhabitants. A large number of the population consisted of workers in paper mills, a special feature of the town. In addition the bourgeois owners of these establishments resided locally, since the capital 30 kilometres away, was too distant, at that time, for commuting purposes.

Before proceeding further, it is necessary precisely to distinguish which people would be considered to be counted among the poor, and which social group would fix the limits for a family to be accepted in the census. Robert Castel distinguishes three areas in society: firstly, the integration area, made up of people with a stable job and with an established residence on the grounds of family and neighbourhood ties; the second area, denominated as an area of vulnerability, an unstable area where work was precarious, intermittent or people were unemployed, and finally the third area, that of exclusion where unemployment and social isolation combined, feeding upon the area of vulnerability.[5] Analysing the situations recorded in the census, it is possible to place the registered families in the area of vulnerability and in serious danger of falling into exclusion. All that was needed were the two factors of unemployment and lack of family and neighbourhood ties to serve as a retaining wall against such a fall. These ties, as such, could be very weak. To be included in the census, it was not sufficient to be poor, to be a humble member of the working class but also to be on the point of ostracism, living in squalor and often with a future in the workhouse or falling into beggary in order to survive. It is important to note that 'professional' beggary, practised by the socially outcast, with no fixed address, and to some extent, cut off from the rest of society (not considered in this presentation), became an aid for the destitute of both sexes as a survival strategy when a working wage was not sufficient to cover basic necessities. There was, therefore, no strict division between beggary and the world of work: when work was scarce, one went out to beg. Moreover, when one member became too heavy a load for the family to bear, they turned to beggary: the old, the blind, the sick and even the children contributed in this way to the family income.

Between 1898 and 1915, dates which correspond to a series of analysed censuses, no wide spectrum social security existed for the working class in Spain, apart from Mutual Aid Societies, organized by the workers themselves, and occasionally, by various enterprises. In 1908 the National Insurance Society was created, initially only to provide some kind of old age insurance coverage. Over the years, or rather decades, new insurance policies were incorporated, such as Maternity Insurance in 1929 but not until 1944 was the National Health Insurance to be set up. At the time of this study, protection for workers of both sexes in the case of death, illness and maternity was almost nonexistent. For that reason, the greater part of the people inscribed in the Census of the Poor came from the queues of the unemployed and the casual workers who worked when they were needed but had no fixed jobs. Alongside these were those who had lost all family support through death or illness; that is to say, all those who, at some time in their lives, found themselves unable to earn a living wage.

During the nineteenth century, social reformers attempted to analyse the phenomenon of pauperism which abounded in populations in the process of industrialization. After Tocqueville published his *'Memoria'* in 1835,[6] it was confirmed that there was a larger number of poor and destitute among the more wealthy and industrialized societies than in the more backward south of Europe, as he himself was able to verify during his journey to Portugal.[7]

These observations were proved correct: industrialization, particularly in its initial stages, created wealth but did not share it, so the numbers of the poor were higher in industrialized townships and regions. In the area under study, in fact, a higher number of poor emerged in industrialized Tolosa than in the tourist and service sectors of San Sebastian, although the difference was not as noticeable as had been estimated. In 1898, 200 families were assisted in Tolosa with some 8,000 inhabitants, whereas in San Sebastian, with just over 34,000, the number was 773, showing that about 11 per cent of the people of Tolosa were already on or on their way to the poverty line while, in the capital, the figure was only 9 per cent. Probably, this relatively low index of severe poverty in Tolosa was due to the industrialization structure in Guipuzcoa: the restricted capital of the petit bourgeoisie impelled the installation of small and medium-sized industry which spread throughout the province, while part of the workforce continued to uphold an agricultural economy combined with factory work. Added to all this, there existed a paternalistic and personal relationship between entrepreneurs and workers.[8]

Nevertheless, this data changes if other realities are contemplated. Both: Booth (1889–91) and Rowntree (1901) estimated that, at the end of the nineteenth century, one third of the British population were deemed to be poor; in the Basque Country, Juan Gracia affirmed that 45 per cent of the heads of family in Bilbao fulfilled the conditions for admission to the Census of the Poor in 1886, which is, somewhat, astonishing.[9] In fact, the differences between the industrialization of Bilbao and that of Guipuzcoa are, certainly, quite evident: Bilbao is connected with mining, heavy industry, blast furnaces, the population concentrated in the suburbs, with high levels of immigration and a rich and powerful middle class; Guipuzcoa, on the other hand, dedicated to the small and middle-sized businesses scattered throughout the territory, with a great variety of end- products, had less immigration and a more petit bourgeoisie: two types of industrialization with different effects upon the make-up of society.

Women in the Censuses of the Poor

Taking into consideration that the head of the household was expected to be the man, in the role of father or husband, the presence of women among these in the Censuses of the Poor, could be considered surprising because of their large numbers. One could even dare to assume that almost all these women who were heads of households were either poor or destitute. In Tolosa in 1896, they made up 54.7 per cent of the Census, in 1897 some 52 per cent and just over 55 per cent in 1898. In San Sebastian, the proportions were somewhat lower but they still clearly show the "feminization" of poverty since in 1898, 41 per cent, in 1907 some 48.9 per cent and in 1915 a percentage of 38.3 were women who were heads of households.

Almost none of the women registered in the Censuses had a fixed and salaried profession, or a job which offered any stable work. When a man had no work, he appeared under the heading of 'unemployed' but this only rarely happened in the case of a woman. It should be mentioned that there existed a certain lack of reliability in the sources of the Censuses with regard to salaried feminine activity and which is in flagrant contradiction to other sources, for example, to the pay books of the factories. The 'invisibility', or disregard of women's activity in the Censuses in the nineteenth century and the first decades of the twentieth was a general phenomenon. Almost all registration under the title 'No profession', corresponded to women. An example of this would be the Census in Navarra in 1887, where 82.3 per cent of the females over twelve years old came under this heading. However, this does not mean that the other 17.7 per cent had a profession: the majority of these were nuns or institutionalized.

An enormous amount of work carried out by women with no fixed hours or as part-time or casual work was not counted. Employment in minor activities was not considered as real work, such as running errands, gleaning, neither was domestic chores, washing or ironing. Very often these same women were unconscious of the fact that they should be considered workers even when they were engaged in activities outside the home, especially if it came under the heading of casual labour. Once established that the real scope of women's work cannot be calculated without recurring to other sources, it is possible, with the data in hand, to evaluate the nature of that work and the living conditions of poor women and, at the same time, outline the survival strategies that they put into practice.

Strategies of Poor Women

The survival strategies engaged in by the women of Tolosa and San Sebastian can be divided into two groups: on the one hand, there are the strategies linked to work outside the home and which brought in earnings, whatever the activity. Domestic work for outside employers could be included in this group.[10] Beggary can also be included which, although not considered as work as such, contributed financially to the family. On the other hand, there were diverse activities carried out in the home itself bringing in income which were not necessarily seen as work. Within this group, three types of activity can be identified: for example, the renting-out of rooms or part of an occupied apartment to other families without other services; secondly, there was the taking-in of boarders, usually single workmen, who received care from the landlady with regard to food, washing and ironing and a room, normally shared with one or more companions. What the English call the 'lodging system' and which had become an 'invisible' job that women have carried out to contribute to the survival of the family, can be considered as housework, although it is preferable to include it in this group because it presents similar characteristics. The lodging system, widely practiced in Bilbao and the surrounding regions[11] which received a large number of immigrants, very often on their own, left little mark on San Sebastian and Tolosa and more on the former than the latter. The third type of strategy was the utilization of family ties. The kinship group could have many shapes and forms, but all were sharing a dwelling place to reduce expenses to be able to pay the rent. The majority of those in this group were widows who lived with sons and daughters and who could, by no means, live on their own, although there existed other types of family groups.

Of the 1,402 heads of households in the Census of the Poor in San Sebastian in 1905, documents for 660 were found, giving complete information about the structure and size of the families at the moment of register, gender, age and descriptions of residence etc. Once these people had been classified according to sex, age and civil status, it was found that few bachelors were present among the families and almost nonexistent after a certain age. That fact can be interpreted in two ways: the first would be that a single man was economically more self-sufficient, and the second (which is not contradictory but complimentary to the first), is that some single and aged men were institutionalized. Added to this was the fact that female longevity could be the cause of the disappearance of single men over a certain age from the Census. If attention is fixed on poor, single women, their number was, in fact, small although their presence was much greater. Among the married men and women, the latter were in a small majority which was often the result of husbands being absent, either because they had left home or because they had migrated to America. This, in some cases, came to the same thing since some of these migrants abandoned the families they had left behind in Europe and formed another family in their new place of residence. As usual, the most representative group of poor women was to be found among the widows. To begin with, there was a vast difference in their numbers: twenty-eight widowers to 210 widows. There are many reasons for this difference but all to do with gender. The men were more likely to marry again, so there were many more widows. These men, although they were widowers, were less likely to fall into the extremes of poverty since their new civil status did not necessarily affect their income or their way of life. Also, in case of necessity and abandonment, they were more easily admitted to sheltered accommodation.

There were two determining factors in the survival strategies of the poor women in San Sebastian. The first was connected with the job market with little to offer in the industrial and manufacturing sector and with temporary work, basically in summer, in the service sector where women were employed as waitresses and cleaning women in hotels, boarding houses and restaurants. These posts were normally occupied by young country girls from the province who wanted to save up this extra money for their dowries, and once the summer was over, returned to their places of permanent residence. For that reason, the figures for salaried women in the capital were very low while, in Tolosa, there were many poor women to be found in industrial work since the job market in the factories was open to women. The problem was, however, a question of remuneration and stability. Between 1845 and 1905, women occupied 40.6 per cent of industrial posts in Renteria, an industrial locality seven kilometres from the capital.[12] In Bergara, another town in Guipuzcoa, the figure was 40 per cent in 1905.[13] Nevertheless, it must be mentioned that in San Sebastian there was a big tobacco factory which permanently gave work to some hundreds of women in coveted posts. In 1915 no less than 400 women were employed. Hardly any of these women, with a fairly stable job, appeared in the lists of the Poor Women's Census. That same year, only four widows, declared themselves as tobacco workers.

The house was often used as a source of income because of two factors: on the one hand, the scarcity of work for women in the capital, and on the other the high price and scarcity of housing. For that reason, the houses of the poor were densely occupied with an average of 7.5 people to a dwelling place. In Table 2.1, the occupation levels can be seen, showing that more than half (55.78 per cent to be exact) were occupied by six to ten people; nearly 15 percent had a population of between ten and fifteen persons and there are even examples (1.37 per cent) of more than sixteen people were living together. Only 33 per cent of houses were occupied by one family unit alone. In the rest, there was more than one family or a family which took in relatives or boarders. However, in general, these residences were undersized and only by living almost on top of one another could the poor survive.

This should explain why the familiar figure of the poor, the lonely, elderly widow does not appear in San Sebastian. Juan Gracia, who had worked on the Censuses of the Poor in Bilbao[14], informs us that of all the homes that had a woman in them, 32 per cent were alone and most frequently they were elderly widows. In Tolosa itself family cohabitation was used as a strategy, a large number of widows shared their homes with married sons or daughters, or with other people, relatives or others, but there were also widows or spinsters living alone, as we shall see later. None of this happened in San Sebastian: in all the Censuses of the Poor consulted, there are only two women living alone, both widows and both concierges (or doorkeepers), who were able to do so since they had the right to a free dwelling. In order for a woman to be able to live alone in this city, she would have to receive an income unobtainable for the vast majority of women.

Table 2.1: Poor people and co-residence in San Sebastian 1815

Number of Persons	Homes		Total number of persons	
	N.	percentage	N.	percentage
1–5	164	27.89	666	15.04
6–10	328	55.78	2550	57.59
11–15	88	14.96	1076	24.30
16–19	8	1.37	136	3.07
TOTAL	588	100	4428	100

Source: San Sebastian, census of the poor 1915

Some authors question the general solitude of the aged:

'there is not much documental proof that the aged in the cities were abandoned... several studies show that the majority of the elderly lived with other members of their families, married or single'.[15]

Later, they insisted in the same idea:

'In areas where townships were growing, it was frequently found that large numbers of the aged, widows and widowers, lived with their married children...following what could be termed as the principle of nuclear reincorporation'.[16]

In the censuses of Tolosa, the majority of women who were heads of households were widows, 86 per cent in 1896, 80 per cent in 1898 and 78.6 per cent in 1899. As commented, although it is true that only a few were able to live alone, in 1896 there were seventeen in that situation compared with fifty-six living with their families and another three boarding in private houses.

The widows with single sons and daughters were to be found in different situations, depending on their age. When the children were old enough to work and bring in a salary, the mother stayed at home. It is noticeable that there exists a tendency to aim for a middle-class domesticity. When conditions permitted, the woman stayed at home to do the housework, looking after those who went out to make a living for the family. The fact that these were found to be among the most destitute was due to the precariousness of their jobs, to the fact that not all the adults could find work and to the fact that among them there were girls and boys under the permitted working age. In addition, it must be added that, in many cases, it was the daughters who had jobs, earning a lower salary than their brothers. In the lists of the Census of the Poor in Tolosa, there appears, in 1898, the name of Ramona Salvide, a widow with two daughters who worked for Arzaá, the tailor; Micaela Antonia Goicoechea, a widow with a daughter who worked in the Elósegui beret factory for 1.50 pesetas and Martina Lizaso, also a widow with a son and a daughter of twenty-two, who was a dressmaker and whose salary was all the money that entered the house.

Widows with small children had, themselves, to go out to earn a living. In the same census of 1898 there also appeared Dolores Rezola, a widow with three small children who made tripe in the slaughterhouse for a salary of 1 peseta, Ignacia Sarasola, a widow with two children working in the Elósegui beret factory for 1.50 pesetas and Antonia Ugartemendia, also a widow with three small children, working for 1 peseta for Arzaá, the tailor.

More desperate cases were unemployed widows without children unable to earn a living, like Micaela Zubeldia, a widow, alone, without work, or Matea Esturo, a widow with seven small children; impossible to imagine how they managed to survive. Teresa Irazusta, a widow with a blind daughter, and both unemployed, could only look forward to beggary or the workhouse.

There were others who had the possibility of residing with their married sons or daughters. They could help with the housework and look after their grand-children, although not always in optimum conditions. Magdalena Otaegui, a widow, lived with her married daughter who had seven children; only her son-in-law and the eldest grandchild were working.

Very few of all these women had jobs which could offer any kind of stability. If they had, they were very badly paid. Josefa Bengoechea, a married woman with a husband who was away from home, earned 1.25 pesetas for herself and her three children. However, she could be considered lucky since she lived with her father and other relatives which fact allowed her to go out to work, leaving the children in the care of one of the family. In the case of Josefa, she had recourse to both types of strategies described since the low income she obtained from her work was combined with a minimum of expenditure, sharing a residence with her father and other relatives. Another woman, also married and whose husband was in Buenos Aires, lived alone with her three children. The eldest was an apprentice. She worked in La Guadalupe paper mill and earned, like the latter, 1.25 pesetas a day. These were difficult times but their future was more promising when the three children had begun working. The widow, Eulalia Martinez, with no children in her care, worked for a peseta and rented a room in a private house. That was the way she would have to survive while she had work and health. At that time, there was no way of making provisions for the future. One lived from day to day.

Many of these women could only hope for casual labour, a fact which placed them in a more precarious and destitute situation. Teresa Gallot was a widow with two children. One of them worked for 0.75 cents and she helped in a fishmonger's for 0.50 cents, but only when there was enough work. Another widow, Trinidad Munain, lived with a family and worked as a washerwoman and in other household jobs. This was a similar case to that of Francisca Oyarzábal who, moreover, had to take care of a two-year old granddaughter. In this case, she did not have a job, as such, but did the washing and other domestic chores, like the latter. These were clear cases of the 'invisibility' of women's work, unrecognized because the nature of the work was domestic, in spite of being carried out for others and being remunerated.

After the widows, a much smaller group of spinsters was examined who, therefore, presented fewer variables as far as strategies were concerned since there were no dependent children to be considered. In the Census of the Poor in Tolosa in 1896, only six single women appeared as householders, although five of those were living alone and were unemployed; the sixth had no work either but lived with her sister who was employed. In the census of 1898, of the 122 women householders, only eleven were single. One of those lived with her sister who worked in a paper mill and she, herself, earned 0.50 cents for each mattress she made. In the same year, Joaquina Casal, a sick spinster was living with her three brothers, only the eldest of whom worked, in the Amaroz paper mill. María Errandosoro, an unemployed spinster of seventy-five, shared accommodation with another elderly woman. Then there was Ascensión Irigoyen, a spinster who lived alone and worked at home sewing espadrilles, earning 2 pesetas...a week! Dolores Ercilla, also a spinster, made a living shrouding corpses, but there is no information about how much she was paid for each.

Already mentioned were the cases of married women who appeared as heads of households because their husbands were away and, therefore, found themselves in the same economic position as the widows. María Angeles Echebeste was married but her husband and was in an institution and so she had to go begging, while Josefa Lete, whose husband was also in an institution, apparently had no work.

Margrita Muguruza, whose husband was in Cuba, had two small children and worked for the Elósegui beret factory for 1.50 pesetas. Faustina Zubillaga was in a similar condition but she had a daughter and, working in the same factory, only received 1 peseta.

Finally, the cases were examined where the householder was the man to find out if the inclusion of some of them in the Census of the Poor had anything to do with the 'feminization' of poverty, that is to say, to establish if the women had to bear the weight of the family economy, thus making them more vulnerable.

In the family of José Domingo Juanagorría, composed of the couple, a daughter and a mother-in-law, the latter went out begging, according to the Census of 1897, and in the case of the couple formed by Miguel Pellejero and his wife, he was a casual labourer and she went out begging. In the 1896 Census, José Lorenzo Pildain, a widower with a daughter, the work was roughly divided up in the same way but, in this case, it was the daughter who worked in a factory while the father was begging in the doorway of the church of Santa María.

In many of the families described, it was confirmed that only the daughters and the wives brought in any earnings, which leads to the question of why they were included in the censuses. With the father and husband unemployed or sick, these family groups hovered on the boundaries of destitution because they had no more resources than those brought in by their women, and also the young, both boys and girls, earned less than adults. For this reason, an important part of feminine poverty was covered up, unless attention is paid to the circumstances of families whose heads were men who had no regular work and who were supported by the women of the family. Since the women were worse paid than the men, the families fell into destitution. The links between women and poverty then became evident.

Manuel Aguirre, with only one arm, was not fit to work. His wife and he lived with their 4 sons and daughters on 1.50 pesetas. In 1897, the couple formed by José Joaquín Alustiza and his wife, survived only thanks to the earnings of their thirty-year-old daughter, who worked in the Limousin factory. The same year, Doroteo Curiel, a married man, was unemployed. The couple had a small son and the wife worked in La Esperanza paper mill for 1.25 pesetas a day. Lucas Elizalde and his wife, José Estívariz and his, survived on the work of their respective daughters: one earned 0.75 cents and the other, 1 peseta. Even more dramatic was the situation of the family of Francisco Ledesma with four sons and daughters with the eldest daughter, eleven years old, who was the only one who had work, in a factory where she earned 0.62 cents. The father had to turn to beggary.

It can clearly be seen that there was no solid barrier between the world of work, beggary and the poor house for these people, between making a living and seeking assistance, and how easy it was to alternate between the two or find oneself in the two areas at the same time.

The source of information – the Censuses of the Poor – gives us an insight into the plight of the most deprived of the poor population, living in inhuman conditions since all the families registered formed part of a group who were without a minimum living wage, which the administration had calculated as one peseta per person per day. This was, for the most part, a female world, in which the greatest weight was borne by the widows and due to the scarcity and precariousness of employment, the irregularity of offer conditioned by the market, the invisibility and subsidiary character of feminine earnings and also, the middle-class ideal of domesticity, the influence of which could be perceived in the sharing of household chores. These are the most outstanding elements which give an explanation for the feminization of poverty.

It is necessary to point out that, in cases of extreme poverty, or near destitution, emphasized by the Censuses, the range of survival strategies to be resorted to or that could be organized, was very narrow. There was not many of them and no variety of ways to combat the crisis. Without the salvation of a stable job, in some cases, the home could be a valuable asset particularly if there was some other source of income to count on. For the rest, the poor house or beggary was the only ways out.

Conclusion

Poor women's survival strategies are strongly influenced by the offer of the work in the labour market. The comparison of two nearby localities has confirmed that in San Sebastian, a town predominantly aiming for the tourist trade, with very limited possibilities of work for women in the scant industry, female strategies were focussed on money making activities using the home.

Although the tourist season was limited to the three summer months, it raised house prices, which compelled poor families to share living space with each other. To be able to pay the rent, when one family rented a flat, it sublet rooms to other families. Another kind of invisible work by the housewife was the lodging of single immigrant workers and providing them with domestic services.

On the other hand, the strategies of poor women in the industrialized Tolosa were connected with work in factories where they received smaller salaries than men, and faced less stable employment. In Tolosa, poor families sometimes had to recourse to begging or to interment in a poorhouse to survive. It should perhaps be emphasized that working poor families turned to begging with the greatest ease. Particularly those in families supported by women and on the margins of survival. Children, the elderly and the disabled with scant chances for regular work went out to beg to contribute to the maintenance of the family, few were inactive.

3 WOMEN, WORK AND SURVIVAL STRATEGIES IN URBAN NORTHERN EUROPE BEFORE THE FIRST WORLD WAR

Beatrice Moring

It is not unusual to come across the statement that women in the past were economically dependent on men. Men have been seen as producers while women and children have been defined as consumers. Therefore a widow or abandoned wife would logically be a person totally dependent on charity and poor relief.[1] Irrespective of if women were the victims of patriarchal society and could not work, or women devoted themselves to the welfare of their family and would not work, the outcome would be the same. Because of lack of property and employment the loss of the breadwinner would spell disaster. While it might be understandable that nineteenth-century middle-class statisticians and census takers held such views,[2] in retrospect they cannot be accepted without reservation. Jane Humphries has highlighted the issue that female input for communities during the industrialization period has largely been ignored.[3] The acceptance of female dependency as a fact by modern research must be seen as problematical. Richard Wall has also demonstrated that the viewing poor relief as a sole income source for widows and other female household heads in nineteenth-century society is totally inaccurate.[4]

Ignored, unrecorded and invisible is how Hill described the economic input of women in the eighteenth and early nineteenth century[5]. The situation did not necessarily improve over time. The definition of work as full time and outside the home in the 19th century censuses ruled out a considerable amount of activity. Some census schedules were generated in a specific way because of prevalent ideologies among statisticians, assuming that married women should not work. The problems with defective registration of women's work can in some cases be linked to misinterpretations of instructions or very literate interpretations of instructions, i.e. if a woman was not working on census collection day, she was not working at all.[6] On the other hand one might ask if the same strict interpretation was applied to the men. If a man had a profession, or considered himself as having a profession, would it perhaps be listed irrespective of if he held employment on the day of the census.

The problems with information about female work have also been affected by a desire for large easily manageable data sets and simple categories, particularly in studies of long-term trends in standard of living. Even after the arrival of sophisticated technologies for statistical calculations, accepting censuses as they stand or using data on male earnings only is less laborious than struggling with corrections.[7] This preoccupation with adult male wage rates as a source to living standards has been severely criticized by Horrell and Humphries and Feinstein.[8] Acceptance of statements about domestic ideology has also made it possible to create scenarios of economic development without having to bother with problematic detective work into the issue of female earnings and the problem of people voicing ideology rather than reality.[9] Some have argued that women willingly gave up work in the late nineteenth century and concentrated on the home.[10] Others have raised considerable question marks around the registration, pointing out that early twentieth century surveys revealed that an overwhelming majority of working class households could not manage without earnings of the wife and children.[11]

While Higgs highlighted the general problems with the registration of female work in the census, it has been demonstrated that there were considerable differences in employment opportunities regionally, and that the recording of female work also depended on local perceptions.[12] It is necessary to remember that while industrial full time work seems to have been well recorded, the same cannot be said of part time activity. Work like washing and cleaning, was particularly defectively registered.[13]

Jane Humphries has demonstrated how making certain activities morally debatable had been used in ideological and political conflicts already in the 18th century. Before enclosure some representatives of the propertied classes harboured a grievance against economic activities that created a modicum of self-sufficiency among the labourers, as it made them less willing to come when called. Such independence was described as bad for the economy and dangerous for the social fabric.[14] While the desire of social reformers to protect women from work seen as demoralizing or physically dangerous, was in many cases genuine, the thought cannot be avoided that the potential independence created by female earnings could also be seen as worrying. The virtue of domesticity was continuously promoted in the second half of the 19th century. Male unions wholeheartedly supported the idea of the family wage brought in by the male household head. Unfortunately, however, many families needed the income of several people to survive and by the end of the 19th century while superficially not in the labour force, an increasing part of married women generated earnings through "secret" home work and sweated activities that were for most part unregistered.[15] As the census takers did not consider part time work to be real work married women were defined as not active.

In the Nordic countries the issue of viewing women as economically non-productive revealed a rift between the rural and urban universe in nineteenth-century political discourse. While the farmers had little interest in increasing female authority, they still saw them as co-producers, heading the female side of production and co-runners of the farming enterprise.[16] Such views were alien to the urban middle classes. When the urban middle class ideology penetrated changes in legislation from collective to male focused individualistic, so did the promotion of the family ideal with female domesticity. Despite rising female participation in industrial work in the 1930s female production was often seen as belonging to the "domestic" sphere.[17] The belittling of this sector caused severe rifts among economists and efforts to raise the profile of domestic economy were made.[18] The issue had far from marginal economic importance in a country with considerable female productivity in the farming sector. However, the ideological impact of the re-interpretation of the female role has governed the analysis of family economy as late as in 1980s and 1990s economic research. The repetition of the mantra that women did not work after marriage in the past has even resulted in anachronistic expressions like "housewife" being used when classifying working class women of the late nineteenth century.[19]

The aim of this study is to correct some misinformation on the issue of the economics of the working class household in Northern Europe, exemplified by Finland, a hundred years ago. Women in the past did work and earn, even though they were often badly paid. Women did run both households and small businesses successfully and managed surprising balancing acts in feeding their families using a combination of strategies. Males were not necessarily the sole breadwinners of a family. While generally registered as having an occupation, men could experience prolonged periods of unemployment, when the family survived of the income of wife and children. One of the problems with the work of women is its defective registration. Some of it was part of a hidden economy, therefore alternative strategies will have to be used to find information about its prevalence or economic impact. We will also discuss the strategies used by women when they had to function without a male breadwinner and what conclusions can be drawn about the effectiveness of such strategies and the ability of women to carry the full responsibility for a family.

We will use censuses, surveys, industrial statistics, household budgets and oral history to penetrate the mystery of female work and earnings and particularly gather information about the keeping of lodgers, washing, ironing and cleaning as sources of income for women in the late nineteenth- and early twentieth-century urban Finland.

Women, Work, Position and Production

In rural Nordic society the female economic input was important. Even though the occupational statistics registered female work defectively, economic and productivity surveys, in addition to production statistics, have revealed that the input of women was crucial until the onset of the modern mechanization process, 50 per cent of most work tasks were performed by women.[20] As a consequence of the organization of work within the family, systems were also in place for security in old age for women of the landholding class. In the early nineteenth century the majority of rural widows either ran the farm or resided with their children in retirement.[21] While the situation for the landless was more problematic, and the proletarian group had increased considerably towards the end of the century, even the widows of crofters retained rights to residence and land use. The methods of work exchange in rural communities could easily convert house rent to a couple of days work at harvest. Supplementary benefits like the right to graze a cow or some sheep on the village land or having the use of a potato patch, could be granted landless widows by the village community or individual farmers and thereby relieve the community from poor relief payments.[22] In an urban environment however the situation was different women had to arrange their survival using work, family collaboration, supplementary strategies and assistance from society or charitable institutions.[23]

  While we find that a considerable proportion of poor relief recipients in late nineteenth-century Finland, were old and infirm women, one must not forget that old men were also in this situation. The numbers of women in receipt of help should be viewed in the light of their greater survival rates. While the number of men and women in poorhouses and hospitals was almost identical around 1900, the number of women alive over the age of sixty-five was 30 per cent higher than the number of men. While men were often institutionalized, women frequently received out-relief and in addition many were relying on a combination of income sources.[24] Even fairly old women could engage in some kind of economic activity. Therefore to be able to penetrate the issue of female strategies it is important to study not only female occupations but female work and options in general.

The Census, Registration and Interpretation

'It was the task of women to assist, always assist, carry mortar and water, sand and filling and clean, endlessly clean, mortar dust, wood shavings, paint splashes, bits of paper until the house was finally finished and smelling of freshness received its first inhabitants.'[25]

Too often it has been assumed or proposed that women in the past were not economically active but lived off the income of their husbands. Where the husband was running a business, just like in the countryside running a farm, assistance from the wife was natural but that did not mean that the husband stated it on the census sheet.[26] The male attitude to female household work as self evident and free is exemplified in a budget where the husband, a barber, paid his apprentice in food and lodging only, but does not declare that his wife made any economic contribution to the household economy, even though her work saved him the cost of a salary.[27] In some cases female employment has been presented in relation to all women, i.e. including babies, toddlers and little girls with the resulting figures indicating low participation.[28] In other cases even students of social history accept at face value oral history statements of questionable reliability. Collections from the 1930s would reflect the then prevalent domestic ideology and it is not unheard of that people suffer from selective memory loss when aspiring to please an interviewer or want to underline working class respectability.[29] The situation has not been improved by such ideologies creating recalculations of existing data. When working on his comprehensive studies of working class northern Helsinki Heikki Waris went back to the original census sheets of 1900 and redefined female work participation. All married women engaged in activities that, according to him, would not bring in all that much money, like washing, ironing, cleaning etc were defined as economically dependant on their husbands and not in employment. Only if engaged in an occupation like being a shopkeeper was the woman accepted as economically productive. Men however were classified as economically productive and family providers, irrespective of type of occupation, disregarding regular seasonal unemployment or other reasons to be sceptical.[30] In actual fact many working class biographies reveal that it was common for married women to engage in permanent or part time work, particularly washing and cleaning. Vera Hjelt found, when collecting budgets in 1908, considerable female activity of so called auxiliary kind but seldom viewed by the husband as an occupation. She also found defects in the registration of earnings by family members.[31]

The instructions for filling in the census forms of Finnish towns in 1900 and 1910 stipulated that the forms are to be filled in by the household head but that the employment or profession of the head and his family members should be registered. Even secondary occupations were requested. If wives were engaging in trade or washing it was to be noted on the form, as was any gainful employment by children or lodgers. The instructions also specified that retired persons indicate that they are no longer engaged in what used to be their occupation. However, a temporary absence from the workplace was not to be defined as unemployment. On the other hand no information was provided about how unemployment should be registered.[32] As most men were or had been in some kind of employment at some stage in life, or had received training for a profession, the logical consequence of the instructions would be that a man would describe himself as a labourer or bricklayer or clerk, irrespective of whether he was in employment or not when the census was taken. Thereby the census recorded social stratification or even occupational structure but not employment and most certainly not economic dependency or breadwinner position in the family.

According to the Helsinki census of 1910, 55 per cent of all women and 67 per cent of all men over fifteen were occupationally active or had an income.[33] 36 per cent of adult women did not have any information about employment or activity, 5.6 per cent were in education or institutionalized while 1.5 per cent were registered as not working. The largest group of the women in employment were engaged in manufacture, the second largest worked as domestic servants, trade and shop work and manual labour also provided a source of income for many women (Table 3.1). A detailed breakdown of these categories revealed that industry included industrial employment and all types of production, in the case of women any kind of textile work would fall into this group. Trade and shop work included shop owners, sales assistants as well as market traders, street vendors and door-to door sellers of bread and milk i.e. everyone irrespective of if they were trading in bulk, selling over a counter or from a basket. Manual labour included building work, garden work, cleaning, washing etc. By 1910 office work was already developing into a female occupation giving work to more than 2000 women in Helsinki. A certain number also lived of a pension or investments, this group also included those who stated that renting out rooms in a house that they owned was their occupation.[34]

Table 3.1: Female occupations in Helsinki 1910.

With occupation	%	No occupation	%
Industry	16.8	In institution	3.2
Domestic service	13.8	Students	2.4
Trade, shop work	7.3	Widows not working	1.0
Manual labour	5.5	Visitors	0.1
Office work	3.8	Unemployed	0.5
Health care	1.9	Others	1.3
Pension, capital, house	2.2	Not in employment	8.7 %
Transport	1.4		
Education	1.4		
Academic	0.2		
Agriculture	0.08		
Administration	0.08		
Janitors	0.1		
Working	55 %	No activity registered	36 %

Source: *Statistisk arsbok for Helsingfors stad*, (Helsingfors: Helsingfors statistiska kontor 1916) Municipal statistics of Helsinki 1910 (57043 women over 15).

With the purpose of getting to grips with female activity, a detailed scrutiny of a sample of the original sheets of the 1900 census of Helsinki was undertaken. The sample, consisting of 242 female headed households, of which 155 headed by widows and 24 by married women, revealed certain interesting points. Only 15.7 per cent had no registered occupation or income. 17 percent gave their occupation as manual labourer, 21 per cent were engaged in service work; 16 per cent in washing and ironing, others working as childminders, in cafes, or bathhouses. 13.6 per cent were engaged in trade or petty trade and 8.6 per cent in textile work. 8.6 percent rented out rooms or kept lodgers (Table 3.2). On occasion statements we made like 'feeds the young men', or 'takes care of the lodgers'.[35] However an analysis of the household composition of the 15.7 per cent without occupation revealed that while 6 per cent had adult children in the household that could be assumed bringing in the money, no less than 8.6 per cent had lodgers, some more than one. Therefore even if no work was registered an economic contribution would have been present.

Table 3.2: Occupations of female household heads in the census of Helsinki 1900.

Occupation, or status in census	percentage	Of whom	percentage
Trade and petty trade	13.6	Shopkeeper	5.7
		Market or basket trader	7.8
Labourer	17.3		
Factory work	6.1		
Craft	3.3		
Textile work	8.6	Seamstress	6.2
		Knitting	2.4
Service	21.0	Washing, ironing	16.1
		Childminder	1.6
		Café, bathhouse etc.	3.3
Clerical, education	3.3		
Earnings from property	8.6	Housework (for lodgers)	4.5
		Owns house rents out flats or rooms	4.1
Pension	0.8		
Poor relief	0.8		
No occupation	15.7	Lodger in household	8.6
		Adult child in household	6.1
Total (242 households)	100 %	No information	0.8

Source: Census of Helsinki, Northern, working class districts, original sheets, The National Archives Helsinki

It is of course impossible to tell whether activities in widowhood were a continuation of the situation during marriage. A comparative sample of 100 married couples from the same census and part of town recorded (sheet filled in by the husband) 12 per cent of the wives having an occupation: ironing, manual labour, trade and petty trade, textile work, factory work and child minding. In addition half of the households kept lodgers. While the occupations in both cases reflect the activity patterns that have been associated with working class women, it is interesting to note that only 16 per cent of the women did not consider themselves having an occupation. However, only 12 per cent of the husbands decided to record an occupation for their spouses. Some husbands specified that their wife was engaged in housework, but the information was crossed over in the census office.[36] It is possible that the men in Helsinki wanted to see themselves as "the" breadwinner or that they reasoned like Waris 30 years later; if the activity of the wife was of little importance economically it did not need to be recorded. In situations of economic hardship, however even small earnings could be of vital importance.

The Question of Earnings

Estimating female activity levels can be difficult but harvesting information about female earnings can be even more complicated.[37] In the late 19th and early 20th century Finnish municipal taxation was linked to the size of earnings. The high earners paid more and had several votes in local elections. In Helsinki those earning less than 800 marks per year were exempt from paying tax and barred from voting. The same basic rule applied elsewhere but the threshold could be lower in smaller towns. Municipal taxation has sometimes been used to measure social stratification and gender inequality. Of the population in Helsinki 1899 only 22 per cent had the right to vote. The presence of women among the voters rose from 18 percent in 1880 to 29 per cent in 1910, but while some very opulent female voters can be found, most of the women co-existed with the labourers in the lowest income brackets. The largest proportion of the male taxpayers were also to be found in the lowest taxation category and the average income of tax paying labouring men in 1899 was 970 marks per year.[38] While anybody in factory employment or working for a business that had to keep accounts would be unlikely to escape tax, the situation was different for the self- employed. Women engaged in washing, ironing and cleaning on cash-in-hand basis were not likely to keep written records. Even if their earnings did rise past 800 marks per year they were hardly going to inform the authorities and be forced to pay council tax. The privilege of voting, especially having one vote in a tiered system, where the rich would have more than twenty votes each, was dubious and would not have been worth the effort or the expense.

Relieving those earning less than 800 marks from local tax was not a chance approximation. Calculations by economists in the 1890s had resulted in a fairly general agreement that a smaller income would make it difficult to keep a family of four afloat, ideally another 100 marks should be available for each additional child. A single person of careful economic disposition was believed to be able to survive on 400 marks per year.[39] These calculations were based on national averages. A study of expenditure in craft men's and skilled worker's households from 1890s Helsinki revealed income levels of 1200 mark for households of couples and 800 marks for single men. Among the lower income groups additional input by wife and children was necessary to balance income and expenses.[40] Income levels also varied depending on location. In the industrial town of Tampere it was quite common for a man to earn between 400 and 800 marks per year around 1900.[41] However, in smaller towns the rents were lower than in Helsinki and even food costs could be reduced, through self- provisioning or interaction with the surrounding countryside.[42]

While a man in full employment could in many cases earn enough to keep a family, those in seasonal employment were at risk of falling under the poverty line. The 1890s experienced a long period of unemployment and the municipality of Helsinki, as well as private charities, were running soup kitchens to keep the families going.[43] Despite improvement in the next decade full employment was not self evident. In 1909 the average unemployment periods could be as short as 0.3 months for those in the paper mills and as long as 1.6 months in the saw mills. While factory workers could be reasonably confident about employment all year round, such was not the case for those in the building trade or engaged in other types of outdoor work. The bricklayers were out of work on average 3.5 months, the painters more than 4 months and the unskilled outdoor workers more than 3 months of the year. In the problematic winter of 1905 the stoneworkers of Helsinki were unemployed for four months.[44] While the earnings of men in manufacture was on average 4 marks per day in 1900 and slightly higher in 1910 and the unskilled workers earned 2.50 in 1900 and 3 marks per day in 1910, the working year, particularly in the latter case, has to be estimated to about 220 days rather than 300. Therefore the income of industrial workers might well have been 1200-1300 marks per year and more for skilled workers and factory hands, the urban unskilled men on the other hand might not bring in more than 550- 600 marks in years with employment problems.[45]

When the standard of living in working class families was measured in 1908, it transpired that unemployment was a common affliction. Earnings from wife and children were commonly present in families with children over the age of 15. Even in families with young children only, the male breadwinner brought in only 83 per cent of the money. Unemployment periods of 2 months or more figure frequently, there were even cases where the husband left the area to find work elsewhere. 18 % of the families in the study were perilously close to the poverty line and 3 % were struggling with seriously insufficient means.[46]

Female Earnings in Surveys and Budgets

While women in Finland were regularly earning less than men, when working in a segregated labour market, as well as when working in the same factory, it was not out of the question for women to earn a reasonable wage. One the one hand the industrial statistics record average female income levels way below 800 marks per year, on the other it is important to remember, that a large proportion of women in industrial employment were young women between the age of fifteen and twenty-five. Surveys of wage levels in industrial work indicate that apart from gender, time in employment had considerable effect on earnings. Adult women with experience could earn from 65 per cent to 85 per cent of a male wage while girls in their teens were paid 25 to 50 per cent. Therefore, the larger the proportion of young women in each sector, the lower the average earnings.[47] Some efforts were made to calculate the income of adult women in connection with a study of female night work in 1911. While averages could not be calculated, because of the reluctance of the employers to provide exact information, it would seem that the majority of women in industrial night work would have been earning between 430 and 700 to 800 marks per year. There were instances of earnings over 800 marks, even as much as 1200 marks. However there were also examples of earnings between 200 and 300 marks among those recently employed.[48]

It has been said that even after industrialization women tended to be engaged in sectors with links to the household production, that had been their mainstay in previous centuries; the production of food, clothes and care[49]. Sewing was indeed a female dominated sector, often practiced at home by married women and at the premises of employers by young unmarried women. The sector suffered from very low wages. In 1890s Helsinki seamstresses were the lowest paid group among those engaged in crafts, earning about 530 marks per year. A survey of the conditions of seamstresses from 1908 revealed that the majority earned between 300 and 700 marks and earnings of less than 300 marks were a reality for 15 per cent of the women. The sector was particularly badly hit by seasonal unemployment. The survey also revealed that one in ten of the seamstresses were badly paid teenage apprentices.[50] However when statistics were collected on small enterprises in 1913 the average earnings recorded by women engaged in textile work at home, such as knitting and weaving, rose to between 600 and 700 marks per year.[51]

One of the sources that can be used to complement the information from censuses is budget studies. While budget studies can be used for correcting information of overall statistics they unfortunately also suffer from certain drawbacks. Turn of the century statisticians had at some point become almost obsessed with what was called "the normal family", to be included in budget studies. Definitions varied but one invariable characteristic was the presence of very young children in the household. In some cases only families with children under the age of ten were accepted as "normal families". In other cases the children had to be under 15 or 18 or not in employment. By necessity it was more difficult for the wife to be in work outside the home under these conditions and the economic importance of the male household head would be enhanced. While it is true that childbearing could continue through most of the marriage and that young children were present in working class households with mothers in their 40s and 50s, the family situation would be considerably different during the first 10 and the last 5 years of the reproductive cycle. The availability of extra earners or childminders from the family circle could make considerable difference to the opportunities of earning for a woman.[52]

Table 3.3: Female yearly earnings in early twentieth-century Finland.

Budget study 1908	Minimum	Maximum	Industrial statistics	Average Female wages
Textile factory	446 marks	1456	Textile industry 1904	514 marks
Paper mill	509		Paper industry 1912	599
Tobacco factory	596	1770	Tobacco industry 1903	598
Cork factory	453	995	Printing1907	668
Shoe factory	883		Glassworks 1913	505
Factory knitter	510	898	Bakery 1905	559
Seamstress	240	826		
Washerwoman	159	614		
Ironing	467	1106		
Bathhouse worker		888		
Manual labourer	562	839		
Garden worker	629			
Market trader	184	865		
Factory worker	727	789		
House owner	1198			
Textile work at home		1296		
Catering	250	415		

Sources : Hjelt, V., *Undersokning av yrkesarbetarnes lefnadsvillkor I Finland 1908-1909*, (Helsingfors: Industristyrelsen, 1911), pp. 29-30, 138, 153-155 (female household heads only); Snellman, G.,*Undersokning angaende tobaksindustrin* (Helsngfors: Industristyrelsen 1903), pp.86-87; Snellman, G., *Undersokning angaende textilindustrin*, (Helsingfors: Industristyrelsen 1904);
Hjerppe, R. and P, Schyberson, *Kvinnoarbete i industrins genombrottsskede ca. 1850-1913* (Helsinki : University of Helsinki, Department of Social and Economic History,1977), p.15.

Individual budget studies show that while some women had very modest earnings, others earned considerably more than the average proposed by surveys (Table 3.3). The mean earnings by female household heads in a budget study from 1908 was 666 marks per year (about half of the male average in the study), 22 per cent earned more than 800 marks, reaching sums of 1456 from working in textile factory and 1106 from ironing. 37 per cent of the women earned between 600 and 800 marks and less than 10 per cent brought in earnings under 400 marks per year. The highest recorded income was 1770 marks and the lowest 159 marks (for males 2700 and 416).[53] With the added income from lodgers the situation improved (Table 3.4). Those in industrial employment generally earned more than the female average recorded by the industrial statistics, other types of employment was more variable. Determining the size of the earnings of married women in the budget study was problematic, as the earnings of different family members were not always separated. However in the families without children, with only young children or in cases where the survey provided information about the earnings of the wife, we find that out of 60 married women 50 per cent earned less than 400 marks but 50 per cent earned more. Lodgers generated a sizable part of this income, and in many cases board and lodging was provided. Even cleaning and washing could bring in 400 marks per year or even more.[54] This would indicate that the earnings of adult women were about half of those of skilled workers and more than half of the unskilled. As the income of the wife was necessary in many families women did not stop working at marriage, they engaged in different types of work.

Table 3.4 Yearly Income (including lodging) of Women and Female Headed Working Class Families 1908

Earnings of female head*	%	Total family income**	%	Earnings of married women***	%
				0-200	20
0-400 marks	7.5	0-400	-	200-400	35
400-600	29	400-600	5.4	400-600	25
600-800	35	600-800	29.7	600-800	10
800-1000	16	800-1000	24.3	800-1000	6.6
1000-2500	12	1000-2000	32.4	1000-	3.3
		2000-	8.1		
Total	66 women			Total	60 women

* including income from lodgers, ** income of all family members plus rent from lodgers (66 female heads), ***earnings including income from lodgers (60 married women) Source: Hjelt, V. *Undersokning av yrkesarbetarnes lefnadsvillkor I Finland 1908-1909* (Helsingfors: Industristyrelsen 1911), pp. 29-30 138, 153-155, 190-200

Three Ways to Earnings for Married Women and Widows - Trade, Washing and Lodgers

Assisting a husband or working independently: Trade and Hawking

While in early modern times trade was a male privilege the guilds accepted widows carrying on the trade of their husband. Indeed in the statutes of 1734 of Sweden and Finland two exceptions were introduced to the male hegemony, widows and poor women engaged in hawking. The widows were expected to have worked alongside their husbands and therefore having the necessary experience. In the 19th century the regulations were eased and by the 1870s widows and adult unmarried women could run shops without restrictions. In the 1880s 12 per cent of the shopkeepers in Finnish towns were women and in Sweden 27 per cent.[55] In the town of Turku, in south western Finland, one half of the women holding a licence for small business in 1910 were shopkeepers.[56] While married women gained the right to control their income independently of their husbands in 1889 they were still subject to his marital authority when engaged in trade.[57] Even though working in the family business was as normal for the wife of a shopkeeper as that of a farmer, such work was not paid for and often not registered. A sample of the original sheets of the 1900 census revealed that some shopkeepers registered their wives as working in the shop but many did not do so. Wives were left without occupational information and in-living shop assistants could be registered as servants. However, in many a small family enterprise it was often the wife who engaged more actively in the day to day work in the shop. Particularly when the husband had a predilection for drink and the enterprise was located at the home/business premises, many a wife had to take over.[58]

Among poor women trade had been a solution for a long time. Even during the period of regulation the urban authorities would often give such women the right to engage in street hawking of homemade textiles, yarn, children's clothes, ribbons, hair pins etc rather than pay them poor relief. In Helsinki poor widows and daughters were allowed to sell homemade textiles and bread from market stalls. While paying the rent for shop premises could be beyond the capacity of a woman, keeping a coffee and sandwich stall, trading at one of the market places or hawking goods from door to door could be an option.[59] Keeping market stalls had by the late 19th century become a female dominated activity. It was also not unusual for working class widows and married women to sell bread and milk door to door to feed their families. Street hawking of bread and milk was remunerated as a percentage of the price (10-14 %) and it would seem that it was possible to make a living on these earnings particularly with the assistance of some out-relief from the authorities.[60] The concept of a woman selling bread from her basket was such a part of normal life that it found its way into literature.[61]

The registration of such activities could vary considerably. While the census does record women engaged in petty trade it is impossible to tell to what extent their numbers reflect reality. For example a budget study from 1908 included the family of a labourer who spent most of his time unemployed engaged in drinking, not even bothering to chop the firewood. All the belongings had been bought with the savings of the wife, and she now kept the family through bread hawking, work that she had been doing for ten years. At the time of the survey the husband was remitted to the workhouse for seven months to the great relief of his wife. The wife earned between 500 and 600 marks per year. The family was still classified as the family of a labourer with the man as household head and breadwinner. In another family with six young children, the wife sold berries, fruit and flowers at the market and did some washing, earning about 200 marks (⅓ of the husbands' earnings) keeping the family going through periods of unemployment.[62]

Washing and ironing - Half registered, unregistered

Washing has been seen as the activity to which women reverted when no other options were available. While working class biographies reveal that many women did engage in washing, the published census does not specify washing but puts it into the large category of "manual work". In addition, the male household heads filling in census forms did not necessarily note that their wives were engaged in washing. Where women operated from a fixed address and applied for a trading licence they can be located, but generally this would indicate a permanent or economically more solid undertaking. In 1894 some women's organizations tried to survey female work. According to this survey altogether 1136 women were registered as engaged in washing or ironing in urban areas. These businesses were in 90 per cent of the cases one- person enterprises with no employees. The authors pointed out, however, that as washing is generally a part time occupation of married women, it would have been grossly under registered.[63] In 1910 10.000 women were registered as occupationally active in the town of Turku. Of these 10 per cent were licensed to run a business, one half were shopkeepers and one in ten held a licence for washing, ironing or cleaning. Five years earlier however, a study of the living condition among poor people in the town found 234 female household heads engaged in washing and ironing in the most marginalized areas.[64] The municipal statistics of Helsinki listed seven laundries with fifty-three female employees in 1905. However a survey of 10,000 working-class households five years earlier registered 1238 female household heads, of whom 39 per cent were engaged in washing, ironing and cleaning, 225 gave their occupation as washerwoman. No information was gathered about the occupation of wives of male household heads.[65] The same survey revealed that it was not unusual for working-class families to engage in crafts or money making activities in the home. Because the aims of the survey were concentrated around hygienic issues the observations were geared to register activities taking place in the dwelling, not occupational activity. As a result washing was never registered as home work, because it usually took place in the washhouse or some other outbuilding. On the other hand the study reveals that 211 women were engaged in textile work and 138 women were ironing in the small, one or two room flats.[66]

While washing and ironing often went hand in hand the combination of washing with cleaning was not uncommon. Women cleaning schools or working on part time basis for wealthy families would however not necessarily have an occupation in the census. For example the Helsinki tram company offered the job of cleaning trams at the depot, in the night, to the wives of their employees. These wives of male breadwinners cleaned trams between 2 and 6 in the morning and then came home to make the family's breakfast.[67]

The nature of the work

Washing was hard work and badly paid but not plagued by the unemployment problems of some other sectors. In general two systems were in operation. In the one case the washerwoman picked up the washing, washed it at home and brought it back clean. In the other she washed at the premises of the employer on washing days, either alone or with assistance from the servant(s) of the house. Many families had an established relationship with a particular washerwoman who came at regular intervals. The families were visited for the "large wash", monthly or 2-3 times a year, in some cases more often. The undertaking could take several days, with soaking, bleaching, boiling, drying and mangling. In such cases it could be customary for the employer to provide nourishing food to help with the hard work. Some houses had a washhouse in the yard with in-built cauldrons and tubs. Many washerwomen who worked from home dragged the sheets down to the sea for rinsing at all times of the year because of water charges.[68]

Working at a laundry was not necessarily easier than work as an independent washerwoman. Oral history accounts have documented children as young as six assisting their mothers in the early years of the 20th century. Often the working day ended so late that the night was spent at the laundry rather than going back home.[69]

Income from washing

The income from such an undertaking naturally varied, the 1894 survey stated that the daily income from washing would vary from 80 penny to 1 mark 50 penny per day with meals included. A survey among workers in 1890s Helsinki estimated the daily income for washing at 1 mark and that of ironing as 1.50 for a 12 hour day (430-450 marks/year), the earnings of a painter and decorator was registered as varying between 1.97 and 3.58 per day.[70] 1898 the washerwomen in Helsinki formed their own union with the aim of raising their daily earnings from 1mk 50 and cutting down their working day. Not everybody acted with solidarity and there were women willing to do washing at reduced prices undercutting the charges of their colleagues. In addition the water costs created a problem when the sea became too polluted for the rinsing of sheets and the municipal rinsing houses were closed down after 1908. The employers did not like the idea of unionization. The middle class women formed an organization, which among other things had the purpose of boycotting all unionized servants. To what extent this also affected the washer women is not however clear.[71]

The information collected by the statistics office in 1913 revealed that of women running a one person laundering and or ironing business, those who provided information about earnings often earned between 400 and 800 marks per year. However, more than one third earned less than 400 marks and only 12 per cent more than 1,000 marks. A collection of working class budgets from 1908 gives examples of washer women earning around 400 marks per year, sometimes more, i.e. half of the earnings of the husband, but in some cases less. Washing was also combined with cleaning and or textile work in the households of manual workers.[72]

"I guess they were rich as they didn't have any young men?" Lodgers and lodging

Lodging had long roots in the rural Nordic society and came to flourish among the urban working class in the late 19th century. It was however not unheard of even among the higher social strata. Kin, friends and men or women with no suitable relations in town or schoolchildren boarded out populated the extra rooms of the middle class families and beds or floors of the working class.[73]

In the year 1900 a survey into working class housing was conducted in Helsinki. In the process 10.000 working class households in different parts of the town were studied. Information was gathered about the size, condition and location of the dwelling, about the availability of heating facilities, access to water, toilets, washhouses etc. In addition information was gathered about the inhabitants; their professions, family circumstances, lodgers and also about economic activity in the home. While it had been known that the working classes provided space for lodgers and that lodging was common in this group, it was a wake up call to those sceptical about the benefits of lodging to find that no less than 38 per cent of the households in the study kept lodgers. The majority of the lodgers were men but women were also present. In some cases whole families or mothers with children took lodging in the household of an unrelated family (Table 3.5). Ten years later another survey of similar size revealed that no less than 50 per cent of the working-class households kept lodgers.[74] If the family had more than one room or a room and kitchen, the second one was almost invariably let out.[75]

Similar co-habitation patterns were revealed when a sample of census sheets of working class households in Helsinki were analysed for this study. One family in two kept lodgers and some had more than one.[76]

Such a situation cannot be considered unusual in a rapidly growing town. Oral history accounts describe a system where the first lodgings of a young person from the countryside, was with a relative or the relative of a neighbour from back home. Later lodgings were found through work mates.[77]

Table 3.5: Survey of housing conditions of the working class in Helsinki 1900.

	Total	Men	Women	Children
Persons in survey	45.947	37 per cent	37 per cent	25 per cent
Lodgers in survey	6829	63 per cent	34 per cent	3 per cent
Lodgers of all persons in survey		25 per cent	13 per cent	2 per cent
Households in survey	10.419			
Households with lodgers	38 per cent			

Source: Sucksdorff, V., Arbetarebefolkningens i Helsingfors bostadsforhallanden, redogorelse for Arbetarebostadsundersokningen ar 1900, (Helsingfors: Halsovardsnamnden, 1904), pp. 33, 244-246

Rent and income from lodging

The survey of working-class housing conditions of 1900 recorded that the most common rent paid by lodgers varied between 4,5 and 6 marks per month, some paid less and some paid more but the vast majority paid about 5 marks.[78] The average rent depended on the size of the flat, the location and to some extent on the size of the family. Landlords saw it as perfectly reasonable to charge more for the same premises if the family had many children as it created more wear and tear. The census of 1900 registered rents of around 20 marks per month, with a variation from 16 to 25 marks in working class areas (Table 3.6). The housing surveys revealed somewhat higher rents depending on location and size of the family.[79] With a rent of 20 marks per month (240 marks per year) a contribution of 60 marks or 120, in the case of two lodgers, could mean the difference between keeping the flat through unemployment or not. Elsewhere in Finland the rents were lower and so would the contribution of the lodger be, but the proportion of the contribution was similar. Documentation on the economic situation of widows on poor relief in the textile town of Tampere in 1900 has revealed that some of the widows kept lodgers who paid about half of the rent.[80] Of 103 couple households in northern Helsinki 1900 50 % had lodgers and 29 per cent had 2 lodgers or more. Therefore in 21 per cent of the families an income of at least 60 marks per year would be available and in 29 percent of the families an extra 120 marks would come in to help with the family spending.[81]

Table 3.6: Size of monthly rents in Helsinki and rents paid by lodgers 1900 and 1910.

Survey 1910 all house-holds	Census 1900 Couples	Census 1900 Widows	Rent paid by lodgers 1900	%
24-27 marks (1room)	23 marks *	21-22 marks**	Less than 4.5 marks	23 %
43-44 marks (2 rooms)		16 marks***	4.5-6 marks	60 %
			More than 6 marks	16 %

* Average for 100 working class households in Northern Helsinki, **Average for widows' households Northern Helsinki in the vicinity of the marketplace, *** average at a greater distance from the marketplace (150 widows).

Sources: Sucksdorff 'Arbetarebfolkningen' 1904, p. 255; Gauffin, A., *Bostadsbehof och barnantal med afseende sarskildt a inneboendesystemet i arbetarfamiljerna i Helsingfors*, (Helsingfors: Foreningen for framjande af allmannyttig byggnadsverksamhet, 1915), pp. 24-26; Helsinki Census 1900, original sheets, National Archives, Helsinki.

If the lodger had only lodgings, morning coffee on weekdays and dinner on Sunday were included in the rent, but other meals would not be forthcoming. Some dined on bread and ham while others bought food from a stall.[82] As in Britain and elsewhere in the Nordic countries keeping lodgers could vary considerably depending on the conditions. Some women held on to large premises and were running veritable guesthouses providing food lodging and washing. In such cases the income of the wife could be considerable, compared to that of their husband.[83] The census sheets mention lodgers with food and lodging and budget studies show examples of cooking for lodgers and the lodgers of others. In the cases where schoolchildren or foster children were cared for it is obvious that the undertaking included food and washing.[84] The income from a lodger wanting board and lodging could vary from 290 to nearly 400 marks per year and with additional washing even moré. As transpired from the 1908 study no less than 415 marks was earned by one of the "housewives" from providing meals to people in lodgings.[85] In some instances services were exchanged, female lodgers provided help in the household or male lodgers repaired shoes in return for having their clothes washed.[86] Estimating the economic value of some of these services is difficult but one has to assume it created a mutual advantage.

While the economic impact for an individual family could be considerable, women also provided a service to the growing urban community. As this was part of the hidden economy calculations of overall turnover are difficult. A cautious estimate for the year 1919 can however be made based on the survey of living conditions in Helsinki and a study of income and expenditure the following year. In 1919 the households in central Helsinki included nearly 19.000 lodgers or boarders which would suggest cash transfers between 6.5 and 13 million marks per year, depending on the percentage boarders and the quality of the lodgings.[87]

Female Survival Strategies

Increasing Income – Collaboration with Lodgers and Children

It has been demonstrated above that the image of women depending on a husband bringing in the money is not correct. In addition to the work registered in the census considerable activity was taking place. The problem, however, when faced with the situation of having full and continuous responsibility for the upkeep of a family, instead of throughout periods of unemployment, was the lower level of earnings. In Britain female earnings have been calculated to represent about 30–50 per cent of male manual workers, depending on activity, the more casual the lower the remuneration.[88] The budget study from early twentieth-century Finland seems to indicate that the income opportunities might have been slightly better. It would seem that it was not impossible for women to reach earnings similar to unskilled males. Even in the analysis of the budgets the question was raised by those compiling the work if this could be typical, as the female earnings seemed higher than had been expected.[89] The difference might have been linked to the fact that the women in the study were adult, unlike the population used for calculating mean earnings for women in industrial work.

Table 3.7: Cohabitation patters of couples and widows in the working-class part of Helsinki, according to the census 1900.

Married couple	Nr	percentage	Widows	percentage
With lodger (s)	50	46	95	61
With relative	10	9	6	4
With employees	8	7	2	1.2
With foster child	3	2.7	11	7
Nuclear family only	35	32	40	25
Married child			11	7
Altogether	109		158	

Source: Census of Helsinki 1900, 109 couples and 158 widow headed households in Northern Helsinki, Original census sheets, National Archives.

Widows 18 % no occupation and lodger, 58 % had an earning child in the household.

Women also developed support networks with workmates and lodgers. One in three of the female household heads in the study gained extra income from lodgers, a rate similar to that of working class households in general.[90] A comparison with data from the 1900 census of Helsinki on the other hand reveals that two thirds of the widows in working class areas had lodgers in their household (Table 3.7).[91] Such variation could be explained by the fact that the budgets were collected from a number of locations including areas with low levels of rent.

Helsinki was an expensive place to live with an average rent of 340 marks per year while in Tampere the mean rent was 206 marks and in the small industrial community of Forssa only 74 marks.[92] The effect on the household income of keeping lodgers was however considerable. While the mean income for female household heads, according to the budgets, was 660 marks, the same budgets reveal that if lodging is taken into account female income rose to 744 marks. The relations between landlady and lodger could also be quite close if the lodger was a friend, in some cases the co-habitation could last for decades and take the parties through very difficult times. Services could be exchanged, particularly child-minding, but also help during unemployment or even child-birth.[93] Even if the relationship was more distant it could mean the difference between keeping the room or not when there were employment problems. The oral history accounts telling about sharing with work-mates is certainly substantiated by an analysis of female households in the 1900 census where finding women sharing an occupation is a commonplace in all female households.[94]

When exploring parts of the hidden economy in the working class budgets it transpired that labourers' wives, in small towns and industrial areas, kept pigs and chickens, even cows providing milk for the family eight months of the year. Potato growing was often practiced when the family owned their cottage and bartering systems involving clothes and other items were also in operation in the local communities. Oral history collections also reveal that those with a particular skill were using it in non-monetary exchanges.[95] In early twentieth-century Helsinki the co-operative movement started making available allotments, for the purpose of growing potatoes and vegetables, available for hire to the working population for a nominal sum. A coastal town like Helsinki also provided opportunities for gathering fire-wood by the seashore, another way of contributing to the household, a job that was often taken on by children.[96]

When widows and abandoned mothers had to shoulder the role of provider they had to keep their children, but the children could also make contributions, as they did in couple headed households. The budget study analysed the budgets of sixty female households, thirty-three of these were headed by widows or abandoned women. The women were all occupationally active and all but one had children in the household. Half of the widows were industrial workers while half were engaged in typically female activities like washing, ironing, sewing form home etc. 36 per cent had another adult, generally a child over eighteen in the household. Even though 63 per cent had only minors in the household some of these managed to generate some income. Working as a paper boy or running errands were common ways for children to earn small sums of money.[97] While the widows earned less than the cohort on average the family income could be reasonable if several children were in employment. Most of children's earnings were absorbed into a communal economy in these families. Pocket money was handed out or small sums kept for lunches etc but where the economic situation was problematical the children would provide a total contribution if they lived at home. In 20 per cent of the families the contribution of the children was more than one third of the family income and in another 20 per cent less than one tenth of the total while in one third oft of the families the contribution varied between 10 and 30 percent of the total earnings. In all female headed households the average economic contribution of children and other family members was 28 per cent, i.e. higher than the 17 per cent in male headed household with children under working age.[98] Women did however not only collaborate with their children. Women's budgets and industrial surveys reveal cohabitation between adult women and their mothers and siblings in widowhood, when abandoned or as single mothers. They also reveal a tendency among daughters to stand by their mothers to a greater extent than sons.[99] No less than 52 per cent of 2500 seamstresses surveyed in 1904 lived with family. Even those heading households showed a tendency to share household with mothers and sisters. Even in the 1920s co-operation between mothers and daughters in industrial work was common.[100] Similar tendencies to female kinship clustering have been recorded in other Nordic towns in the late nineteenth and early twentieth century. While working-class men in Stockholm were found to occasionally assist mothers economically even after marriage, daughters tended to remain in the parental household, if the mother was widowed, and pool their income with her. Frequent examples can also be found of cohabitation between a widowed mother and a widowed, abandoned or unmarried daughter with children. Widows with young children seem to have sought the company of kin or taken in lodgers for the purpose of economic survival or assistance with childcare.[101] Kinship contacts with relatives in the countryside were not necessarily lost, children could be sent to relatives for the summer to eat and help with farm work, or food items like potatoes could be sent to relatives in town to help with the upkeep.[102]

Female Strategies – Reduction and Re-structuring of Spending

While increasing income through keeping lodgers or sharing with family was a popular female strategy, the other way to approach existence on lower income levels was through cuts in spending.

Female headed households can be found to live in cheaper accommodation than families with a male head. Of the families in the budget study so called normal male headed households paid on average 196 marks per year in rent while female headed households paid 144 marks. Similar differences could also be detected when comparing rent costs of couples and of women in the Helsinki census (Table 3.6). While staying within reasonable walking distance from the central part of town, with its employment opportunities, widows sought the cheaper flats further out rather than the more expensive ones near the market place in northern Helsinki. Even when taking up residence more centrally, they tended to rent the cheaper rooms rather than the larger and lighter locations. While couples often tried to rent two rooms or a room and kitchen, for the purpose of renting out one, widows and single women shared their only room with the lodgers.[103] An even cheaper option could be taking lodgings with a family, which did happen even when the widow or unmarried woman had a child. Single women could even get board and lodging for 300 marks per year.[104]

The cost of living also depended on the size of the family and the sex and age of the family members. While the average food cost for all families in the budget study of 1908 was 927 marks per year, a family of two spent only 587 mark and one of three 678 mark. On average the female headed households were smaller than those headed by men.[105]

Traditionally studies of standards of living have assumed that all family members have equal access to family resources. Therefore wage levels and GDP have been viewed as satisfactory sources to the life of families in the past. However, already in the nineteenth century social reformers were aware of the fact that wives and children could suffer deprivation when efforts were made to satisfy the needs of the household head.

In urban working class households the economic position of the wife could be weak, her earning potential bad and chances to care for her children without a husband problematic. Hence many working class wives disregarded their own welfare in their efforts to keep the family together. The gender in-balance in food distribution within poor working-class households could, in the worst cases, result in conditions of female starvation. However, it was far from extraordinary that household heads allowed themselves considerable 'top shaving' for alcohol and tobacco, at the expense of their families.[106]

The assumption has often been made that a household with more income was a household where the family member had a higher standard of living. The labour market gave systematic advantages to male workers in the shape of higher earnings. However males were perennial consumers of pricey items like meat, butter and alcohol. The idea that a man 'needs' such things was ingrained in the mental landscape of the working class.[107] Working-class budgets do not always reveal the costs to the family. Drink taken outside the home was often not included in the budgets or it could be hidden under the heading miscellaneous expenses. Sometimes both husband and wife conspired against giving outsiders information on drink. At times, however, the wife was ignorant about actual expenditure as it was taken out of overtime perks or even raises.[108] It is however obvious that with considerable amounts being spent on alcohol in society, the working classes cannot have been sober. Hirdman estimates that about 12 per cent of an urban Swedish working class budget was spent on drink.[109] In Helsinki the breweries were turning out 8 million litres of beer per year around the year 1900, but the working class budgets records expenditure of 1-2 per cent. Oral history collections reveal that it was commonplace for men to send out for beer from work, particularly on Saturdays, but even at other times drinking at work was not unusual. The police statistics of people being drunk and disorderly reveal a town with alcohol problems.[110]

Adult sons could use up almost half their contribution to the household budget in meat while contributing less than their sisters. Unlike men, women tended to adjust their consumption to fit their means.[111] The other family members could be second class citizens when food was distributed, to the extent that wives and young children could be malnourished while the household head was in the rudest of health. The male share of the budget was not restricted to the period of employment but a male privilege. Therefore adult males could prove to be a burden to a household instead of an asset.

Table 3.8: Expenditure in working-class families 1908–9, Finland.

Items	Expenditure per family Male headed households* Mean %	Female headed households minimum %	Female headed household maximum %	Expenditure per family Female headed households** Mean %
Bread, flour, grain	25.7	17	40	27.4
Milk	17.8	12	33	21.2
Butter	13.9	5	20	11.9
Meat	11.3	2	15	7.6
All meat and fish products	16.8	5	26	12.6
Potatoes	4.5	1	7	3.3
Sugar	7.4	5	14	4.7
Coffee	4.6	2	14	9.7
Of total on food	54	39	71	56
Of total on rent	12	7	25	17
Household size	5.3	2	9	3.7

Source: Hjelt, V. *Undersokning av yrkesarbetarnes lefnadsvillkor I Finland 1908-1909.* Helsingfors: Industristyrelsen 1911), pp.79, 86, 140-201

A comparison of the male and female headed households of the budget study reveals that the household without adult males had no expenditure on alcohol and tobacco. In families headed by a man more money was spent on meat and butter (Table 3.8). Because of lower income levels the share of food of the total budget was slightly higher in female headed households (56 per cent) than in male headed households (54 per cent). The amount spent per person and day was 47 pence in women's households and 50 pence in male headed units. The structure of the spending was however different. Where women did not have to cater for the male taste less meat was bought and a larger share of the food budget was spent on bread and milk. Women bought less butter but slightly more cheese and considerably more vegetables. While the Nordic porridge and rye bread consumption made its mark in both male and female diets, women satisfied their families with a higher proportion of these commodities. On the other hand the presence of larger quantities of milk gave the children some decent sustenance. A calculation of available calories per person and day in 34 female headed households gives a result of 2050 calories per person. Converted to consumption units the result would be 3200 calories. The figures for male-headed households would be 1830 per person and 3700 per consumption unit (Table 3.9).[112]

Table 3.9: Consumption of foodstuffs per year in male headed and female headed working-class families 1908–9, Finland.

Items	Male head per family/year 210	Male head per person/y 1113	Female head per family/y 34	Female head per person/y 127
Bread, flour	512 kg	97 kg	442 kg	120 kg
Milk	1079 lit	203 lit	845 lit	225 lit
Butter	44 kg	8.3 kg	31 kg	8 kg
Cheese	13 kg	2.5 kg	10.6 kg	2.8 kg
Meat	80 kg	15 kg	44.6 kg	12 kg
Sausage	16 kg	3 kg	12.8 kg	3.5 kg
Fish	31 kg	5.8 kg	20.5 kg	5.5 kg
Potato	399 kg	75 kg	238 kg	64 kg
Vegetables	13 lit	2.4 lit	39 lit	10 lit
Sugar	60 kg	11.3 kg	44 kg	12 kg
Coffee	19.5 kg	3.6 kg	17.6 kg	5 kg
Calories/day	9728 cal	1834 cal	7729 cal	2050 cal

210 male headed households,113 individuals, mean size 5.3 persons, 34 female headed households, 127 individuals, mean size 3.9 persons.
Source: Hjelt, V. *Undersokning av yrkesarbetarnes lefnadsvillkor I Finland 1908-1909* (Helsingfors; Industristyrelsen, 1911), pp. 79, 140–201

The basis for the consumption unit is uneven distribution. One assumes that children and teenagers need less food than adult males. In some cases radically less. That children did get less in the working class areas of Helsinki is evidenced by the health surveys in primary schools of the early twentieth century.[113] The redistributed spending of women had however the consequence that by replacing expensive meat calories with cheap milk calories the protein intake could be kept at a reasonable level. The higher intake of vegetables also provided some assistance to health and development. Feeding a family on a lower income did demand skill and acumen. One way was buying old bread from the bakery or reduced items from rural traders on their way into or out of the marketplace.[114]

Despite their best efforts the income did not always match the expenditure. While 40 per cent of the women who supported family members were able to balance their budgets, almost 60 per cent were in deficit. The problem was one that faced the working class in general, 53 per cent of the households with male heads were also unable to meet their costs. In the case of single women the situation was slightly better, only 37 per cent were spending more than they earned. In some cases, however the overspending was less than 10 marks per year. The shortage of funds was covered through borrowing, trips to the pawnbrokers, the use of savings and owing the tradesmen.[115] Women did also approach the poor relief authorities and private charities for assistance, particularly on a temporary basis.[116] While women were still able to work or could be part of a kinship network such assistance proved to be only a part of a bundle encompassing work, family collaboration, lodging and auxiliary income generation activities. Only when old age brought a situation of incapacity combined with lack of family and or friends did assistance from society as main support become a realistic option.[117]

Conclusion

Women's work has been badly registered in the past, in addition, they were often not given credit for work like caring for lodgers, apprentices, foster children and adult family members. Censuses, designed by middle class statisticians based on information provided by male household heads, are often unreliable in their registration of married women's work and should if possible be complemented with other sources of information. 1930s studies of working class life have also been found to downplay the economic input of women. While the middle classes were obsessed with the domestic role of women, the glamorizing of motherhood, the home and the romantic notion of domestic bliss also penetrated the ideology of the working classes. At a time when in reality sweated homework decreased and more women entered the labour force, the domestic ideal had been internalized by many male unions as well as 'good' working class mothers.[118]

The unfair wage structure is a historical fact going back into rural society. Urbanization did little to close the wage gap. However, while turn of the century (1900) studies highlighted the plight of some women when trying to survive on low wages there is no doubt that many women in employment supported not only themselves but also other family members.[119] The reckless classifying of women (and children) as passively living of the earnings of a male breadwinner in early 20th century urban Finland is far from the historic reality. All men were not able to support a family but were dependent on an economic input from wife and children. The problem for married women was the presence of household duties and the effect of pregnancies and child-care on the ability to participate in employment outside the home, the only work that was registered.

Therefore they would work at low paid tasks such as washing and ironing and brought in sums that in many cases provided the rent and food in families with unemployed or absent so called bread-winners. It is also necessary to include all income sources, not only wages, when studying coping mechanisms, in the case of married women and widows lodging provided a considerable share.

Unlike for married women, work of widows was acceptable and respectable. There are even examples of special bonuses instituted to carry widows and bread-winners through difficult times.[120] Widows also registered their own occupation and had therefore higher participation rates in the census. The level of earnings depended on profession and considerable variation was evident. However, wages were usually linked to time in employment and widows did not have to take time off for childbirth, which contributed to the chance of earning a living wage. The income information in budget studies confirm that the female household heads earned on average 50 per cent of the wages of a skilled worker and other studies have revealed that this comes close to the yearly earnings of an unskilled man. Although widows were to be found frequently among the recipients of outdoor poor relief and their children could benefit from the efforts of private charities, such income only formed a fraction of the family budget. A scrutiny of the household composition of widows reveals that multiple strategies were in operation. Co-operation with family members like sisters and mothers was in evidence. When the children reached the age to contribute economically the situation improved and delayed departure by daughters or even intermittent or continuous co-residence in mother-daughter systems was frequent. Lodgers were another option. Widows could run households with more than one lodger and in some cases board and lodging was provided. While young single lodgers could move frequently, examples have been found on family like systems where the lodger stayed for years or even decades.[121]

Women also cut down on expenditure by avoiding things like alcohol and tobacco. They spent more on milk and less on meat than families headed by adult males. Women rented smaller or cheaper flats in less desirable locations. Another option was sharing or taking lodgings, which happened even when the woman had children to support. While their budgets were indeed modest they had the ability to cope. In doing so they provided the growing urban areas with their labour, officially in the market or in the unofficial service sector

It is highly unlikely that we will be able to find exact data on the working life of married women, we might be permanently left with 'married women did not work' and 'everybody went out washing and cleaning'. The paradox remains that a married woman who washed and cleaned was a housewife but a widow who washed and cleaned was a washerwoman or cleaner. What we have been able to do, however, is to reassess the assumption that when women did work they only earned insignificant sums and had to depend on family members or the poor relief authorities for support. Women assisted in providing for their families but they also successfully acted as breadwinners. The question should also perhaps be raised whether their economic input in the lodging sector should not be noted when making calculations about the economic output in growing urban centres like Helsinki.

4 WOMEN, HOUSEHOLDS AND INDEPENDENCE UNDER THE OLD ENGLISH POOR LAWS

Susannah Ottaway

I thank God I am indeed endued with such qualities that if I were turned out of the realm in my petticoat, I were able to live in any place of Christendom. – Queen Elizabeth I, 1566[1]

I have been the more particular in describing the Management of this School, because the Ladies, who have the Oversight of it, seem to have carry'd it to the utmost Perfection, so as to enable the Children to shift honestly by their own Industry, if it should be their lot to be cast into any Part of the Kingdome where they might be friendless. – A Letter from a Gentleman at Greenwich to his Friend in London, regarding the Girls School at that Place, 1724.[2]

These quotations are separated by a chasm as wide chronologically as socially, but they express a common ideal of early modern English society: every person, regardless of circumstance, should be able to support herself independently. This valuing of self-sufficiency has important implications for the lives of poor women, especially in relationship to their household and family. As recent research has demonstrated, family economies were essential to the maintenance of independence, and that independence was the essence of the aspirations and self-image of even the lower classes.[3] And yet, of course, it could be extremely difficult for poor women, especially, to develop effective strategies for self-reliance, and it may seem problematic to assume that the poor shared the well articulated ideals of their economic 'betters'. In fact, some historians have even challenged the notion that the poor had 'household economies' in the early modern era.[4]

Moreover, coinciding with this valorization of independence was an equally evident mistrust of disconnection from family and friends.[5] Hence, in the quotations above, we note that the ability of the women to support themselves away from place of origin, and without friends, was presumed to be a great achievement. We can begin to get some insight into the fear of isolation from the case of Ann Bowman, a pauper woman from Cumberland whose letters Steve Hindle has used to illuminate the family life of the poor. Bowman pleaded with her local overseer of the poor in 1710:

'I being old and feeble and infirm desire I may not be confined to an old ruinous house which is without the cry of any neighbours and of which the officers in [the parish] were speaking: for that unmerciful and savage behavior would have pined me to death with hunger...[they] would confine me to a dismal corner where none might relieve or help me ...'[6]

While Hindle has used this and other pauper letters to argue convincingly for the place of neighborhood and community in the lives of the poor, Bowman's words also beg the question of the importance of location, reminding us to look both at the space in which poor households were located and at the people who occupied those homes. Thus in order to understand the choices of poor women in regards to their housing and co-residents, we need to spend considerable time unpacking the nature of household form and formation that we find in the context of English communities.

For all that we know about the poverty of women and children in the European past, there has been a relative lack of historical work on early modern English women's place of residence: their lives as mothers, members of households, and independent agents, using their domestic resources and personal connections to make their way in the world.[7] Historians of the poor in Europe have relied upon the concept of the 'economy of makeshift' to explain the patchwork economies of workers and paupers, but few have taken the time to ask, 'What did poor men and women seek to make shift *for*?'[8] This chapter argues that it is important to consider place of residence and household make-up as a central concern of poor women in eighteenth-century England. The powerful ideal of residential independence, alongside the evident mistrust of isolation, shaped the worldview of poor women who had profound disadvantages in meeting these ideals. The comparison of these ideals with the experiences of poor women makes for a fruitful arena to address the central themes of this collection. Here, I will make particular reference to the different experiences of women in disparate stages of the life-course, highlighting the importance of adult children to women in their middle-age and beyond.

Several decades ago, Olwen Hufton noted that poor widows and spinsters in eighteenth-century France often formed 'clusters', using shared housing as an important strategy for survival in urban areas.[9] There is evidence of similar co-residence patterns in England, too, but unlike in France, we know that some of the choices that the English poor made in regards to their place of residence were forced upon them by local authorities under the aegis of the poor laws. Overseers of the poor and churchwardens, unpaid men who controlled the distribution of England's locally collected and distributed poor rates, could and often did insist that they would only assist a poor person who moved into another home, almshouse, or even workhouse.

Household listings, pauper letters, poor relief distribution lists, and many other sources can shed light on the issues at hand. It is easy to see, for instance, that gender (as well as age) affected the residential patterns of parents and children, and several case studies have shown the ways in which pauper women positioned themselves relative to relieving authorities.[10] This chapter focuses on the evidence that concerns place of residence for women who were in danger of, or were suffering from poverty in two rural Dorsetshire parishes in the eighteenth century. Because the presence of a spouse obscures the view of women's particular patters and experiences, we will consider women without co-residential spouses. While no one could argue that the parishes were 'typical' of all pre-industrial England, the residential patterns that they reveal serve as an important comparison to studies of the urban poor, and they help to remind us to look beyond employment and welfare when examining the survival strategies of poor women in the European past.[11] After examining the household listings, the chapter turns to a brief exploration of women's position in workhouses as a way to deepen our understanding of the plight of poor women and their agency in shaping their experiences of the poor relief system. We will see that poor women used a range of strategies, and faced an array of possible outcomes in their efforts to maintain both residential independence and connection to family and community.

Women's Households: Corfe Castle, 1790

Earlier studies have demonstrated some of the ways in which gender and socio-economic status influenced the structure of households and families in pre-industrial England.[12] A closer look at residence patterns in one of the most detailed pre-modern listings – that of Corfe Castle, Dorset, from 1790, gives us a particularly vivid picture of the make-up of households in a rural community.

The Corfe Castle household listing is like most early modern censuses in that it clearly divides the residents of the parish into their household groups, but unlike most, it provides more specific information on co-residency, and the nature of the relationship amongst household members, as well as on income and employment. Corfe's listing was created under the direction of Sir William Moreton Pitt, M.P., and is indicative of his general interests in issues of work, population, housing and poverty.[13] As well as the usual range of employment in agriculture, spinning and weaving, this Dorset parish of 1239 residents benefitted from the work provided by clay extraction, thanks to its location in the Purbeck Hills.

Corfe residents were typical of early modern populations in their tendency to avoid isolation; out of 256 inhabited houses, only 10 contained solitary women 'housekeepers'(as the heads of household were labeled in the Corfe listing), and only 4 men apparently lived alone.[14] Interestingly, 3 of the 10 lone women were on parish pay, but none of the men were. These 3 women, however, were hardly living in isolation; Sarah Jenkins, for example, a 66 year-old widow on parish pay, lived in the house listed next to Ann Rolle, a 38 year-old baker, and the other two lone paupers, Elizabeth Dams and Julian Webber, a widow and spinster in their sixties, lived on the apparently crowded High Street, with just two houses listed between them. This tendency for solitary poor women to live close by one another in densely populated parts of the town may suggest that they lived in parish owned houses, or even perhaps in separate dwelling spaces within another's house. It also highlights for us the surprising difficulty of defining what qualifies as solitary dwelling, when one is using a source that is not perfectly clear on the nature of the categories used by the census taker, and where the relationships among people in different houses is never spelled out. Thus, for example, we could perhaps classify some other individuals as 'solitary' in the sense that they are seemingly isolated from kin, as in the case of a 56-year old poor widow who is probably paid to house the 12 year-old pauper girl who lives with her, or in the cases of the five people (one woman and four men) who lived just with servants. But these people seem to occupy a household type halfway between residential isolation and a spinster-widow cluster.

There were many more houses that clearly contained 'clusters' of widows and spinsters, and widowers and bachelors (though still no where near the number of complete nuclear family households, which remained by far the most common household type in Corfe Castle). Table 4.1 shows two calculations. In one column, we count as 'clusters' not only homes where unrelated single people cohabited, but also those households in which a man or woman lived with a child whom we would normally expect to have moved out of the parental dwelling, and to be capable of significant contributions to the household income (so boys and girls over age fourteen). There are twenty-two female-headed households, and twenty-five male-headed households of this nature. Of these, thirteen female clusters (59 per cent) contained one or more residents on parish pay, while only four male households were poor (16 per cent). If we narrow our definition and exclude those households where the cluster comes from cohabitation with adult or nearly adult children, thereby only including households that cluster non-nuclear kin, or unrelated individuals, then the figures shrink to fifteen female and seventeen male clusters. Of these, nine female and four male-headed households had residents on parish pay (60 per cent and 24 per cent, respectively).

Table 5. 1: Solitary and Clustered Living Situations: Corfe Castle, 1790.

	All Females	Poor Females	All Males	Poor Males
Solitary	10	3	5	0
Clusters (incl. children>14)	22	13	25	4
Clusters w/o family clusters	15	9	17	4

Source: Corfe Castle Listing, Copy at Cambridge Group for the History of Population and Social Structure.

In sum, if we look at how women without spouses were making shift in this Dorset parish, we find that ten women housekeepers were solitary, and twenty-two were part of clusters of other women (and sometimes men) in similar circumstances. An additional four female-headed households contained their married children and grandchildren (two with married sons and two with married daughters). Finally, five women housekeepers were lone mothers with young children, at least three of whom were on parish pay. The evidence from Corfe Castle highlights the importance of shared housing for the poor in this Dorset parish. While only one third of the solitary women were paupers (and these may actually have been women who lived in shared housing with their close neighbours), almost two thirds of clustered women received parish poor relief. We do not know to what extent their housing was determined by the overseers of the poor and churchwardens, but it seems very likely that this was the case, and in this regard, the women stand in strong contrast to the men, who tended to cluster with others in their occupations, and to stay off the poor relief rolls if they lived in shared housing.

One more aspect of the Corfe evidence bears mentioning. Although it is clear that children of both sexes were important co-residents for Corfe Castle poor women, we find that daughters played a particularly significant role, especially for elderly women. While men aged sixty or more who headed households lived with sons fairly often (twelve with daughters, six with sons, and five with both), older female householders lived overwhelmingly with daughters rather than sons. Six women housekeepers in their sixties through eighties lived with a daughter, and only one with a son; none lived with children of both sexes. (In percentages, 30 per cent with daughters, and 5 per cent with sons, of all households headed by women over the age of fifty-nine). In Corfe Castle, then, the older a woman grew, the less likely she was to use the presence of an adult son to make shift, and the more likely she was to turn to co-habitation with other women.

Households and the Poor, Puddletown, 1724

A helpful comparison to Corfe Castle, and a source that allows us to deepen our understanding of the ways poverty and poor relief shaped poor women's households, is an even more detailed account of a population in the nearby parish of Puddletown, Dorset. In 1724, Puddletown's extraordinarily active vicar, Henry Dawnay, compiled a house by house record of his parish, an area of mixed farming with a population at the time of 612, who lived in just over 150 household units, 115 of which were located in the town, proper, and on which we will focus here, since the outlying areas were recorded at a different date. Because the list has gaps in its records of some houses, ages and household information, it has not been used by those who have pursued quantitative analyses of early modern household listings. But the 'Dawnay Census'is exceptionally useful in its detailed account of poor households, and, because I have completed a partial reconstruction of the parish, here I can cross-reference the listing with the parish registers, vestry minutes and overseers' accounts to shed much light on the residential situation of the parish poor.[15] Of particular interest for our purposes is one street in the parish: New Street, which forms an arc in the Southeast of the parish, and still exists, abutting fields, a short walk from the town center.

New Street was the slum equivalent of this sleepy southwestern parish. The twenty-three households counted up by Dawnay (four of which were located in shared houses, but which were nevertheless counted as separate 'families") contained fourteen families who received some assistance from the parish overseers. Six of these households were on full parish pensions; six received help sporadically, but were clearly vulnerable to poverty (as many got help later in life), and two others were in receipt of a variety of small payments primarily in kind. Of the remaining nine households that stayed free of overt dependence on the parish overseers, four received charitable assistance from the Churchwardens through either Bradish's Charity (which gave coats to men, Bibles to children, and money to women), Lady Walpole's charity, or another unnamed parish charitable fund, which also distributed small cash payouts. Thus only five of these twenty-three homes appear to have been entirely self-supporting in the 1720s and 1730s. How did their poverty and dependence affect the living situations of these paupers, and in what way did the poor women fare differently from the men?

One aspect of the poor households that sets them apart from the other neighborhoods in Puddletown was their impermanence. According to Dawnay's census, seven of the families on New Street moved away before a year had passed. Six of these were complete nuclear families and included at least some young children; the other was an older couple living without other co-residents. All seven of these mobile families were relatively free of dependence on the parish; three of them remaining completely off the parish books, and the others in receipt of only occasional assistance. It looks, then, like most parishioners were eager to get away from this part of town if they could, and that the removals were, for at least a few families, a part of an upward social mobility (even if of a very modest sort). Female headed households, in contrast, tended to stay put; there is no evidence for any of them moving away from New Street in the years following Dawnay's 1724 census, and they thus give us a sense of more permanent attachment to their neighborhood than do the men's households.

Table 4.2 outlines the basic household structures of Puddletown's population in 1724, and it allows us to compare the residential patterns in New Street to those in the parish as a whole. Not surprisingly, in both cases, most people lived in nuclear family households, about 60 per cent in complete nuclear households, and 15 per cent with spouses but without children. It is important to remember that many women, whether rich or poor, had co-resident spouses in this parish, but this seeming dominance of the nuclear family household – such an essential element in our historical understanding of the English past – should not distract us from the rich variety of living situations evident in the Puddletown listing. Almost every imaginable residential pattern can be found in the 115 households of this parish.

Table 5.2: Residence Patterns in Puddletown, Dorset.

	Male House-hold Head	percentage	Female House-hold Head	percentage	New Street Male Hhh	percentage	New Street Female Hhh	percentage
omplete uclear (w/ or /o other non-..n)	52	60		0	10	63	0	0
pouse (w/ or /o other non-..n)	13	15		0	2	13	0	0
xtended	8	9		0	3	19	0	0
olitary	6	7	9	32	0	0	0	0
one Parent w/ hild[ren] <14	1	1	9	32	0	0	4	57
Widow or pinster Cluster may inc. Chil-ren>14)	6	7	11	39	1	6	3	43
otal	86	100	29	100	16	100	7	100

Sources: see note 15.

The distinguishing feature of poor women in New Street, in contrast to their fellow parishioners, is a pronounced tendency to cluster together, or to live solely with their young children, surviving on parish pay. No one in New Street lived alone, and, in fact, even the lone mothers who lived on New Street lived in exceptionally close proximity to one another. Three of them lived in (respectively) the first, fourth and fifth houses on the left side of the street, and the fourth lone mother, Ann Gold (or Short) lived 'within the yard' of a young couple, six houses down, on the same (left-hand) side of the road. Thus this situation looks very much like what we observed in Corfe Castle, where we also observed poor women without husbands living in close proximity to one another.

With intriguing symmetry, three of the four co-habiting clusters of women lived across the road. On the right hand side of New Street, female-headed households were unusually common, featuring in the second, fourth and fifth (of six) families. Only one of those clusters was clearly arranged by the parish over-seers: one lame widow and three elderly spinsters (two of whom were sisters), all parish pensioners, were placed into the house, with their rent and fuel paid by the parish. In contrast, the other two female-clustered families were among the mere five households that received neither parish poor relief nor charitable assistance. The second house on the street was subdivided, with the widow Mary Tyler in one half, sharing living space with her granddaughter and (most unu-sually in this era) great-grandson, while her husband lived out in service with one of the most prominent families in the parish, Mrs. Rolle. A young couple and their baby girl lived in the other part of the house, at the 'Sign of the Chec-quer'. The last cluster on the right side of New Street was comprised of an elderly maiden, Elizabeth Lovelace, (aged about sixty-five) 'In moderate circumstances' who lived with an apparently unrelated twenty-three year-old woman, Mary Boyce, daughter of Lawrence. Lovelace is something of a rarity: an elderly single woman with no evident relations in the parish, who (at least as far as we can tell) managed to retain complete self-sufficiency. While Boyce and her immediate kin never appear on the overseers' lists or charity distribution rolls in the 1720s and 1730s, her grandfather's house rent was paid by the overseer in 1716; a woman who appears to be her maiden aunt received money from charity in 1728; and her two adult brothers were living at home still with their artisan father, so this living arrangement for Mary may have been a convenient housing and economic strategy for a family that might have found itself vulnerable to economic chal-lenges, even if not to poverty. It was almost certainly a boon for the otherwise isolated old woman with whom she lived.

It appears from Table 4.2 that the women of New Street were unusual, in Puddletown, for their avoidance of solitary living, but we need to look more closely at the seeming prominence of solitaries amongst female headed house-holds in the areas outside of New Street, for it is unusual, in early modern censuses, to find so many women living alone. Indeed, closer attention to the circumstances of the seemingly solitary households outside of New Street reveals a more nuanced picture. Henry Dawnay might have recorded these women as living 'Alone', but in fact most of them were far from isolated.

Four of these solitary women lived alone in our modern sense of the word. These four, however, shared some interesting characteristics. Sarah Talbott, Jane Flambert and Mary Daw, all widows, occupied independent dwellings com-pletely on their own, and although Flambert and Daw received charity money in the 1720s, none of these women were given poor relief. The fourth independ-ent solitary woman was Mary Clerk, a maiden, who received neither charity nor poor relief, and instead earned a living by 'entertain[ing] lodgers accidentally or people that work in the Town and are Strangers.'[16] It appears that these women were making ends meet on their own, and that their isolated status was likely something that they preserved because of their economic stability, suggesting, perhaps, a preference for this form of living.

Two other female solitaries were in situations that suggest the temporary nature of their solitude. Sarah Sherwing (or Sherring), a widow who had been given a parish pension when her children were younger in the 1700s and early 1710s, lived in a house on the West side of the moor on her own. She likely had co-residential children shortly before the census was taken, and when she died in 1725, her son Thomas moved into her house with his wife and daughter. There was also another Sarah Sherring who lived up the road with her sister and brother-in-law at the same time. Mary Bassett was living alone in 1724, but by 1725 she had moved just across the street (from the third house on the South side of Northbrook Street to the third house on the North side) into a house with the pauper Elizabeth Stroud and Elizabeth's adult daughter. Mary Bassett was given fairly regular assistance in cash and kind (though not a pension) from 1704 until her death in 1729, when the parish paid for her burial.

Three more 'solitary' women actually lived in a range of cohabitation, but must have kept independent housekeeping facilities, or enough of a separation amongst residents for Dawnay to consider them to be 'alone'. Two of these, the older maidens Edith Phippot (or Philpot) and Joan Wellstream actually lived in a house with two lone mothers with young children. All of the four women received parish relief, the most going to Joan Wellstream, who was also the only one who was recorded as having her house rent paid at this time, and to Elizabeth Lavender, whose young children required significant parish assistance. In contrast, Edith Philpot was the only member of the house who received charity money, and she seems to have remained relatively free from dependence on the parish until the 1730s, despite her advanced age. We might consider this to be a widow/spinster cluster, even if there was significant independence amongst the inhabitants, but it is also clear that each woman had developed her own relationship with the parish officers and churchwardens, who considered their cases entirely separately in determining assistance.

Finally, in this category, Mary Boyce was an old Quaker Maiden who lived in one end of the house occupied by the young family of John Butt, and she also lived two houses down the street from Lawrence Boyce, who appears to have been her brother. The sole contribution the parish made to Mary's care was to grant her a small amount of charity money in 1728. Mary was considered by Reverend Dawnay to be living 'alone', but her case highlights the flexibility of this category, and, once again, reinforces the apparent importance of the proximity of friends and relatives for women without spouses.

It is clear that a complex variety of residential strategies, often manipulated or enforced by the overseers, were at play to minimize women's dependence on formal parish poor relief in Puddletown. The circumstances of these nine women supports the view that the overseers would not pay rent for poor women unless they were prepared to share housing with another person or family. The tendency of the more economically secure women to live alone rather than with strangers or extended kin suggests that despite the apparent willingness of poor women to share their homes, there may have been a general preference for more solitary dwelling where this was economically feasible.

There is also an interesting comparison to be made with the men who lived in solitude. Unlike the women, these 'Alone' men actually did generally live in residential isolation; none of them had any co-residents at all. Only one of the men, John Hardy, a widower born around 1658, received poor relief, including house rent paid in 1719 and 1721, perhaps at a time when he still had dependent children living with him. A separate case that highlights once again the complexity of the category of living 'alone'is that of John Genge, an old Anabaptist (aged 86 or 87 by the time of his death in 1727), who lived 'Alone', but 'Within his Yard, lying South of the House, live two of his Grand Daughters, Martha Leveridge, born in 1701, and Eliz. in 1705. Fatherless and Motherless, both unbaptized.. Since they were known to be 'very poor,' it is not surprising to find house rent being paid for the 'Leverage Maid.' We cannot know the exact nature of these living arrangements, but the women certainly benefited from the provision of lodging, and they are quite likely to have provided assistance for their grandfather, illustrating the reciprocal benefits of multigenerational ties in the eighteenth century that we often see with the ubiquitous co-residential grandchildren in both Puddletown and Corfe Castle.

We saw in Corfe Castle that female household heads who lived with their adult children tended to live much more frequently with their daughters than sons. Puddletown's widows and spinsters followed this pattern as well; eight female-headed households contained adult daughters, while four had both sons and daughters, and only three had solely sons. In contrast, the two widowed men who lived with their adult children both had co-resident sons and daughters.

It is fascinating to correlate these residential patterns with the level of poverty these women experienced. Five of the fifteen female household heads who lived with their adult children were on significant parish poor relief (four of the five on pensions at this time). All five of these women lived with adult daughters, and had no sons present. Of the other three women whose co-resident adult children were female, one, Elizabeth Bartlett, began receiving poor relief in 1733, and charity by 1726. Another, Joan Genge, lived with her brother, a painter and glazier, who also stayed free of charity. The third, Ann Nightingale, was actually a landowner who was paid rent by the parish to house other old women in some of her properties. Once again, we see the marked tendency of mature poor women to cohabit with their adult daughters, and this residential pattern coincides with parish relief. It is impossible to identify cause and effect here; the parish officers did not necessarily force these women to reside together, nor did residence with an adult daughter necessarily contribute to dependence on the parish. But it is at least clear that poor relieving officers would have seen this type of widow-spinster cluster as a norm amongst the poor, and that one strategy employed by poor women to make shift was mother–daughter co-habitation.

These conclusions sit easily alongside our current state of knowledge about the households of the poor, supporting assumptions amongst historians of the family that those most vulnerable to poverty were also those more likely to live in complex and changeable households. Tom Sokoll, for example, found that pauper women were more likely to live in extended families than the better-off in the Essex communities that he studied.[17] Indeed, it seems clear from work on poverty, as well, that the poor would have had to be more flexible and strategic in their residential patterns than were those of the middling sorts.[18]

Attitudes of the Poor Regarding Place of Residence

It is more difficult, however, to determine the attitudes of the poor towards their households and family. Our evidence from the household listings highlighted the ubiquity of co-residence with adult children for those vulnerable to poverty, and in Puddletown, especially, we saw the poor substituting clusters for solitary or independent living. Pauper letters are one source that help us to determine whether such residential patterns occurred by choice or by parish officials' pressure. Letters written by (or for, as in many cases the poor were illiterate and relied on an amuensis) the poor have revealed intense ties amongst family members, ties that extend beyond the immediate family to include the bond between grandparents and grandchildren, another characteristic of the Dorset parishes studied above. A particularly vivid example of this is Jane Cross's 1755 letter from Canterbury to the overseers of the poor of her home parish of St. Botolph, Colchester, Essex. Cross explained:

> I beg leave to acquaint you I Gott safe to cantubery and was loveingly received by my dear mother who was doubtless Glad to see me and is very willing to help me in what is in her power but her acent years makes it not in her power to do Greatly for me neither do I of my self desire to be incombant on my dear mother but desire to labour for my self and my child but its not in my power to subsit with my own labour I therefore appeall to your dear Goodness to consider my case and be please to allow me some small allowance to help bring up my dear baby – my mother is willing to Give me a bed and some sl small triffle to help furnish a room but I <can> <n>ot undertake to pay house rent and maintain my self and child therefore I beg Gentlemen you please to consider it and soon to send me your answer and I hope you will not deny me so small a subsistence as six pence a week which to be sure is but a triffle and my hands must labour hard to do the rest.[19]

Here, Cross utilizes a range of strategies to make shift: the overseers have apparently helped her to move to Canterbury, where she can save on the cost of housing by living with her mother, but neither woman is positioned (in the letter, at least) as dependent upon the other. Instead, Cross paints a self-portrait of anxious autonomy. While this was undoubtedly part of a greater strategy to appeal to the relieving officers, the letter does at least speak to a willingness of the poor to adopt such a position, and Cross's situation rings true. It was common in such letters for the poor to claim the importance of family members to their care, and to assert strong preferences for their current place of residence, even using the threat of their return as helpless residents to their home parishes as leverage to get assistance.

We can see this strategy in a letter Ann Clark wrote to her home parish from Bermondsey, London, after her husband was injured in 1768. She claimed, 'That with industry imay bee able to git my bread or Else mut bee oblidgd to com don and my family upon The paresh.'[20] Letters like Clark's and Cross's demonstrate women's potential to use family connections, and show their desire to live in places where they can most easily earn their own bread, but some women lacked even these options, and lived simply at the mercy of their parish officers.

Increasingly, over the eighteenth century, such officers were likely to seek to 'solve' the residential problems of the poor by placing them in parish workhouses. Thus, especially after a Parliamentary Act of 1723, women in Cross or Clark's plight might find themselves subjected to the 'Workhouse Test'; that is, they would have been forced to enter the workhouse in order to benefit from any assistance by their parish. How was such an option viewed and used by poor women in this period, and what effect did it have on the nature and range of their options regarding place of residence? In fact, poor women's attitudes towards the workhouse, as well as discussions in the press about these institutions, reinforce the themes that we have already noted in regards to poor women's residence patterns, showing both the desire to be independent, and the preference to remain in close proximity to friends and family.

The Last Resort? Workhouses and Poor Women

Workhouses were never, in the eighteenth century, the main locus for poor relief when considered nationally, but they were quite common, and in localities that adopted this method of poor relief, they could dominate the lives of the poor. There were some 600 workhouses in place by the 1740s, serving around 30,000, and according to statistics collected by Parliament, there were as many as 2000 in 1776–7, and around 4000 by 1815.[21] These institutions occupied a disproportionate place in debates over poor relief, serving as a main focus for discussion. Finally, by the passage of the 1834 'New Poor Law', workhouses were designated as the principal form of assistance to the poor, and all other manner of relief was strongly discouraged, as England was divided into regional 'Unions', each with a massive institution for the care of the poor.

Revisionist historians have gone a little way towards modifying the common view of these workhouses as Dickensian horror houses, but we can still be sure that they were loathed by the poor, and that the chief reason for parishes' adopting them was to diminish poor rates, not to provide a more 'humanitarian' social welfare option.[22] The fact of pauper women's (and men's) rejection of the workhouse reinforces this chapter's argument about the centrality of residential independence to the household ideals even of the poor and helps us to understand some of their strategies for guarding this independence.

In some parishes, it is clear that pauper women simply refused to enter the workhouse when ordered. In Terling, Essex, where overseers occasionally used the workhouse as a deterrent to keep the poor off the parish rates, the vestry decided in 1796 that Isaac Wager's wife should be 'taken off 6d. a week in her allowance or go into the workhouse.'[23] Commentators on the poor laws, such as a gentleman in Inkborough, Worcestershire, noted, 'There is, however, still remaining, among many of the Poor, a degree of pride; who, though they would willingly receive an unjust allowance at their own dwellings, would scorn the relief afforded by the parish work-house...'[24] Isaac Wager's wife fit this pattern; she apparently was willing to forego her pension rather than enter the workhouse after the vestry's order.

Once in the workhouse, women could express their dislike through running away, refusing to work, and acting up in numerous other ways, as in Hampton, Middlesex, where the female inmates, 'are not content with the ample allowance of food that is furnished them, and would be riotous without tea every morning.'[25] Thus it is clear that even within the workhouse, poor women did have scope and various strategies for improving their situations.

Some workhouse rulebooks even demonstrate parish officers' acceptance of the norms of residential independence, and seem positively apologetic. An elaborate example of such thinking was found in Liverpool's workhouse. Here, the old inmates were given separate quarters, specially furnished, so that 'being thus detached from the rest of the Poor, [they] may consider themselves as comfortably lodged in a secluded cottage; and thus enjoy, in some degree, (even in a work-house) the comforts of a private fire-side.'[26]

Not only the poor, but also some elite commentators and politicians expressed profound disapproval of workhouses as a method to house the poor. William Moreton Pitt, of Corfe Castle, was convinced that there was a dire housing shortage. He articulated an ideal of residential independence for the poor that seems to mirror their preferences, as well as to reflect a typical late-eighteenth-century concern with hygiene and privacy. Pitt described with disgust how the families of the poor were often forced to seek to share houses 'seldom calculated to contain two families.' But he saved his worst vitriol for country workhouses, decrying the cases where the rural poor were 'taken into a wretched poor-house there to associate with the old, the infirm and decrepid, idiots and insane persons, the idle and dissolute, loathsome from filth and infested with vermin... crowded together without discrimination of sex or character.' Even for the destitute, Pitt opined, the parish should fulfill not only its obligations, under the terms of the Old Poor Law, to provide 'convenient houses of dwelling for the impotent poor' but for '*any* poor in want of houses.'[27] Indeed, Pitt made a special point of stipulating that for the sake of decency, as well as convenience, each cottage should have separate sleeping rooms for boys, girls and parents. This Member of Parliament was not alone in his preoccupation with the need to separate different kinds of poor, nor in his opposition to the workhouse, which was shared by many both within and outside of Parliament.[28] Opponents of the workhouse attacked along many lines, including scare-tactics regarding its supposed effect of effeminizing male labourers, but the specific experiences or expectations regarding female paupers were seldom explicitly discussed.

Coincidentally, there has been a real lack of attention to the issue of gender in studies of the English workhouses under the Old Poor Law. This is, in part, a reflection of the eighteenth-century records' silence on this issue. For example, the immensely detailed 'Report from the Committee Appointed to Make Enquiries Relating to the Employment, Relief, and Maintenance of the Poor...' from 1776, is primarily concerned to display information regarding workhouses (and far less interested in outdoor relief), but not a single column in its massive tabulation of information relates to gender. One can comb the comment columns for information on women and see some material, but there is not a way to attain systematic information because it was not collected.[29]

Indeed, the lack of attention to gender in workhouse records, rulebooks and dietaries is, itself, quite striking. Historians have assumed that amongst the poor, women ate significantly fewer calories than men; yet no workhouse diet I have seen discriminates between men's and women's food allowances. There was a dramatic discrepancy between men's and women's average wages; yet no workhouse ever charged different amounts for keeping men and women if they worked with a contractor. Even those documents that are concerned to give a general sense of the poor in workhouses (like the publications of the Society for the Promotion of Christian Knowledge in the early eighteenth century), usually simply recount the number of 'men and women' in the workhouse, and only a handful of accounts enumerate men and women separately.[30]

Still, it is very clear that women did live in eighteenth-century workhouses, and that they generally slept in separate rooms from the men and children, as well as often doing different work from the other residents. Where the gender of inmates is given in the 1725 'Account of Several Workhouses'(a publication enumerating and promoting houses of industry), only in one case are there more men than women among the adults. Sir Frederic Morton Eden's State of the Poor, at the end of the eighteenth century, collected similar data and reveals similar trends. Only at the oldest age group do men tend to equal or outnumber women as inmates.[31] Local studies can add nuance to this picture. In the parish of Terling, Essex, for example, the workhouse started out primarily as a place for middle-aged women and young girls in the 1770s, but by the end of the century, when as many as 14% of Terling's aged population lived in the workhouse, it was housing almost equal numbers of old men and old women.[32] More typical was the pattern in the West Yorkshire township of Ovenden, in the parish of Halifax. Ovenden's workhouse became increasingly feminized at the end of the eighteenth century, fluctuating between an equal and a masculine gender distribution in the early part of our period, but housing primarily women by 1801.

Tim Hitchcock has argued that women in London workhouses sometimes took an instrumental approach to these institutions. His work, which demonstrates that young women had an 'in and out' relationship with the workhouse, has been especially important as a way to highlight the agency of poor women relative to workhouse masters.[33] Alysa Levene's study of workhouses in London seems to echo Hitchcock's findings, but very little work has been done on rural workhouses.[34] One suggestive finding to support Hitchcock and Levene comes from Ovenden, where an unusually rich set of workhouse books from 1775–80, which detail 228 entrances into the workhouse, reveal that there were many cases where women (and men) entered the workhouse on more than one occasion even during this relatively short time span. Twenty-six women and sixteen men entered at least twice, and four women and seven men came into the workhouse on at least three different occasions.[35]

There are two cases where women appear to be echoing the behavior Hitchcock and Levene found in London: William Smith's wife Betty entered and left the house on her 'own accord'in both 1776 and 1778 with her two daughters, one a newborn. Susan Bartle or Battle went into the workhouse in 1779 and was out quite quickly, only to return in 1780 to bear her bastard son. Both then left on their 'own accord'after only one month. Was Battle forced to have her illegitimate child in the workhouse, or did she take advantage of its medical facilities as a deliberate strategy? Her quick and voluntary exit suggests that the latter may be a plausible explanation. In addition, while adult men almost never entered the workhouse as lone fathers, a majority of women who entered the workhouse as part of a family unit did so with just their children: fifteen women entered with their children, while only one man – a very old man with an adult daughter – entered as part of a family that was not either a complete nuclear family or a couple. Strikingly, many of these women left the workhouse with their families intact. Even in relation to the workhouse, then, we can witness poor women's efforts to control their residential situation, adapting old strategies of combining and recombining households, and shifting place of residence in order both to maximize their own independence, and to best utilize the resources available to them under the Old Poor Law. Still, workhouses would have taken women away from both the neighbors and the residential independence that they treasured, so that we must view these institutions as negatively affecting and limiting the lives of poor women in the eighteenth century.

Conclusion

This chapter has highlighted the complexity of poor women's households in eighteenth-century rural England. Looking at the household listings, and setting them into the context of the attitudes and realities of the period has confirmed, in the rural setting, the importance of co-habitation, in widow-spinster clusters, to females who were vulnerable to poverty. It seems that both economic pressures and the interference of overseers of the poor reinforced a tendency that was already likely to have existed, for vulnerable women to group together in shared housing, and to live in close proximity to one another in neighborhoods where those in similar living situations lived close-by.

At the same time, however, the seeming preference of economically well-to-do women, especially in Puddletown, to live alone, or solely with someone who would be a servant or companion, is striking, as is women's determination to stay out of workhouses, or to use them as stop-gap measures. In most of the literature on early modern and eighteenth-century families, the need to 'train... sons so that they could maintain themselves in employment' is contrasted to the family obligation to 'see...daughters suitably married'.[36] But the quotations at the beginning of this chapter, along with the evidence from these Dorset household listings, and our brief discussion of workhouses, suggest that we may need to look harder at the ways in which women and girls, too, strove to meet ideals of residential autonomy.

5 THE ECONOMIC STRATEGIES OF WIDOWS IN SWITZERLAND FROM THE MID-NINETEENTH TO THE MID-TWENTIETH CENTURY

Anne-Lise Head-König

Introduction

The change in life expectancy and mortality, combined with the economic changes which took place in society between the middle of the nineteenth and the middle of the twentieth century, also had an impact on widowed females. This is true both for the group of younger widows (under forty-five), which represented 13.2 per cent of all widows living in Switzerland in 1860 and had declined to only 6.4 per cent in 1940, as well as for the group of older ones (sixty-five years old and more), which increased considerably from 35.8 per cent in 1860 to 53.8 in 1941.[1]

The population of widows was in no way homogeneous and the older widows, often frail and lacking adequate financial resources, had different material needs from those of the younger ones, especially those who had lost their husband and had children not yet able to be engaged in gainful employment. Up until World War 1, widows with dependant children figured prominently in the assistance registers of local authorities. This was because when a widow's relatives were unable to assist her in kind or with money her commune was obliged to provide the necessary help. Conflicts were frequent as many local authorities were unwilling to assist the poor adequately or could not meet the rising cost of expenditure resulting from the provision of assistance as their own budgets were very limited, especially in upland and rural regions. Until the implementation of the first Swiss Civil Code in 1912, which unified the heterogeneous cantonal civil codes, in many cantons a widow had often only a very limited share of her dead husband's property – in some cases only a child's share – which naturally created an extremely difficult critical situation in regions where fertility remained at a high level and many offspring survived.[2] Also, her legal position with regard to her children was far from uniform. Often she had only limited parental authority over her fatherless children since she had to share legal authority with an officially appointed guardian. Thus, recourse to public assistance from the commune meant constant interference in a widow's life and the upbringing of her children, as frequently there were regular house visitations by an individual appointed by the local authority. This was the case especially in some German-speaking cantons, such as that of Zurich, where at the beginning of the twentieth century rules concerning official legal guardianship were reinforced at the expense of the individual's rights. In an urban context, the problems encountered by widowed mothers with under-age children were often complicated by the specific rules prevailing in respect of assistance to be given to people who did not possess local citizenship and thus did not belong to the commune in which they were living. Strict rules with regard to settlement often considerably limited eligibility for poor relief. It was only after World War 1 that the situation improved slightly as a result of intercantonal agreements on assistance and due to the implementation of a Federal program specially designed to help widows and orphans in need.

After World War 1 apprehension of the needs of the group of older widows was also growing rapidly. In proportion to the total population, older widows were more numerous in towns – in 1920 they made up 11.2 per cent in the seven main towns – than in the small towns and the rural regions – 8.9 per cent – and many of them lived in poverty. Paradoxically, in the countryside and mountainous regions they were more often without sufficient income, due to the more limited possibilities of living with relatives and pooling available resources. This factor was aggravated by the marked trend to emigration to towns or abroad on the part of the younger generation common in several upland regions, such as Ticino and Graubünden. In 1920, 16.6 per cent of widows lived alone in the seven main towns in Switzerland, but 23.6 per cent in the rest of the country. On the other hand, large households (6 persons and more) headed by widows were proportionally more numerous in the less urban and more rural regions where farming still prevailed – 12.4 per cent of all households – due to a combination of various factors, such as higher fertility, the presence of relatives, of agricultural labourers and of boarded out children, whereas in the main towns this type of household represented only 9.8 per cent of the households headed by a widow.[3]

The sources concerning widows are few and far between, with the exception of the existent communal and assistance registers. There are little micro data on widows' households and their income in the first half of the twentieth century and family budgets were always biased towards the traditional family (a parental couple and two children). But the official macrodata, too, often amalgamated all non-married women - single, separated from their husband, divorcees and widows. Thus, apart from a few exceptions, there is a general lack of data concerning the structure of the households widows lived in as well as with regard to their presence in the labour market. In respect of the amount of poor relief given to widows' households, their demographic structure and the number of persons who were involved, a number of difficulties arise. Practically all Assistance Boards mention only the number of cases which were concerned, and hardly ever indicate the age at which widows entered widowhood, whether their lived alone, whether they had children and, if so, how many.[4]

The specific manner in which assistance was organized in Switzerland also contributes to the difficulty when it comes to obtaining an overview of the situation of the widows. In most urbanized cantons, until the second half of the twentieth century, two separate entities in each commune were responsible for assistance: one had to provide poor relief for the commune's own citizens and the other for those who did not belong to the commune. Unfortunately, the data of these two institutions when they relate to widows and the relief they received are not in the least compatible.[5]

In this paper I shall examine the changes which occurred in the general attitude towards the gainful employment of widows, whatever their age, the changes brought about in the assistance policy affecting persons who were considered not to belong to the local commune since they did not possess its citizenship, the shift from kinship responsibility to that of the commune of origin and finally the general improvement brought about by the creation of the Old Age and Survivors Insurance in 1948.

The Family Economy of Widows: The Insistence on the Obligation to Work for the Period up to the End of World War 1

Until World War 1, the widows' problem was that whatever their age, the state of their health, their duty towards their young children, and the availability of work on the labour market, they were always expected to earn their living and provide for those who depended on them. But most widows' income was inadequate for such purposes due to the poorly paid employment available to them. In order to survive they were forced to rely on supplementary income provided either by relatives, according to the legal obligation these had to help their kin, or by the local authorities of the communes to which they belonged. Even when elderly widows were no longer able to work full-time because of their infirmities, they were still expected to work part-time in order not to become a burden on the resources of the communes or those of their relatives. Elderly widows (sixty years old and over), even when too frail to work full-time (as domestic servants, in factories, and so on), were frequently refused assistance, local authorities insisting that in summer they could work as day labourers or laundresses.[6] The insistence on the need to be engaged gainful employment up to World War 1 is one of the most striking features of the poor relief policy. The moral value ascribed to work continues to be evident even in the Interwar period: some kind of work was expected of most inmates of old people's homes as a contribution to the cost of their upkeep.[7]

Before World War 1 a widow with few or no qualifications living in a Swiss town was severely limited in her choice of employment: she could work in a factory, from home, accept casual work or be self-employed in the retail sector. The latter possibility explains why, in a quickly expanding town such as Basle, widows were overrepresented as shopkeepers, especially as grocers.[8] New, better-paid openings in commerce and trade only appeared after World War 1, but often widows lacked the necessary training or experience. Factory work meant reorganizing the household, since very long working hours would prevent widowed mothers from working in factories when no relatives or paid help could be obtained to supervise the children. Domestic work and the labour market for domestic servants offered only limited opportunities before the 1920s, since living-in was the rule and the presence of children often precluded many widows from this activity except when they were able to board out their offspring, which is a problem we shall address later. After World War 1 there were more opportunities to work in this sector as a daily, since the prevalent scarcity of accommodation also affected the middle class and prevented them from employing indoor servants and, by the middle of the twentieth century, 19 per cent of the working widows in Zurich worked in the domestic sector, but only 6 per cent of them indoors.[9]

Keeping the Family together while Working from Home

Most widows tried to keep the family together. To get an income or to supplement it a widow with or without children could often resort to new activities after her husband's death, such as taking in lodgers or increasing the number of individuals she had lodged previously. This was especially the case, being an alternative to outside work in the quickly expanding towns where accommodation was scarce and landladies were still very much in demand until the middle of the twentieth century. Amongst the working widows in the Zurich 1950 census, 13 per cent described taking in lodgers as they main activity,[10] whilst in the 1958 survey 16.2 per cent mentioned it.[11] However, to maximize the income from this activity often meant that the widow and her family lived in dire circumstances themselves, as the case of a Basle widow shows. After the death of her husband in 1898 she decided to take in an additional lodger to the two she already had and turned her living room into an additional bedroom. The consequence was that she had to use the kitchen as a bedroom for herself and her children and, since space was scarce, she was obliged to sleep on an old carpet.[12] Taking in lodgers was also not without its risks either, and as Barbara Koller has shown for

Basle, there was always the possibility that neighbours would use the argument of overcrowding or of promiscuity to lodge an official complaint with the local authority in order to get rid of an unwanted neighbour and this, if successful, would entail her being evicted from her flat.[13]

Up to World War 1, domestic industries, such as embroidery and silk production, were one source of income for the population of the eastern part of Switzerland, and in the Jura region it was clock- and watch-making. In most main towns, elsewhere, working from home was important for widows. It is, however, difficult to assess exactly how many widows worked in this sector, because the censuses did not pay particular attention to female home workers or to their civil status. Thus, because of statistical inconsistencies, the proportion of widows calculated to be in this sector can vary considerably. It is obvious, though, that domestic industries were on the decline after the 1880s. In 1905, widows made up 20.6 per cent of female home workers in Zurich and it was 17 per cent in 1894.[14] But the extremely poor wage conditions of home workers, together with the irregular working hours and fluctuating income are part of the reasons for the very rapid decline of this form of production during the first half of the twentieth century.

A welcome opportunity for widows to earn a living while at home was to take in children boarded out by their parents or the local authorities. For a long period local authorities considered that boarding out provided a satisfactory solution for two problems: finding a cheap boarding place for children whilst at the same time giving some employment to widows who otherwise would probably have had to be assisted.[15] The consequence of this was that the mortality rate of boarded out children was higher than that of the children living at home, as was the case in Zurich in the last decade of the nineteenth century. Such children were often badly looked after as some widows took in up to three or four children in order to increase their income. The situation only improved during the Interwar period with a better selection process applied to families wanting to take in a child. In the town of Zurich over a period of twenty years (1914–35), the proportion of widows with boarded out children and earning money from such an activity fluctuated between 9 and 13 per cent of all families with boarded children.

The Boarding out of Widows' Children

However, as mentioned above, most widows with dependant children were obliged to work because their income from other sources was almost always inadequate. This partly explains the very high proportion of children who, having lost their father, were then boarded out in the whole of Switzerland. Even in the 1930 Census, 24.2 per cent out of the 70'672 children under eighteen who had lost their father did not live with their mothers[16] and this was at a time when the Swiss state was taking the first steps to give financial help to widows and their orphaned children and thus to keep women out of the labour market. As late as the middle of the twentieth century, in a survey of widows' households and their income in 1958 Zurich, 13 per cent of their children under eighteen were boarded out.

In fact, the motives leading to the boarding out of children were very ambivalent because they were the result of two conflicting conceptions. On the one hand, women, and among them quite a significant proportion of widows, decided against keeping their children or some of their children at home with them either because they had to work, or because they knew that their income would be insufficient to provide for their whole family. A typical example is that of a widow in the canton of Basle Country. In 1880, she put two of her four children into the care of the local Poor Board, which had to pay for their upkeep and she promised to finance the upkeep of the other two herself. One she placed with relatives in Basle, where she found work, and the other child she left with her parents-in-law, promising to pay for its upkeep. But her meagre earnings did not allow her to do so, and despite her asking the local authorities to help her with this payment, she met with the total refusal of the communal Assistance Board[17] to do so, arguing that no other widow had cost them so much.[18] But, at the same time, there was also an explicit policy of interference on the part of the local authorities in respect of the upbringing of a widow's children. Widows were permanently under suspicion as it was thought that without a man in the family they would be unable to deal with money matters properly and thus the upbringing of their children would be unsatisfactory. The cases where the local Assistance Board proceeded to take away the children from their mother under the pretext of bad upbringing or a harmful environment were numerous. The practice in these occurrences varied widely, but in some cantons it was drastic and this is why up to World War 1 so many children whose parents were assisted did not live with their own parents. In 1887, in the town of Bern, of the 823 children belonging to permanently assisted families only 15.8 per cent lived with their own family, 74.4 per cent were boarded out with strangers living outside the town, 2.6 per cent were boarded out in the town and 7.3 lived in institutions.[19] The chances of success that mothers had when appealing against arbitrary decisions similarly varied widely. In some cantons, such as Zurich, the changes occurring in the law of guardianship at the beginning of the twentieth century even reinforced the power of the state institutions to curtail legal parental rights.[20] As was noted by a contemporary observer in the 1930s, the risk of interference from the Assistance Board also explains the reluctance of many widowed mothers to ask for additional and much needed material assistance as they feared this would be used as a pretext to separate them from their children.[21]

The Problem of Older Widows

Intergenerational support of widows, when old, was taken for granted both from the point of view of the law and from that of society. The support, however, varied widely depending on the place where widows lived.

In the countryside and upland regions, where farms were transferred inter vivos to one son, up to the second half of the twentieth century the transfer contract nearly always included a retirement contract for the old farming couple or the survivor of the couple, with a detailed list of the subsistence needs and services the old couple had to be provided with on the farm premises. However, in regions where partible inheritance and the fragmentation of the farms were the norm, the material situation of the widows was much less favourable. Often, when no sufficient supplementary income would contribute to the already meagre income from the children's partitioned rural household, the widowed mother had to move in with whatever child (mostly a daughter) could be made to take care of her.[22]

For widows in an urban environment, support could take different forms. There was the support with money when the adult children did not live in the same place as their widowed mother, the money being sent home, even from abroad. Or, when children lived in the same town, support was given in two ways, as can be seen from some of the few data on urban residential patterns which exist for the end of the nineteenth century, such as those for Winterthur and those for Bern at the end of the 1920s. Co-residence with unmarried adult daughters was frequent, especially in towns like Winterthur, where economic activities such as trade and industry influenced the migration pattern of the sons. The citizens' list of Winterthur of 1890 reveals a significant proportion of sons who were temporarily absent from the town or living elsewhere in Switzerland or abroad. Consequently, there was the obligation for a daughter, sometimes for two, to remain single and to look after their mother and nurse her when old whilst at the same time earning some income for the upkeep of the household. When the widowed mother had no unmarried daughter on whom to rely and was unable to manage to live alone due to lack of resources or physical infirmity, she co-resided with married children and became a member of the household either of her married sons or her sons-in-laws. Elderly widows were much less likely to live in a rented room or in an institution than single or divorced women of the same age group, as can be seen in the table below (Table 5.1).

Table 5.1: Non-married females over sixty and their living arrangements, Bern 1929 (per thousand).

Living arrangements	Single	Widowed	Divorced
Own household	458	506	522
Living in the HH of relatives	145	384	257
In a rented room	135	47	106
At their employer's	76	7	18
In an institution	185	56	98
Total per thousand	999	1000	1001
Total females	801	2072	113

HH: Household.

Source: 'Die Altersbeihilfe in der Stadt Bern. Ergebnisse der Zählung der über 60 Jahre alten Einwohner vom Juli 1929', *Beiträge zur Statistik der Stadt Bern*, **14 (1930)**, p. 23.

In exchange for their livelihood, widows living with relatives often provided services, such as the minding of grandchildren, which in turn allowed the daughter or the daughter-in-law to be engaged in some part-time activity. Such help on the part of the older generation in exchange for being looked after materially are difficult to document. However, a survey made in the 1950s in Zurich (in 195⅞) gives some glimpses of the intergenerational exchanges which allowed widows with few resources to supplement their income. Confirmation for this type of help is provided by details of a widowed grandmother living with her widowed daughter who was the head of the household.[23] One should, though, not forget the material difficulties encountered by some couples in Swiss towns at the end of the nineteenth century and the beginning of the twentieth century when attempting to lodge a widowed mother. Shortage of affordable accommodation was common and even young couples were sometimes forced to board out their children due to the fact that they themselves were lodging in a single room, as was sometimes the case in the 1920s in Zurich.[24]

The Legal Obligations towards One's Kin

Until the introduction of the Swiss Civil Code in 1912 all cantonal constitutions made it legally binding for kin and siblings to assist their elderly parents and relations. Depending on the legal system of the relevant Swiss canton, the obligation to support kin could be defined very broadly. In most cantons, the obligation to assist kin in need ran not only through a three-generation chain of responsibility of the nuclear family, but it included a much wider set of kin. It extended not only to unmarried adults and married males but also obliged 'allied' kin connected by marriage to help out with older people. The responsibility of a woman to maintain her elderly parents or her widowed mother was similar to that of her brothers even when she was married. All daughters, even when married, were indirectly liable for the care of an older parent, since it was a husbands' obligation as son-in-law to maintain his mother-in-law. Up to the middle of the nineteenth century legal obligations remained very extensive in some cantons as can be seen from some cases in the canton of Glarus. There, the circle of assistance liability extended to the fourth degree of parenthood, the family being considered as the natural circle within which all members should help each other. This system functioned until 1849 and lists of relatives obliged to assist their poor relations were established regularly, with the relative financial means of the contributing relatives being taken into account. Regarding the 112 assisted persons mentioned in the cantonal lists of 1849 we learn that a total of 7,353 persons had to contribute to the upkeep of their impoverished relatives and that of these compulsory contributors there were 4,853 persons who were only related in the third and fourth degree of parenthood to them. This broad conception of the family's obligations had some advantages, since some better-off members of the family were also included in these lists. But people in the third and fourth degrees (66 per cent of those mentioned in the 1849 lists), on the other hand, often did not know those they had to assist at all well, or even had to assist people quite unknown to them because these had emigrated, or were themselves so poor that they were hardly able to contribute to the maintenance of those poorer than themselves. As a first step, it was decided in 1849 to limit the obligation to the first and second degree of consanguinity and affinity and, as a second step, the *Landsgemeinde* decided in 1879 to change the Glaris Poor Law and to drastically limit the obligation to provide assistance. It was decided that assistance to the poor was primarily the obligation of the family, but restricted to the mutual assistance of the parents, children and siblings, secondarily that of the commune of origin, and thirdly that of the State (the canton).[25]

Such assistance could include the cost of food, accommodation, or also medical care, which in the case of assistance to elderly parents could vary according to their age and illness. But, aid had not necessarily to be provided in cash, it could be given in kind, such as by providing shelter, food or clothes.

The Changes in Relatives' Legal Responsibility for the '*Dette Alimentaire*'

At the end of the nineteenth century, two changes occurred. The former extensive circle of kin liabilities became legally less extensive in some parts of Switzerland. Where the strict rules were still theoretically in existence, they were not applied as systematically as before, so distant kin were not asked by the communes for the reimbursement of the financial support already given by the commune. The second change was that the liabilities ('*l'obligation de la dette alimentaire*') tended to be reduced or even rescinded when a household was too poor to contribute to the upkeep of their destitute kin. Nevertheless, the obligation for in-laws related by marriage (in affinity degrees) to assist the members of their spouse's family was still in evidence until the introduction of the Federal Civil Code in 1912. An example of this obligation can be seen in the decision of the Swiss Federal Court in a court case of 1913. In 1909, a widow Henriette Bippert-Gottraux, living in the canton of Vaud, brought proceedings against her daughter and her son-in-law in a district Court in order to receive the payment of a monthly alimony pension of Frs 60. The Court granted her request and the son-in-law had to pay her a pension of Frs 40. However, with the introduction of the Swiss Civil Code as from the 1st of January 1912, the number of those obliged to support elderly kin was limited to the blood relatives. When the son-in-law in question, Henri Menthonney, refused to pay the pension from then on, his mother-in-law instituted legal proceedings to recover this money. He lodged an appeal in the Federal Court against these proceedings and the Court then confirmed that the new rules had to be applied in the whole of Switzerland.[26]

The Shift of Support to Local Communal Authorities

The new limitation regarding support for family members created a change in assistance to the elderly. There was also the additional factor that life expectancy was increasing and numerous families were thus unable to assist their elderly parents. The obligation regarding assistance to be given was then often transferred from the family to the commune of origin to which these parents belonged. According to Swiss law, the commune of origin always conferred rights to assistance to its citizens and these were passed on in turn from fathers to their sons and daughters. When a woman married she acquired both the local and the cantonal citizenship of her husband, so that it was up to his commune to assist them both when in need.[27]

The shift of support to the communal authority when the family was unable to support a widow in need had several significant consequences, since the communal authorities had a large autonomy in their decisions concerning poor relief. They were free to decide whether they wanted to assist a widow and her children in her own family household or not. Up to World War 1 the result was often the dissolution of the widow's household, especially in rural regions where there was no longer any communal land to provide her with a meagre income. Since in rural areas the budget of many local communities was limited, the objective of the Assistance Board was to find the cheapest solution in the circumstances. Poor children were often placed with families which hoped to benefit either from the allowance they were paid, but more often from the work the children were obliged to do. They were placed either with relatives or with strangers. In the latter case, up to the beginning of the twentieth century, the auctioning of these poor children was frequently the means for the commune to be able to pay the lowest pension. As a rule, siblings were separated. And it was not infrequent that the mother was also auctioned, a practice which existed till the 1920s in some communes of the canton of Fribourg. In the case of elderly widows, who had no relatives to care for them, until the Second World War one can observe the practice in some cantons of boarding them out with strangers, either because there were never enough old people's homes available to take them or because the cost of their upkeep in an institution was too high.[28]

The transfer of the obligation to provide support to the commune also had another consequence which in the course of time affected the poor population to an ever greater extent. With the increase of the mobility of the population, litigations as to which commune was responsible for assisting the poor also increased. Was it the obligation of the commune of residence or that of the commune of origin even when the relevant citizen had never ever lived there?

As mentioned above, residence without local citizen's rights brought no entitlement to assistance. Often widows were confronted with the fact that a commune or a town where they had never lived had to assist them when the nearest relatives were unable to do so. Two solutions existed in such cases. One was that the place of residence granted a certain amount of financial support which it subsequently requested the commune of origin to reimburse, the other was that the commune of origin – often one in rural regions – refused to defray the costs for the upkeep of its citizen living outside the commune and demanded that such citizen should be sent back, as it was considered to be cheaper to board a widow out with a local family or to put her in a local institution. It is only in the Interwar period that some cantons concluded agreements regarding assistance in order to regulate assistance for those not possessing local citizenship and to reduce the number of persons transferred back into their commune of origin against their will. However, as the practice of the town of Geneva shows, only a minority of cantons concluded such agreements. In Geneva, in the 1920s, the Bureau de Bienfaisance had to assist poor Swiss who did not have Genevese citizenship, and to ask for the reimbursement of its outlay. The system worked very well with the communes of the cantons of Vaud, Berne, Neuchâtel and Zurich but, as was reported several times, the Genevese Bureau de Bienfaisance encountered the total opposition of rigid communal officials in the cantons of Valais and Fribourg, so that it had to have the citizens of these two cantons sent back 'home'.[29] In the 1930s, the phenomenon of forced removal (*'Heimschaffung'*) was still in evidence, despite the occasional exceptions the authorities of some towns began to make in the 1920s out of compassion for a small number of elderly widows who had lived in their town fort a long time: they gave some supplementary aid in order to allow such women to stay where they had lived for most of their adult life. In fact, forced removal correlated with the state of the

economy, as the data collected for Basle for the period 1910–48 confirm. Years
of crisis with high unemployment, such as the years 1913–15 and 1933–8, show
a drastic increase of in the removal of non-citizens, that is those Swiss who did
not possess the local citizenship.[30] In 1946, in their yearly meeting the cantonal
directors of public assistance complained that the practice of removal was still
in force and that it often concerned persons who had no contact at all with their
canton of origin and who had often never lived there and did not even speak the
local language.[31]

The example of Basle illustrates the difficulties with which some of the major
Swiss towns were confronted when seeking to obtain the reimbursement of the
sums paid out for the relief of Swiss citizens who did not possess local citizenship, but whom they had assisted. In 18⁹%₁, other Swiss cantons reimbursed only
24 per cent of the relief given to those Swiss of different origin who were assisted
by Basle, but with huge differences in the willingness of such cantons to pay for
the upkeep of their own poor living in Basle. The most helpful canton (Zurich)
agreed to reimburse 55 per cent of the sum, and the most unhelpful (Lucerne)
only 6 per cent. In 1905, total reimbursements were slightly increased to 53 per
cent of the total sum spent by Basle (77 per cent for the most helpful canton, and
32 per cent for the least helpful).[32] However, in towns, and especially in times of
crisis the fear was omnipresent that they could be overcrowded with people who
were not citizens of the local community. For people of all ages, migration was a
standard means of escaping unemployment in their own regions, and in addition
migration to a town was a means to insure a higher level of support than was possible when living in the countryside. The result was that in the Interwar period a
new urban policy emerged, particularly in the larger towns. Long- term stability
of residence became an essential requirement for those non-citizens who wanted
to be supported by the town they were living in and to avoid the risk of being
removed to their commune of origin.

The Old Age and Survivors' Insurance (Assurance Vieillesse et Survivants) and the Improvement of the Material Welfare of Widows

After 1920, the continuing discussion about the aid to be given to widows, both
to older widows and to younger widows with children, has to be seen in the
context of the acrimonious debate relating to the pauperization and insufficient
income of older people of both sexes and the protection of the family, where the
first duty of a mother was to assure the welfare of her household and the satisfactory upbringing of her children. The debate became even more virulent after
World War 1 for two main reasons: the increasing pauperization of the older
generation, whose life expectancy had increased but which had been unable to
make sufficient provision for old age and the general economic situation with

its high rates of unemployment. The tendency to expel women, and especially women with children, from the labour market was very much in evidence in Switzerland as indeed it was in other European countries, too. For trade unions, in the Interwar period a reduction of the size of the female labour force was viewed as a way to provide more work for males, while at the same time putting pressure on employers to increase the wages of these male breadwinners. According to the official statistics the proportion of widows in gainful employment was as follows: 29.5 per cent in 1930, 24.6 per cent in 1940 and 24.7 per cent in 1950. But, as already stated, in fact many more widows worked than those mentioned in the official statistics, not only because those working part-time or who had a second job – the first, according to the statistics, being to manage their household[33] – were not included, but also because a large proportion of widows working did not declare their income in order to avoid paying tax, especially when they worked from home as seamstresses or as dailies or as landladies.[34] So there is a marked underevaluation of the proportion of those working in gainful employment. But, despite being in gainful employment, a large number of widows were unable to provide a sufficient income for their family, since most of the sectors in which they were employed paid much lower wages than those paid to males. For a working class widow, an additional problem was that she had few qualifications, that her husband had often been able to make little or no provision for his family. When a widow had to re-enter the labour market on the death of her husband, she often had to accept an occupation other than that she had had before marriage. The result was that not only widows over 65, but also a considerable proportion of widows under 65, lived in dire circumstances with their children and had to be assisted.[35]

In the Interwar period, apart from relief given sporadically by the philanthropic sector, poor relief for widows was provided from three sources, since a first attempt to introduce a compulsory Old Age pension for those aged over 65 was rejected by popular vote in 1931. Besides the communes, the Federal Government also provided poor relief, and for older people there was in addition the Foundation for the Aged (*Pro Senectute*), created at the end of World War 1. We have only sporadic data relating to the proportion of widows who received relief. Unfortunately, no data according to marital status exist for the aid given to all widows by the Foundation for the Aged.[36]

With regard to the assistance provided by the communes to their widows aged 60-65 and on the basis of federal sources which exist for the year 1927, we can calculate that the proportion of assisted widows was as follows: about 4.4 per cent in the canton of Basle, 4.8 in St.Gallen, 7.3 in Neuchâtel, 8.8 in Bellinzone and about 9.5 in the canton of Geneva. These differences are due partly the fact that divergent criteria were used with regard to the necessity for providing relief, but more especially to the fact that in some cantons there already existed either a compulsory or a facultative old pension scheme.

As for the widows younger than sixty-five assisted with the aid of the Federal Government, these represented 11 per cent of all widows in 1937 and 15 per cent in 1944.

With the adoption of the Old Age and Survivors' Insurance (AVS) in 1948, there was a marked improvement in the economic situation of widows. Essentially, the system of the AVS was also intended to protect the family as such. In the experts' discussions of the modalities of widows' pensions great importance was attributed to the role of the mother as well as to the traditional conception of marriage with the husband being the breadwinner of the family. Even a widow without children had to be financially protected after the loss of her husband. The main points concerning marriage as defined by the Swiss Civil law which was introduced in 1912 and which prevailed up to 1988 were that the husband was the provider for the family and the wife was responsible for the household and the education of the children. A married woman needed her husband's consent to be in gainful employment, but in the case of refusal, the judge could allow her to work if it were in the interest of the marriage or the family. The very first discussions concerning the survivors' insurance in 1929 had already stressed the importance of the role of the husband as the breadwinner of the family and the necessity that this should always be taken into account.[37]

In its discussion of the details of the section of the pension dealing with widows and orphans, the Federal Government insisted on the fact that the amount of financial assistance provided should be at such a level that it would permit the mother to stay at home as long as she had the care of children under 18.[38] But it was also stressed that the combined pensions of the widow and her orphaned children should not exceed 90 per cent of the income the father earned in the last three last years before his death.[39] The question as to the age at which a widow should be entitled to a pension when she had no children younger than 18, gave way to lengthy discussions, and the experts could not agree. Ultimately it was decided that widows who were not yet forty or who were older than forty but had yet not been married for five years should get a lump sum,[40] since 'it could be reasonably expected of them to work in gainful employment'.[41] It was also stressed that a widow without children could be expected to retrain in order to find employment, hence the partial pension paid out to her. The mention in the official text that in some cases it was not a question of retraining, but simply of training reflects the fact that before their marriage few women of these generations had had a training which would enable them to enter the labour market with satisfactory qualifications.

The Income of Widows' Households

Swiss statisticians seem to have taken little interest in the way incomplete families managed to survive in straightened circumstances. There are few data and such reliable data as they have emerged in a few urban surveys dating from the first half of the twentieth century. For rural regions one often has to rely on the qualitative evidence showing the extreme and frequent poverty into which widowhood plunged many elderly women, as is apparent in the short descriptions of individual cases given for mountainous regions in the reports of the Swiss Foundation for the Aged ('*Pro Senectute*') in the 1930s.

One rare insight into the impossibility of making ends meet is provided in the 1905 report of the *Allgemeine Armenpflege* in Basle, an institution which assisted people who were not citizens of that town. The situation of a widow with three children aged 6-10 years who lived in a two-room flat with two beds was as follows: as a seamstress she had an income which covered only 43 per cent of the expenses of the household; the rest, 57 per cent, had to be found by other means. In her case her commune of origin added 19 per cent to her income, the orphans' institution (*Landwaisenhaus*) 23 per cent and 15 per cent had to come from elsewhere. The expenditure on food represented 55 per cent of the household's outgoings and the rent of the flat 29 per cent. Compared to the cost of food per head that the factory inspector regarded as a minimum, the family's expenses were 29 per cent lower, and were even 13 per cent below the amount spent on the inmates of the local prison.[42]

Also in Basle, a detailed survey made in the 1940s of the help provided by the town for its own citizens gives some insight into the households of widowed mothers and the help they received. In 1941, the assisted widowed mothers made up 15.4 per cent of all cases of assistance and 20.3 per cent of all assisted citizens. On average they had 1.6 children. Of these assisted widows 74.8 per cent had only under-age children, 6.0 per cent under-age and grown-up children, and 19.2 per cent only grown-up children. On average, the relief paid out to a widow with children was Sfr 1,115.[43] But the scale of help varied from an average of Sfr 865 for a widow with one child to Sfr 3300 for a widow with seven children, though it is evident that the amount of help provided was only partially dependent on the number of children. The main criteria was the total income gathered together by all members of the family, which in turn depended on the situation of the labour market, the sectors they were employed in, the age and the health of those who had to earn the money.[44] In the 1930s the rule was that those adult citizens who were entirely assisted received Sfr 2.5–3.0 per day per person for their food and daily expenses, plus an allocation for their lodging, new clothes and so on, but the precise amount of this help is not specified, and in the 1940s this amount was increased to Sfr 3.50–4.00. The Basle data also provide some insight in the fact that many widows living in Basle who were not citizens of the town were in a difficult financial situation. The statistical data provided by the *Allgemeine Armenpflege* in Basle which had to help them out shows that their group is over-represented. In 1905, the widows made up 38 per cent of the assistance cases and in 1922 still 22 per cent.[45]

As already mentioned, the purpose of the introduction of Old Age and Survivors' Insurance in 1948 was to allow the widowed mother to stay at home as long as her children were younger than eighteen years of age. However, despite periodical adjustments to the cost of living, the pensions paid out provided only an inadequate income for some widows' families.

In Zurich, in 1950, nearly one fifth of the widows with children under eighteen had to work and more than one quarter of the widows without children (Table 5.2).

Table 5.2: Proportion of widows in gainful employment with and without children: Zurich 1950.

	Widows	
	With children under 18	Without children
In gainful employment	18.4 per cent	26.8 per cent
Not working	81,8 per cent	73.2 per cent
	100 per cent	100 percent
Number	3,800	14,900
Average child per mother	1.43	–

Source: Biske, *Zürcher Mütterbefragung.*

Unfortunately, the detailed data provided for the town of Zurich in 1958 concerns only a fraction of the widows' families, that is those widows who had children younger than eighteen and who were in gainful employment. We have no data for the vast majority of widows who in the 1950 census were mentioned as having children (81.8 per cent) and nevertheless were mentioned as not being in the labour force, nor for the widows who had no children under 18, whether they were in gainful employment or not. It is obvious, however, that for a number of years after its introduction, the benefits paid out according to the Old Age and Survivors Insurance were unable to provide the oldest widows with an adequate pension, even if they had no children under eighteen years of age. Hence it was necessary for them to continue working if they were able to do so. The problem was that those nearing retirement at the time of the introduction of the Insurance, in 1948, would not have paid in enough yearly contributions, sometimes not even one full year, to qualify for any of its benefits. It was subsequently decided that there should be a transition period over which benefits would be slowly scaled up to full value. And during this period, such older citizens, among them many widows, would only be paid out a *'pension de besoin',* which was needs-tested and which represented only a fraction of the normal old age pension. For this reason even at pensionable age a considerable proportion of widows were still working: in the age group sixty-five to sixty-nine, 15 per cent; at age seventy to seventy-four, 8.3 per cent.[46] Their presence in the labour market, however, differed widely according to professional status: among the employees: 6.1 per cent worked, among the workers: 12.2 per cent, and among the self-employed: 35.4 per cent.[47]

It is also evident that the age structure played an important role when one considers that a large proportion widows without children under eighteen did not work. In Zurich, 10,823 widows of sixty-five years and older were mentioned in the 1950 census. Their income was mostly derived from the Old Age Insurance, perhaps a pension from their husband or both combined when this pension together with the supplementary allowances which were handed out in many Swiss towns was not sufficient. More intriguing is the fact that 81.6 per cent of widowed mothers with children under eighteen did not participate in the labour market, at least officially. This is probably the consequence of three factors. The first was that some of them were entitled to a widow's pension after their husband. The second was that, as they were on average older than the other mothers, they often had older children able to contribute to the income of the family,[48] and the third factor – which I have mentioned before – was that undoubtedly not all part-time work was declared in order to avoid taxation or a reduction in the complementary benefits which some towns provided. These hypotheses seem to be confirmed by an earlier census. In 1920, amongst the households headed by a widow, 27.8 per cent of the widows in Switzerland were mentioned as not being in gainful employment. However, nearly a quarter of these households had children of fifteen to seventeen years of age, a large majority of them probably contributing to the upkeep of their widowed mother's family. A more detailed analysis of these widows , 'not in gainful employment', reveals also that 4.3 per cent of them were paid for taking in boarded out children (often more than one), that 19.2 per cent had lodgers (often more than one) and that 12.3 per cent lived with relatives who probably also contributed to their upkeep.[49]

A survey made in Zurich in 1958 of more than a thousand working mothers provides some information in respect of the income of 68 working widowed mothers with children under eighteen (Table 5.3). The family income was drawn from multiple sources: the wage they earned, the survivors' pension, the income from the other adult members of the family living with them and in addition some smaller income from other activities. The wage they earned contributed between 66 per cent and 45 per cent of the family income, depending on the number of children living with them (66 per cent: one child; 57 per cent: two children; 45 per cent: three children). The combination of their State widow's pension and that of the orphans' pension amounted to 17 per cent of the family's income with one child, 27 per cent with two children and 45 per cent with 3 children. But, as most widows did not live alone with young children, other adults – on average 0.85 adult persons – either adult children or other kin such as the widow's own mother, receiving Old Age Insurance money, also contributed to the income of the household. The pooling of incomes contributed 14 per cent to the family's income (families with one and two children) and 9 per cent (with the three children). The rest of the income was often made up from other resources such as the renting out of rooms to lodgers (about 16 per cent of the households).[50]

Table 5.3: Average family income according to number of children and civil Status of the widowed and divorced, Zürich 1957/1958 (in Sfr).

Widowed Mothers

Nb. Children	Own Income	Income of other family members	Alimony	Pensions	Other Income	Total
1	567	117	–	147	31	862
2	500	120	3	240	9	872
3	567	111	–	562	30	1,270

Divorced Mothers

Nb. Children	Own Income	Income of other family members	Alimony	Pensions	Other Income.	Total
1	540	33	91	14	23	701
2	512	64	154	14	20	764
3	485	15	179	-	38	717
4	401	65	70	-	71	607

Source: Biske, *Zürcher Mütterbefragung*, p. 14.

It is clear that relief provided by the AVS was insufficient for many widows with children, and in the 1950s this led to the adoption of several revisions of the legislation in order to increase the pensions paid out as well as of additional measures to improve the economic situation of those born before 1883 but who had been unable to contribute to the AVS. So, from the start with the introduction of the AVS widowed mothers were much better off than divorced mothers. They had 18.7 per cent more income with one child, 12.4 per cent more with two children, 43.5 per cent more with three children.

Conclusion

Three distinct periods can be observed when considering the economic situation of the widows. Up to World War 1 it was always expected of them that they should enter the labour market after the loss of their husband, irrespective of their personal circumstances and the number of children to be cared for. The local assistance board played an important role – often a negative one – in the breaking up of the family when widows were not able to assure the material well-being of the family or were considered to be morally unfit to look after their children. In the Interwar period, a different concept of the role of the widowed mother emerged with a governmental policy which stressed the importance of good motherhood but with the implicit aim of withdrawing mothers from the labour market. At the same time, the improvement in the financial situation of old people mostly benefited older widows. Finally, after World War 2, the introduction of the Old Age and Survivors' Insurance represented a marked step forward in the material situation of the widows. In fact, the material difficulties of widows almost ceased to exist after having been the object of successive legis-lative revisions of the AVS. From the middle of the twentieth century onwards, the deficiencies in the material well-being of the divorced mothers and one-par-ent families have become the major problem.

6 MEXICO: WOMEN AND POVERTY (1994–2004): PROGRESA-OPORTUNIDADES CONDITIONAL CASH TRANSFER PROGRAMME

Verónica Villarespe Reyes and Ana Patricia Sosa Ferreira

Introduction

This presentation will analyze and reflect on the socioeconomic status of low-income households headed by women in Mexico, particularly with regard to inequality in the workplace, salary and educational discrimination. In addition, the government's *Progresa-Oportunidades* Programme, designed to provide support for poor women, will be scrutinized.

Currently, several poverty-remediation programmes involving conditional cash transfers are in operation in Mexico. An example of these programmes is the Food, Health and Education Programme (Progresa-Oportunidades) launched at the end of the 1990s. This Programme is centred on the concept of *maternalism*, a vision of the traditional, social and biological roles of women, and it offers poor women cash in exchange for *good motherhood*. In order to ensure success, women are incorporated into the design of the Programme in a way that deepens gender division. Progresa-Oportunidades ultimately also reinforces social division, with the resulting replication of gender asymmetries, even though the management of the support resources to some extent empowers women within the household. Underprivileged mothers often participate in the Programme in the hope that their daughters will gain access to opportunities to improve their lives. In other words, the programme is used as a female survival strategy.

Poor Households Headed by Women

Over the past thirty years, economic transformation, characterized by unstable employment and a broad process of increasingly precarious labour circumstances, has taken a heavy toll on women in terms of living and working conditions. Gender inequality, underpins the relative stability of men in the labour market vs. the fluctuations of the entry and withdrawal of women.

While women have made significant inroads into the job market, they generally do so at a disadvantage, often taking jobs that are unstable, piece-meal, part-time or temporary in nature. This common condition of sub-employment is exacerbated during the reproductive years and leads to a general state of impoverishment, to taking on marginal work, which affords time for child care, and/ or to outright joblessness. Therefore, the cycle of impoverishment is etched ever deeper, and more so when these women are the heads of households. The generally lower degree of basic schooling among such women reinforces the prevailing trend marked by lower wages and sub-standard workplace conditions.

Simultaneously, women have seen their personal development constrained by the domestic and extra-domestic workload. Even into the 1990s, the idea persisted that a female head of household could not properly maintain a family and provide for its well-being. This view, among others, is very likely the rationale behind government intergenerational poverty prevention programmes. Programmes of this type, including Mexico's Food, Health and Education Programme (Progresa-Oportunidades), attempt to break the cycle of transmission of poverty from generation to generation through the human capital investment model. This is the vicious cycle of poverty. The World Bank supposes that low schooling, precarious health and malnutrition produce low performances, little productivity and low income; in other words, a low quality of life. In order to transform this cycle into a virtuous cycle it is necessary to invest in human capital.[1]

In 1994 in Mexico's urban areas, twenty-five of one hundred households headed by women were either poor or indigent. By 2002 this figure had risen to twenty-seven of every one hundred households. In rural areas in 1994, thirty-five of every hundred female-headed household lived in poverty. By 2002 the figure stood at 30 per cent (see Table 6.1).

Table 6.1: Mexico: Rural vs urban poverty broken down by gender of head of household with comparison to segment deemed 'not poor' (1994–2002).

			Urban areas						Rural areas			
Year	Indigent %		Poor but not indigent %		Not poor %		Indigent %		Poor but not indigent %		Not poor %	
	Women	Men	W	M	W	M	W	M	W	M	W	M
1994	4.0	6.7	21.3	23.2	74.7	70.2	13.7	21.3	21.1	26.6	65.2	52.0
1998	6.3	6.9	20,0	25.1	73.6	68.0	16.5	24.4	27.8	25.2	55.7	50.4
2002	5.4	4.6	21,4	21.1	73.1	74.2	14.5	17.1	15.2	27.5	70.3	55.4

Source: *Las metas del Milenio y la igualdad de género. El caso de México*, (Santiago de Chile: ECLAC-Inmujeres, 2005), p. 30.

In the period under consideration (1994–2002), the female-headed households in Mexico increased nationally from fifteen to twenty-three per cent of all households.[2] If households are divided by type, gender differences become even more evident. Of female-headed households, 41.3 per cent were single parent, 38.1 per cent were extended or compound families, and only 1.3 per cent corresponded to two-parent, nuclear families. For 2004 the corresponding figures were 39.7 per cent, 35.4 per cent and 7.1 per cent, respectively. As can be seen, among the two-parent households there was an increase in the percentage of those headed by women. This suggests that women take on this role when the husband or companion is out of work or earns less than the wife. The data on extended or compound family households headed by women indicate a decline in terms of percentage, while those headed by men have remained almost the same. This indicates that a high percentage of women take on the duty of caring for extended family members in addition to their own direct descendants (see Table 6.2).

Table 6.2: Mexico: Distribution of female- and male-headed households by family type (1994–2004).

		Single person	Single parent nuclear family	Two-parents nuclear family	Extended or compound family
Women	1994	19.3	41.3	1.3	38.1
	1998	18.0	45.6	2.8	33.6
	2002	18.6	41.7	4.2	35.5
	2004	17.8	39.7	7.1	35.4
Men	1994	3.9	1.3	73.4	21.4
	1998	5.3	1.6	75.1	17.9
	2002	4.4	1.7	74.4	19.5
	2004	5.5	2.0	71.5	21.0
TOTAL	1994	6.2	7.2	62.8	23.9
	1998	7.5	9.4	62.4	20.7
	2002	7.2	9.7	60.4	22.7
	2004	8.4	10.8	56.5	24.3

Source: *Estadísticas para la equidad de género. Magnitudes y tendencias en América Latina*, (Santiago de Chile: ECLAC, 2007), table 11 of the statistical appendix.

The percentage of single women, without a spouse or without the spouse present, who were heads of households, was quite high: in 1994 the figure reached 98.9 per cent and declined to 88.6 per cent in 2004. In the case of male heads of households, these proportions were reversed.[3] For women to survive as heads of households, they are largely forced to work in any job they manage to find. For example, from 2000 to 2004 the economically active population grew by 7.7 per cent, an increase of 3 million people seeking employment. In that period, the country's economy was unable to produce the formal jobs required to absorb the expanding workforce. To a large extent this can explain the increase in informal employment[4] and the concomitant instability these jobs entail. In 2004 formal urban employment increased by 0.7 per cent while the number of informal jobs rose by 4.3 per cent.[5]

The participation of poor women in the formal labour market is constrained by their deficient education, household responsibilities and sexist prejudices that consign women to the role of economically dependent housewives. Additionally, programmes for overcoming poverty, such as Progresa-Oportunidades in Mexico, reinforce women's role as mother, in what has been labelled *the welfare-oriented family model.*[6]

Employment Inequalities between Men and Women

In Mexico, the figures for female participation in the labour market show an increase from 34.0 per cent in 1998 to 37.5 per cent in 2004[7] (see Table 6.3). This growth in the rate of participation can be attributed to the emergence of new family models, in which the number of single female parent households continues to increase and the birth rate decreases, a phenomenon that has seen women move from a single-provider to multiple-provider strategies in order to make up income shortfalls.[8]

Table 6.3: Mexico: Percentage of participation [a] in economic activity by gender (1998–2004).

	1998	2002	2004
Men	81.5	75.1	75.5
Women	34.0	35.9	37.5

Source: *Las metas del Milenio y la igualdad de género. El caso de México,* (Santiago de Chile: ECLAC-National Women's Institute, 2005), Series on Women and Development 67, p. 31.
A Percentage participation is based on the population of working-age persons fifteen years and older

Basically, women have entered the labour market out of necessity, but also to secure greater independence and autonomy, a phenomenon connected to the fundamental human right to work. In today's world, this issue should be considered when public policies are extended. As ECLAC has pointed out in order to ameliorate the lot of the poor, public policies are required addressing employment opportunities that reconcile attention to household duties and paid work.[9] If the rate of economic participation is broken down by the degree of poverty (measured in terms of income), urban/rural locality and gender, one can see a greater gender gap between poor men and poor women than that which exists between men and women who are not poor (see Table 6.4). Poverty in Mexico and in Latin America generally is most prevalent among indigenous populations and peasants.[10] More specifically, because of their limited access to all types of resources, indigenous women face the greatest difficulties in overcoming poverty.

As illustrated in Table 6.4, from 1994 to 2002, the rate of participation in the labour market by rural poor women increased by a higher percentage than that of urban poor women, largely due to the weakening of the rural economy and consequent reduction in income levels.

Table 6.4: Mexico: Percentage of economically active men and women[a] – poor/not poor, urban/rural (1994–2002).

| | Urban | | | | Rural | | | |
| | Poor | | Not poor | | Poor | | Not poor | |
Year	Women	Men	Women	Men	Women	Men	Women	Men
1994	31.1	80.7	40.1	79.2	27.8	85.3	39.2	86.5
1998	35.2	80.1	46.8	80.9	35.7	89.1	43.4	86.8
2002	34.7	81.1	49.3	79.7	33.6	87.5	44.8	85.6

Source: Information provided by ECLAC based on the National Surveys on Household Income and Expenditures (ENIGH) 1994–2002.
a [(Women/men economically active)/Total population of women and men fifteen years of age or older]*100.

In the early 1990s Mexico underwent significant growth in informal employment, mainly in urban areas, a process that intensified in the first decade of the twenty-first century. The gap between the availability of jobs and the growing workforce, made up of persons reaching working age and women entering the labour market, fuelled the informal job market. In terms of available jobs, the fall in real wages since the 1980s and structural readjustment processes contributed to the expansion and deepening of this phenomenon.[11]

With regard to type of employment, in 1994, 10.9 per cent of the women worked in salaried informal jobs, while for men this figure stood at 30 per cent. It should be noted that workers in the informal sector of the economy do not enjoy the protection and benefits provided under current Federal Labour Law. In the category of unskilled self-employed workers, 8.7 per cent of women belonged to this group, a percentage that increased slightly by 2004, while for men the figure for the same period declined from 13.5 per cent to 10 per cent. In the decade under consideration, 3.4 per cent of women worked in family businesses and did not receive wages, while the tally for men fell from 5.1 per cent to 2.7 per cent. In terms of salaried workers in the formal sector of the economy, the situation of women has not undergone significant change and remained at around 8 per cent. In contrast, the figure for men fell from 14.7 per cent to 12.3 per cent. From 1994 to 2004, for every one hundred employed women, an average of fifteen worked within a collective bargaining agreement or under contract for an undetermined period of time. In 1994, 11.6 per cent of the women workers did not have any type of contract. This percentage increased to 15.7 per cent by 2004; in the case of men, the figure fell from 35.9 per cent to 30.4 per cent. Increased labour flexibility, as can be construed from these numbers, has a greater impact on female than male workers.

The data above reveal the gender-role based occupational segregation of men and women in the country, that is directly associated with the lack of child rearing services and an inequitable distribution of these duties in the home.[12] Arriagada argues that the presence or absence of women in certain occupations cannot be explained merely as a market function that weighs the relative costs of hiring women *vs.* hiring men.[13] In his view, the distribution of work in the family and the labour market, the assignment of jobs and tasks based on gender, is also an important factor. Though some portion of this differentiation by gender of jobs is apparently voluntary, the availability of services such as day-care can motivate women to enter the workforce, while constituting an effective instrument for confronting gender-role driven labour division. Indeed, the segregation of men from women in the labour market persists largely because of the lack of day care services, forcing women to gravitate to occupations that allow them to combine their work and child rearing responsibilities.[14] In Mexico, this gender-based segregation is most starkly illustrated by the high proportion –standing at 90.4 per cent– of low-wage female domestic workers against the percentages of men operating agricultural machinery and driving trucks, which stand at 100 and 99.6 per cent, respectively.

Salary Discrimination

In terms of income brackets, as gauged by base minimum wages earned, for 1994 and 2006, 5.9 per cent of female heads of household received between zero and two times the minimum wage, while for male heads of household the figure was between 23.5 and 20.3 per cent. There was a slight uptick in the percentages, from 4.5 to 7.1 per cent, of female heads of household who received between two and four times the minimum wage. The figures for their male counterparts were 26.5 and 20.3 per cent. This indicates that there was no improvement in households from the lowest income stratum headed by women.

Another telling point is the gap in wages earned by men and women in the workplace. Table 6.5 illustrates that there are more women in the workforce who receive no income: 13.4 per cent *vs.* 9.1 per cent for men. On the other end of the spectrum, among the population earning more than five times the minimum wage, the percentage for women stands at 7.5 *vs.* 11.7 per cent for men.

Table 6.5: Mexico: Percentage of employed men vs. women by income level as gauged by minimum wages earned (2000).

Income level	Women	Men
Does not earn income	13.4	9.1
Up to 2X the minimum wage	50.8	41.4
More than 2X and up to 5X the minimum wage	26.0	34.5
More than 5X the minimum wage	7.5	11.7

Source: *Encuesta Nacional de Ocupación y Empleo*, (Mexico: INEGI/STPS), 2000.

The following data also reflects the income disparity between men and women. For every one hundred wage earners, thirty-four were women and sixty-six were men. Moreover, for every 100 pesos earned, women received 28 pesos and men slightly more than 72.[15] With regard to meeting household expenses, among women earners from 30 to 39 years old, almost 70 per cent contributed all of their revenue. For the male breadwinners in this age range, the percentage fell to 60 per cent. In the over-sixty segment, the percentage for women was 84.3 while for men it reached 76 per cent.[16]

These statistics generate several considerations: a) There are more women than men who live alone, either because they are single, widowed or abandoned by a partner. As a result most or all of their income is devoted to cover household expenditure. b) Among older women, this tendency is even more manifest. Considering that women's wages are generally lower than those of men and that women are most widely employed in the informal sector, it is clear that women face a daunting outlook of poverty, precariousness and vulnerability, which becomes worse as they age. At the end of their lives, when employment opportunities are replaced by loneliness and abandonment, poverty may well be catastrophic. Poor women can adopt diverse survival strategies during the course of their lives. Elderly women often find shelter with their families in exchange for help around the house (or simply because this arrangement is part of the societal mores) or they rely on social programmes for assistance.

Use of Time, Income and Education

In the study of social reproduction processes, the analysis of domestic work is central. Because workers typically combine domestic and extra-domestic activities and the elasticity of the former vis-à-vis the latter, it is difficult to accurately determine the hours devoted to each. In Mexico indicators have been developed that attempt to account for domestic work by going beyond factors of gender inequality and the trade-off between work and leisure. These indicators involve statistics on the use of time, while focusing on the power and authority structures emerging from income and spending decisions negotiated in families.

According to the National Survey on the Use of Time (2002), when both spouses work, the average number of hours each week dedicated to diverse activities is 83.3 for men and 99.4 for women.[17] Over the seven-day week, this works out to an average of 11.9 hours of activity per day for men and 14.2 for women, leaving an average of 12.1 hours for men and 10 for women free for leisure, relaxation, rest, eating, sleeping, etc. (see Table 6.6).

Table 6.6: Mexico: Average number of hours per week devoted to activities by men and women spouses in family households and their respective participation in the labour market (2002).

	Both spouses participate in the labour market		Only the husband participates in the labour market	
	Men	Women	Men	Women
Work in the market	51:42	37:18	50:54	NA
Cooking and food preparation	4:18	12:00	3:30	15:30
Assistance in the kitchen	1:48	3:24	1:42	4:30
Cleaning	4:18	15:00	3:30	20:48
Cleaning and attending to shoes and clothing	1:36	8:24	1:18	10:00
Household purchases	3:48	4:06	2:54	4:24
Running the home	2:12	2:18	1:54	2:42
Paying for services and related paperwork	1:48	2:12	1:30	1:30
Home construction and repair	3:42	2:12	5:06	3:18
Raising children and supporting other members of the household (1)	7:54	12:24	7:24	16:18
Attending to children and family members with physical or mental disabilities (2)	9:00	16:18	8:24	19:48

NOTE: The average number of hours is presented in hours and minutes.
NA: Not applicable.
(1) Includes the activities of attending to children, the sick and family members with physical or mental disabilities.
(2) These are activities that can be carried out simultaneously with other tasks.

The data of the Table 6.7 supports the hypothesis that women have less time for themselves than do men. This can be explained partially by women's lower levels of educational achievement resulting from the limited time they have to attend school or pursue education. This generally lower level of achievement is mirrored in lower salaries and, moreover, serves to justify discrepant salaries paid to men and women. It also explains why so many women work in the informal economy under precarious conditions.[18] A comparison of the participation of men against women in the informal economy shows it is married women who have the highest rates of participation. This trend could reflect the fact that there are still no major barriers preventing entry into the informal economy. As such, there is greater flexibility in the use of time either for earning or household activities. Again, the weight responsibility for domestic tasks and child rearing continues to fall on women, who survive under precarious conditions of employment and meagre social protection benefits.[19]

Table 6.7: Mexico: Number of men and women participants in and hours devoted to 20 household activities.

Activity	Number of participants		Percentages in Hours worked	
	Men	Women	Men	Women
Sewing	1.48	98.52	0.87	99.13
Paying services	45.58	54.42	45.43	54.57
Bank paperwork	55.38	44.62	56.46	43.54
Purchases	30.41	69.59	23.92	76.08
Taking children places	24.25	75.75	22.76	77.24
Cleaning house	21.65	78.35	12.09	87.91
Washing dishes	11.26	88.74	6.80	93.20
Washing clothes	7.93	92.07	4.02	95.98
Ironing	9.58	90.42	5.63	94.37
Cooking	12.92	87.08	4.89	95.11
Taking out the garbage	34.75	65.25	37.51	62.49
Bringing water	44.31	55.69	41.10	58.90
Bringing firewood	71.36	28.64	75.99	24.01
Caring for children	29.10	70.90	17.09	82.91
Caring for the elderly	24.11	75.89	18.19	81.81
Caring for the sick	25.56	74.44	23.51	76.49
Repairs	83.85	16.15	90.93	9.07

Source: *La encuesta de uso del tiempo y sus potencialidades para conocer las inequidades de género, Instituto Nacional de las Mujeres,* (Mexico: Inmujeres, 2003), p. 65.

The Mexican gender salary discrimination index is calculated as a function of a) the pecuniary income that salaried women do not receive in compensation for their labour in the production of goods and services, and b) the concomitant skills, training, labour market insertion, job type and the length of the work day.[20]

The salary discrepancies are greatest among professionals, with women earning 5.6 pesos per hour less than male counterparts; supervisors and industrial foremen, where women stand below men by 5.2 peso per hour, and female public officials and managers of private sector companies, who lag behind by 4.4 pesos per hour.

Moreover, the 1994 data show that of the total number of female heads of households, 54.7 per cent had either no education at all, some years of elementary school or had finished elementary school (basic education in Mexico consists of six years of elementary school and three years of secondary school). For male heads of household, the corresponding figure was 42 per cent.

For 2006, the respective figures for women and men were 41.2 per cent and 29.8 per cent. This suggests that even when female heads of households attained higher educational achievement; it did not translate into receiving higher income. In contrast, male heads of household, in fact, enjoyed a positive correlation between educational achievement and income.

The data for 2002 reinforce this view (see Table 6.8). Therefore, the inability of female heads of households to improve income is not simply a product of their generally lower levels of education, as defenders of investment in human capital argue. It also entails structural economic conditions. As a result of these disparities, the income of families with female breadwinners is lower than those of the male-headed households. Income is considered to be the variable with the greatest effect on the situation of women, their families and socio-economic status.

Table 6 8: Mexico: Years of schooling and average female and male income (2002).

Years of schooling	Average male income (A)	Average female income (B)	(B)/(A)%
0	1600.48	1099.41	68.7
1	1872.20	1421.77	75.9
2	1855.47	1082.81	58.4
3	2364.28	1578.69	66.8
4	2085.01	1494.93	71.7
5	2139.85	1308.85	61.2
6	2472.90	1762.25	71.3
7	2878.45	2118.42	73.6
8	2842.90	1794.02	63.1
9	2935.82	2098.55	71.5
10	2851.31	2162.64	75.8
11	3086.37	2381.34	77.2
12	4229.75	3399.99	80.4
13	5188.89	4564.91	88.0
14	4571.99	3843.38	84.1
15	5363.14	4750.05	88.6
16	7211.42	5624.72	78.0
17	10012.92	7415.03	74.1
19	13057.08	10016.00	76.7

Source: Inmujeres, reprocessing ENIGH data, 2002. *Only income from salaries, wages or daily pay among population 15 years and older were taken into account.

Income is a key factor for explaining the gap between female and male economic power, since the lack of access to income as a social resource affects the potential it has to underpin women's general well-being.[21]

Government Support to Poor Women: The Progresa-Oportunidades Programme

The National Solidarity Programme (Pronasol or Solidaridad) was launched in 1989 and ended officially in 1994. Its objectives were to overcome extreme poverty and establish the basis for economic development. To these ends it undertook infrastructure projects, promoted productive activities and developed other socially beneficial projects. The approach of this Programme viewed poverty as a function of deficient economic development. After 1994 and before 1997, Pronasol was decentralized and placed under the auspices of the state and municipal governments. In August 1997, the Health, Education and Food Programme (*Progresa*) was launched, and in 2002 it was renamed *Oportunidades*.[22] In Mexican social-political discourse it is referred to as Progresa-Oportunidades, that is, a single programme, given that the name change did not alter its content or conception. We will also refer to it as Progresa-Oportunidades.

As a federal programme, Progresa-Oportunidades addressed both overcoming poverty and the intergenerational reproduction of poverty. In other words, it seeks to break the so-called 'vicious circle' of poverty. Poverty is no longer seen as a function of economic development, but rather as a problem of enhancing a person's skills and abilities. Thus, Progresa-Oportunidades emerged from the conception of investing in human capital and posited the poorest stratum of the population as its target. While Pronasol had been universal in scope, Progresa-Oportunidades is focused on specific sectors.

The monetary support involves cash transfers of monies conceived as investment in human capital. That is to say, these transfers are conditional. As such, Progresa-Oportunidades falls under the umbrella of *Conditional Cash Transfer Programmes* (CCT).

It is important to clarify that poverty in Mexico is measured as a function of three variables: food, skills and assets (see Table 6.9). Progresa-Oportunidades is aimed at those who experience skills poverty. Poverty in Mexican households, however, is most prevalent as a variable of asset poverty. Moreover, per capita income of these households is below that needed to cover the basic threshold for food, clothing and footwear, housing, health-care, public transport and education.

Table 6.9: The evolution of poverty in Mexican households (1992–2006).

Year	Percentages			Number of households		
	Food [1]	Skills [2]	Asset [3]	Food	Skills or capabilities	Asset
1992	16.4	23.1	44.5	3,041,113	4,287,508	8,248,539
1994	16.1	23.2	43.6	3,177,666	4,566,826	8,589,084
1996	29.1	38.0	60.2	5,963,972	7,784,969	12,336,372
1998	26.3	33.9	55.7	5,844,388	7,531,472	12,371,439
2000	18.5	25.2	45.7	4,384,487	5,972,949	10,821,786
2002	15.6	21.4	42.4	3,825,260	5,242,179	10,407,370
2004	13.8	19.9	39.7	3,535,944	5,089,169	10,155,906
2005	14.1	19.5	39.6	3,614,648	4,999,913	10,178,614
2006	10.6	16.1	35.5	2,813,874	4,269,023	9,410,821

Source: CONEVAL estimated on the basis of ENIGH data from 1992 to 2006.
* These figures are taken from new databases incorporating INEGI and CONAPO modifications reconciling demographic data.
(1) Food poverty figures correspond to households whose per capita income is below that needed to meet nutritional needs under INEGI-ECLAC 'staple basket' guidelines.
(2) Skills poverty or abilities poverty figures correspond to households whose per capita income is below that needed to meet basic food, health and education expenses.
(3) Asset poverty figures correspond to households whose per capita income is below that needed to meet basic expenses for food, health, education, shoes and clothing, housing and public transportation.

Progresa-Oportunidades expanded its coverage by stages. At the end of 1997 it involved 400,000 families; in 1998 the number rose to 1.9 million families; in 1999, to 2.3 million; in 2002, to 4.2 million; and in 2005 it served almost 4.5 million families. The programme is operational in every Mexican state, providing both monetary support and resources in kind.

The aim of monetary support is to supplement family income and boost levels of consumption. The support that a family receives, however, has been contained under a monthly cap of 550 pesos in 1997; 605 in 1998; 722 in 1999; 945 in 2003 and 1,055 in 2005. These sums include food deliveries and monetary support for eligible school-aged children (third grade through the third year of secondary school). The maximum monthly amounts per family in 1997 represented 75 per cent of the nominal monthly minimum wage; in 1998, 72 per cent; in 1999, 75 per cent; in 2003, 76 per cent; and in 2005, 78 per cent. The Programme's official prospectus stresses that the maximum amount of the Programme's monetary support is set so as not to discourage families from overcoming their poverty through their own efforts.[23] In this statement one can hear the echo of the seventeenth and eighteenth century discussion that took place in

Great Britain, which debated the merits of providing monetary assistance to the poor and whether it might not discourage their efforts to seek gainful employment. That debate moreover centred on making a distinction between poor families worthy of such help and those that were not. Progresa-Oportunidades is also gender-targeted on two levels: 1) the monetary support is given to the mother of the family, and 2) the scholarships for girls are slightly higher than those provided for boys.

The Progresa-Oportunidades Programme exemplifies *maternalism* as indicated by Maxine Molyneaux.[24] Women are incorporated in its design in such a way that the Programme's success depends on clearly established distinctions between gender roles. Although women may be marginally empowered by managing the financial assistance funds, the structure and operation of the Programme reinforces the social division that reproduce gender asymmetries. These asymmetries are evident in the traditional roles and social responsibilities performed by women. Thus, the Progresa-Oportunidades Programme targets those responsibilities habitually attributed to motherhood, with the cash transfers made on the condition of the recipient's 'good motherhood.' Men are not contemplated in any sense and there is no effort to promote the principle that men and women might share responsibilities in finding common objectives, which could allow, primarily, for more equitable distribution of child care responsibilities.

As such, women receive support provided they are mothers and are raising a family. The Programme seeks to counteract the incidence of teenage pregnancy and promote higher educational achievement among young women through slightly higher grants to school-age girls. For example, in 2003 there was no difference between monetary support for boys and girls enrolled in primary school, but by the time they reach secondary school, these monies gradually tip in favour of girls. For the first year of secondary school, male stipend recipients received 300 pesos while females received 315 pesos; in the second year, the boys received 315 pesos and the girls 350; in the third year, the boys received 335 pesos and the girls 385 pesos. In middle and junior high school (which last three years and are compulsory in order to enter the university) there are also differences in the amount of monies targeted for boys and girls.

The calculation of the categories of poverty in per capita terms is shown in Table 6.10. Food poverty is calculated, using the cost of a staple food 'basket', with 1998 as a base line, and a household consisting of an average of 4.4 members. The calculation demonstrates that an urban family would need a monthly income of 2,307.58 pesos simply to cover their food needs. The nominal monthly minimum wage for that same year was 839.70 pesos, which contrasts with the 524.45 pesos that the basic staple basket costs per person per month in the country's urban areas. As such, a single minimum wage was only sufficient to purchase 1.5 staple baskets. Therefore, we suspect that the scholarship funding granted by the Progresa-Oportunidades Programme for education was more often than not used to buy food. In this light, the Programme's effectiveness in terms of human capital investment –in this case education to overcome intergenerational poverty – is questionable at the very least.

Table 6.10: Mexico: Per capita calculation of the poverty variables in current adjusted pesos in August of each year.

Domain	Poverty lines[1]		
Year	Food[2]	Skills[3]	Assets[4]
Rural			
1992[5]	124.75	147.49	226.37
1994	142.87	168.92	259.25
1996	289.47	342.24	525.28
1998	388.13	458.89	704.31
2000	463.36	547.83	840.81
2002	494.78	584.97	897.82
2004	548.17	648.10	994.70
2005	584.34	690.87	1060.35
2006	598.70	707.84	1086.40
Urban			
1992[5]	167.96	206.00	336.99
1994	193.40	237.21	388.04
1996	388.81	476.87	780.10
1998	524.45	643.24	1052.25
2000	626.62	768.55	1257.26
2002	672.27	824.54	1348.85
2004	739.60	907.12	1483.94
2005	790.74	969.85	1586.55
2006	809.87	993.31	1624.92
Engel coefficients[6]			
Rural		1.1823	1.8146
Urban		1.2265	2.0064

Source: CONEVAL estimates based on information from Banco de México, at http://www.banxico.org.mx.
(1) Per capita net monthly income in current adjusted pesos in August of each year.
(2) Food poverty: Minimum net monthly income per capita to cover basic food needs.
(3) Skills or abilities: Minimum net monthly income per capita to cover basic food, health and education needs.
(4) Asset poverty: Minimum net monthly income per capita to cover their basic food, heath, education, clothing and footwear, public transportation and housing needs.
(5) Adjustment was made for the change to new pesos for the years prior to 1993.
(6) Estimates were made for 2000 using the Engel coefficients.

Although the Programme's support measures are important to poor families, they do not lead to a transformation in living conditions. As one can glean from Table 6.9, even when women have the same years of schooling as men, salary disparities persist. With six years of schooling, women receive 71.3 per cent of the average income of their male counterparts; with nine years, the percentage hardly budges (71.5 per cent); with 12 years (basic education and middle and junior high school), it advanced slightly, reaching 80.4%.

The Progresa-Oportunidades Programme attempts an integral approach, whereby a higher educational achievement is the precursor to improved use of health care services, adoption of hygienic practices and prevention of illnesses. Moreover, education is expected to underpin better health in infants and children, which would create a feedback into better educational performance. Improved nutrition is expected to aid the development of skills and abilities. These interrelated factors constitute the government's official hypothesis for breaking the vicious circle of poverty and replacing it with virtuous circles of development.

From this flows the conclusion that education –understood as educational achievement facilitating the acquisition of skills and abilities– is a strategic underpinning of the Progresa-Oportunidades Programme. Although the social benefits of a better educated population are evident, Luis Fernando Aguado points out that education in itself is not sufficient to enable individuals to overcome the conditions of poverty in which they live, because if the market is not capable of absorbing the poor population, the individual, although educated, would continue to live in poverty since he or she would not have the income to surmount such conditions.[25]

Thus, poor women who are mothers make use of the Progresa-Oportunidades Programme in two senses: objectively, the scholarships are often used to buy food; subjectively, mothers have the expectation that their daughters will have access to a better life than their own. In other words, it is a female survival strategy.

At the same time, the economic support provided by the Programme focused on women leads to a reproduction of the workforce under better conditions, but it does not guarantee overcoming intergenerational poverty.

In order to overcome poverty, women need a source of reliable and unbroken income, not the *maternalist* options they are frequently offered. The limits of programmes such as Progresa-Oportunidades are clear, not only due to their targeted focus in dealing with social needs, but also in their narrow vision of how to overcome poverty. The financial support that the Programme grants does not resolve structural economic problems nor does it address all the needs of poor households. Given that the transformation of the socio-economic structures underlying poverty is not a purpose of Progresa-Oportunidades; the Programme is ensnared in the social aid or charity paradigm that it officially claims not to recognize.

Conclusion

Poverty is inherited from generation to generation. This vicious cycle cannot be broken or replaced with a virtuous cycle within the system that engenders it and favours its reproduction. The poor generally come from poor families that assign low priority to school because of the need to incorporate young children into earning activities for the household's immediate subsistence. This phenomenon becomes a significant brake on intergenerational social mobility, as the sons and daughters enter the labour market before securing the educational achievement that correlates with higher income. More importantly, programmes based on conditional cash transfers (CCT) do not, in our view, serve to transform the structures that give rise to poverty. Anti-poverty programmes remain persistently detached from other spheres of economic policy. Such programmes treat the poor as if they existed outside the economic domain of production, distribution, exchange and consumption. This view places the poor in isolation from the system that produces them, rather than viewing them in their genuine condition: immersed in the system itself. Because poverty is a functional element of the system, the implementation of programmes to combat poverty emerging from it cannot exert an effect on the broader conditions driving poverty; although they can, perhaps, alleviate or significantly improve some factors these conditions entail. Often politicized, the idea of combating poverty, moreover, is treated as a question of necessity, but always as an endeavour lying outside of the realm of the economic and social structures that produce it.

Poverty is also separated from the gender relations that contribute to its reproduction.

For women living in poverty, the current programmes, such as Progresa-Oportunidades, appear to offer both risks and potential. The cash transfers are welcome in the household, but they offer scant consolation to the poor who subsist in a context of deep inequality, unemployment and otherwise precarious income flow. The caps on these transfers are set in order to avoid undermining the poor family's aspiration and energies to overcome poverty through their own efforts. Although women managing the monies provided within the structure and operation of Progresa-Oportunidades are marginally empowered, the Programme's vision and mission serve to reinforce the social roles that drive replication of gender asymmetries over generations.

Women occupy a central role in the new configuration of poverty; they contribute with their time and effort to their children's future, but they need education and training to expand skills and abilities demanded by the labour market. This needs to be done indiscriminately so that each and every woman can build a future. Whether the poverty in question is of the intergenerational sort or not, all this would imply substantial transformation of the socioeconomic structure and relationships lying beyond the scope of anti-poverty programmes.

Acknowledgements

The authors are grateful to Bernardo Ramirez Pablo for his valuable assistance and technical support in preparing this paper. They would also like to thank Hilda Caballero and Susana Merino for their valuable opinions.

7 GENDER AND MIGRATION IN THE PYRENEES IN THE NINETEENTH CENTURY: GENDER-DIFFERENTIATED PATTERNS AND DESTINIES

Marie-Pierre Arrizabalaga

Introduction

Pyrenean emigration to America in the nineteenth and twentieth centuries has been the object of great attention and extensive research in France and in America, because of the size and length of this movement from a French perspective, and the rich data set available to analyse the trans-continental migration.[1] Documentation indicates that these French Pyreneans envisaged overseas migration in the same way as other French groups (from Alsace, Aveyron etc.) in the same period, but they left in greater numbers and during a longer period of time.[2] The movement did not, however, parallel that of some other European countries, the English, the Germans, the Swiss migrated to America in much greater numbers and proportion. The comparatively small migration which characterized France was actually linked to the French adopting Malthusian demographic practices as early as the eighteenth century, while other Europeans did not start reducing births until the next century. Consequently, in the nineteenth century, the French did not experience a demographic explosion on the scale of other Europeans. Fewer people were forced to envisage overseas migration as a solution to excessive population, shrinking economic opportunities in rural areas, and slowly emerging urban industrial development.[3]

French migration to America was definitely less significant than elsewhere in Europe. The only areas with sizable overseas migration were the border regions of France: the Pyrenees (along the French–Spanish border), the Alps (along the French-Italian border), and Alsace (along the French–German border). This was due to pervasive single inheritance practices or the transmission of the family assets to one child, despite the egalitarian laws of the Civil Code in 1804. Indeed, families refused to abide by the new law obliging the partition of all assets between all children. Instead, they continued to select one child to take over the family farm or business forcing the other children to exclusion or migration; hence massive overseas migration from these border areas of France and in particular from the Pyrenees.[4]

Not only was French migration smaller than elsewhere in Europe, but more is known about male than female migration, researchers have assumed that the women generally followed the men and that their migration patterns and strategies resembled those of the men. That is why the historiography on Pyrenean female migration to America in the nineteenth and twentieth century (like that of other French and European female migration), is so scarce, women being rarely ever discussed and their migration patterns and strategies often being unknown or undifferentiated from those of the men.

The scarcity of female migration studies has not only characterized French research on the subject, but other nationalities as well. This is due to the various approaches which have been used to study migration. The macro-structural approach of migration has rarely led to the study of gender-differentiated patterns and behavior. Indeed, scholars have striven to discern large processes which highlight common global patterns rather than individual, gender differences.[5] In such a perspective, gender has been considered a marginal subject of analysis. This is probably due to the nature of the sources, such as censuses which register men (the household heads) rather than the women, and to the legal and political legislation depriving women of personal representation and status in society and therefore in documentation.[6] By contrast, the micro-longitudinal analysis of migration (deriving from family reconstitution, among other methods) has led to greater gender-differentiated analysis of migration patterns, strategies and destinies, an approach often chosen by researchers favouring the methods of historical demography. Those specialized in gender and migration studies, whether historians, anthropologists or sociologists, have oriented their analysis towards women and their contribution to the labour market.[7] More recently, the above-mentioned approaches have led the way to new queries which discuss concepts such as 'agency', 'human and social capital', 'empowerment' and, 'transnational cultures', an approach most favoured by sociologists (and now by historians) who highlight women's capital and empowerment, analyse their decisions, strategies, and behavior in order to explain why their migration patterns differed from men's.[8]

In the research presented here this particular perspective and approach will be used. It aims at studying Pyrenean women's migration strategies in the past two centuries. It will uncover gender-differentiated migration destinies, highlighting women's capital and capabilities to devise migration strategies and patterns of their own. This analysis will attempt to draw a more complete picture of the complex reality of the phenomenon. Despite the difficulty to trace women's life cycle events in the Pyrenees and in America, the sources used for the purpose of this analysis provide extensive documentation and possibilities for richer analysis on gender and migration. This study on Pyrenean women, the Basques in particular, aims at demonstrating that these women had migration patterns and destinies which differed from their male counterparts, that they made more autonomous decisions than the historiography has traditionally assumed, and that their marriage strategies shaped their specific migration priorities and reflected their peculiar migration objectives. Some women envisaged migration as a way to live a better life, one which secured them status and wealth while others sometimes preferred to relinquish marriage and status altogether for an independent, autonomous life. Overseas migration to America did offer great opportunities for a good marriage, yet Pyrenean women did not necessarily consider this destination as a good strategy. As a matter of fact various options could be available in their village of birth (as heiresses, heirs' spouses or celibates) or in cities. Many preferred these conditions rather than overseas migration, until perspectives improved. They could not be lured to accept higher status and wealth overseas knowing well that life in the wild open spaces of the new American continent could be one of isolation, remoteness, and of very hard work. Instead, they made specific choices, different from those of men, as they settled in towns and cities in greater numbers than men, and lived alone.

Using Basque families as case studies on the Pyrenees, I will first attempt to determine women's options for a living in the past two centuries. In what circumstances did they envisage a sedentary life in their village or nearby, an urban life by themselves or overseas emigration? What were the conditions acceptable for marriage in the village, in cities and overseas? Why did so many of them prefer celibacy at home or in cities rather than a decent and perhaps good marriage and status overseas? According to the data, Pyrenean women's migration patterns and marriage strategies sometimes differed from men's, decisions leading some of them to favour lower social mobility, a more modest life, and greater economic instability. They seemed to prefer the latter conditions because of the sacrifice which marriage and migration imposed. Instead some women remained single, celibacy being the price for greater independence and liberty, especially in urban settings?

Methodology

The method used involved family reconstitution and the use of the civil registers and of the succession records of the nineteenth and twentieth centuries. The consultation and the cross-analysis of these archival sources made it possible to determine men's and women's migration patterns within families. The 120 genealogies were completed in six different villages, all scattered in the three French Basque provinces, four villages being located in the Pyrenean highlands (Sare, Les Aldudes, Mendive, and Alçay) and two in the lowlands (Isturits and Amendeuix). I first selected 120 couples who married in the early 1800s, twenty in each of the six villages. I then reconstituted their life cycle events and those of their children (second generation) and their grandchildren (third generation) by identifying them in the civil records (births, deaths, and marriages records) of their village of birth and of all surrounding villages on a twenty-mile radius around each village and of all district towns, and finally in the regional cities of Bayonne and Pau. This three-generational family reconstitution research work involved the tracing of the individual life cycle experiences of about 3000 people in the period which started in 1800 for the 120 couples and ended in the 1980s for the third-generation descendants, some of whom were born in the early 1900s and died in the 1980s. I thus systematically consulted the birth, death, marriage records of the entire population residing in 150 Basque villages and towns from 1800 until 1980.

Once the family reconstitutions were completed, I searched through all the public land records available on the six villages and all neighboring villages. I focused my attention on the official land records of the *Cadastre*[9] which list each village's land ownership titles by identifying property owners' names and land value from the 1830s or 1840s until the 1920s. Not only did I consult the *Cadastre* of the six villages of the sample, but also those of the villages around the six villages, a total of 38 villages. I thus found traces of the 120 couples' and their descendants' property value as well as that of all the people who lived in the six villages and the five villages around each one of them, for comparative purposes.

For this particular study, I made a specific choice to only consider propertied families, that is about half of the population.[10] Indeed, the data on these families were the richest as opposed to landless families whose descendants could not afford property and overseas emigration. The latter therefore could only be traced in civil registers, hence the scarcity of information about them. As the research progressed, I collected precious information from the succession records (*Enregistrement*)[11] in order to find the official transcription of the sample population's property settlement upon succession. In those records, state officials identified the value of the family property, the heirs, the earlier marriage contracts and testaments which benefited one or several children, and other contracts (purchase or donations) which clearly defined families' property evolution and property redistribution prior to the donors' death. In addition, those records identify the single heir and the strategies which the families elaborated in order to benefit one or several children before others and to keep the property undivided. More importantly, the records indicate the names, professions and places of residence of all the direct descendants, as well as their compensations, the ones they received before their permanent departure from the family house to other villages, to towns or cities, or overseas. These were highly significant sources as they helped to locate and identify all family members, especially those who resided in remote areas of France, Europe and America.

The outcome of this long research work is a rich data set which highlights Basque women's strategies and migration patterns in the nineteenth and twentieth centuries. This paper will demonstrate that women's destinies differed sometimes from men's, not because they had fewer chances and opportunities than men, but because they made choices of their own, which sometimes differed from those of men. Their social and professional background or capital led them to favour very different destinies, depending on their priorities, for social mobility, status and/or independence.

Pyrenean Women's Migration Patterns

Among Basque propertied families in the nineteenth century, women did migrate but in smaller proportion than men and to different destinations. Looking at the destinies of the children and grandchildren of the 120 couples, it appears that almost two thirds of the women never departed from their village of birth while fewer among the sons and more importantly among the grandsons of the sample families remained. The data indicate that 61.3 per cent of the daughters and 57 per cent of the granddaughters of the original married couples of the sample never left their villages of origins or their vicinity while 61.2 per cent of the sons and 45.9 per cent of the grandsons did (see Table 7.1). The purpose of this paper is to understand why men migrated more than women. Were women denied opportunities which men had at the time? Actually women were not all so much more sedentary than men. They did not shun migration and their decisions were not made out of necessity. We will see that in reality, they had a number of options in their village or nearby and in towns, destinies which did fit their professional, marital and social priorities.

Table 7.1: Migration destinations among the children and grandchildren of the propertied families of the sample, percentages.

Residence\ Generation Sex	Second Generation Women	Second Generation Men	Total	Third Generation Women	Third Generation Men	Third Generation Total
Rural	61.3	61.2	61.3	57.0	45.9	51.7
Urban	15.5	3.7	10.0	17.2	4.1	11.0
Abroad	12.9	22.4	17.3	12.3	30.6	21.0
Unknown	10.3	12.7	11.4	13.5	19.4	16.3
Total	53.6	46.4	100	52.4	47.6	100
			(N=289)			(N=466)

Sources: Arrizabalga: Data base collected through a three-generational family reconstitution of about 3000 people starting in 1800 for 120 couples and ending in the 1980s for the third-generation descendants, based on birth, death, marriage records of the entire population residing in 150 Basque villages and towns from 1800 until 1980. The dataset was then combined with succession records including the names, professions and places of residence of all the direct descendants, as well as information on property and inheritance.

When women did not reside in their village of birth or nearby during their whole life, they seemed to prefer settlement in towns or cities rather than America. The men by contrast showed opposite trends. When they left their village of birth permanently, they preferred long-distance migration to America rather than settlement in local towns or French cities (as Bordeaux and Paris). I will later show that men's and women's motivation for urban settlement differed and so did their socio-professional destinies and mobility. The data clearly corroborate these findings. They indicate that 15.5 per cent of the daughters of the sample couples and 17.2 per cent of the granddaughters settled in towns and cities while only 3.7 per cent of the sons and 4.1 per cent of the grandsons did (see Table 7.1). Cities were definitely less popular among the men than the women. America on the contrary attracted more men than women. Indeed, the data show that 22.4 per cent of the sons and 30.6 per cent of the grandsons (and perhaps more)[12] resided in America while only 12.9 per cent of the daughters and 12.3 per cent of the granddaughters did (see table 7.1). The discussion below will attempt to explain the reasons for these gendered-differentiated migration patterns and men's and women's motivations for them.

Men and women therefore had different migration destinies, women preferring urban settlement in local district towns, Basque coastal towns, or regional cities while men preferred overseas emigration to Argentina and Uruguay for the early settlers of the mid nineteenth century, then to Bolivia, Cuba, Chile, and Mexico for those who emigrated in the second half of the century, and finally to the United States and Canada for those who departed at the end of the nineteenth century or the early twentieth century.[13] This paper will later address the question on whether these different migration patterns and destinations had an impact on men's and women's marriage patterns, their destinies, and their social mobility.

Not only did Basque men and women have different migration patterns but they also had different marital strategies and destinies. Contrary to what one might expect, celibacy was not a fate most frequently observed among the women. Contrary to our preconceived idea that the desperate, destitute conditions of celibates were generally women's lot, our data show different trends. Tables 7.2 and 7.3 indicate that more men than women among the propertied families in the Basque Country in the nineteenth century ended up celibate. Why did 30.5 per cent of the sons of the selected propertied couples and 36.7 per cent of their grandsons remain single in America or in French cities, while only 19.2 per cent of the daughters of the selected original couples and 27.9 per cent of the granddaughters never married, especially in cities. One might argue that high celibacy in cities was due to the unbalanced sex ratio which characterized French cities at the time and which remained unfavourable to women. Celibacy was known for being the lot of many urban women as a result of French cities having a larger female population than a male population in this period, and therefore a marriage market favourable to men. This alone however does not fully justify the high female celibacy rates in cities and certainly not the high celibacy rate among the men of the sample. Other reasons must be taken into consideration. I will later show that Basque women in cities seemed to refuse marriage because it did not fit their personal standards and/or priorities. Men by contrast had a greater celibacy rate than women, for different reasons, hence gendered-differentiated destinies.

Table 7.2: Marital status of the female descendants of the propertied families of the sample, percentages.

Residence/Generation Marital status	Second Generation Celibate	Second Generation Married	Third Generation Celibate	Third Generation Married
Rural	13.1	86.9	20.0	80
Urban	47.8	52.2	53.7	46.3
Abroad	12.5	87.5	28.6	71.4
Total	19.2	80.8	27.9	72.1
		(N=130)		(N=183)

Sources: See Table 7.1.

Table 7.3: Marital status of the male descendants of the propertied families of the sample, percentages.

Residence/Generation Marital status	Second Generation Celibate	Second Generation Married	Third Generation Celibate	Third Generation Married
Rural	25	75	33.3	66.7
Urban	25	75	80	20.0
Abroad	60	40	28.6	71.4
Total	30.5	69.5	36.7	63.3
				(N=120)

Sources: See Table 7.1.

Female Destinies in Basque Villages

Contrary to what one might expect, women's social destinies in the French Basque rural environment were not inferior to those of men. Indeed women from propertied families did not live in their village of birth or nearby out of necessity or desperation. In addition they did not always enjoy lower status than men. Finally their lot was not poorer or more desperate than men's. On the contrary, they benefited from local family traditions and privileges, some of which dated back to the Middle Ages or earlier and prevailed despite the Civil Code.[14] In the Basque Country, as in other parts of the Pyrenees (as in the nearby provinces of Lavedan and Barreges in the Modern period), women inherited family assets and the family house in the same way as men even when they had brothers. The House system which prevailed in the Pyrenees and which imposed single inheritance and the stem family household form obliged families to consider the house above individuals.[15] It imposed rules supporting the indivisibility of patrimony (imposed by the Civil Code). As a consequence, at each generation, families selected one child to inherit the family house and land and excluded all the others. While male primogeniture was dominant in most Pyrenean provinces, as in Bearn and the Baronies, and male inheritance no matter of birth rank in French Catalonia, strict primogeniture, irrespective of whether the first-born child was male or female, characterized inheritance practices in the Basque Country, Lavedan and Bareges.[16] In these circumstances, first-born daughters had equal rights and power in relation to first-born sons, more so than younger sons and daughters who were systematically excluded from inheritance and forced to face migration and/or celibacy.[17]

In the nineteenth and twentieth centuries, these practices continued even though the Civil Code of 1804 imposed equal partition of family assets between all male and female children. Families in the Basque Country (as elsewhere in the Pyrenees) elaborated new strategies to get round the law and continued to transmit the family house and land to only one child. In practice, in the nineteenth century, women began to inherit more often everywhere in the Pyrenees, and in the Basque Country in particular where they actually took on headship more often than men.[18] As new opportunities opened in cities and overseas, more and more Basque men, and Pyrenean men in general, started to focus on migration to cities or overseas for better employment and economic improvement. They sometimes left the family house even though they were entitled to inheritance as first-born heirs. In their absence, their sisters assumed headship and ownership. The data corroborate these findings because among the children of the propertied couples of the sample, more than half of the heirs were women and among the grandchildren, the proportion reached about 60 percent.

Thus, the data indicate that women were not more immobile than men out of necessity, destitution, or out of fear for their future, but because they had the opportunity to secure headship as first-born daughters or as young daughters replacing their older brothers residing in America. Because of migration and new urban opportunities, families had to adapt, their children tending to consider more different and diversified destinations as time went by. As long as the departing children accepted to relinquish their rights to the house and that parents were secured qualified heirs among the younger children, the system survived over time (and it did until well into the twentieth century). To make sure that one of the children could inherit, parents raised and trained all their children (first-born or younger sons and daughters) as potential heirs or heiresses and later chose one of them (the most able and the most willing perhaps) to succeed them. This education constituted a real asset, a human, social and professional capital which both men and women employed in order to secure themselves a stable or better life in the village, in town or in America. As sons and daughters originating from propertied families, they had acquired professional skills as farmers and managers of a family business which opened doors to great opportunities for both men and women in cities and in America. They had grown up in an environment where property was symptomatic of status and longevity within the community. They therefore used their social and professional capital to make specific life choices, elaborate strategies to fulfill their dreams, and maintain or improve their life. And women did almost as well as men. Rather few of the children envisaged a more modest life and status. When they could not reach their professional objectives and when they could not enjoy such standards or better, the men did not hesitate to travel all the way to America to settle comfortably and women to urban areas.[19]

When women were unable to inherit (as only one child could in each family), they sometimes married heirs. Most of the women of the sample who resided in the Basque rural environment were either heiresses or heirs' wives. Their marriage patterns were endogamous as they married into their own professional and social group. These were the positions of highest social status in the village or nearby for women. While heiresses received a quarter share of the family assets upon marriage, heirs' wives received a cash dowry equivalent to a quarter share of the assets which the heir or heiress received upon marriage. These dowries were entrance payments into the family house, which guaranteed them status, care, and well-being until death. It is no surprise that women welcomed these favourable conditions. By marrying into the house, they maintained their social status as property owners in the community and had the security to be taken care of until they died.

The data thus indicate that the men and women in the Basque Country (and elsewhere in the Pyrenees) had equal status, power and rights whether they inherited family patrimony or married someone who inherited patrimony. Similar to men, women could become heirs' spouses and enjoy the authority and powers linked to that position. At first glance, men and women received equal treatment in equal position. One must not be lured by the data though. Succession data indicate that at equal status and rank, men and women did not enjoy the same authority and power in the house. A close analysis of succession records highlights gender-differentiated treatment and inequalities. Indeed, while heirs remained sole decision-makers in the house, heiresses had to share their powers with their husbands. Similarly, while heiresses' husbands shared decisions with the heiresses in the house, heir's wives did not. Thus at equal status and position the men had rights which the women did not enjoy equally. Correspondingly, when marrying heiresses, men brought a dowry that served as an entry payment into the house, under the condition that they gained legal rights of co-ownership with their wives on the inherited patrimony, as the Civil Code entitled them to. Heirs' wives however could not enjoy any co-ownership rights despite their dowry being absorbed into their husbands' assets, in the same way as heiresses' husbands' dowry did. As a consequence, heirs' wives lived and died owning their dowry only, while heiresses' husbands owned their dowry and a part of their wives' assets. In the end, heirs made all the decisions in the house while their wives entered the house as secondary decision-makers who had more limited power in the house. Heiresses' husbands by contrast used Civil Code prerogatives to demand partnership in the house as a result of their dowry being used to acquire the heiresses' siblings' share of the property. As heiresses' husbands and co-owners, they had greater powers than heirs' wives, and these powers were guaranteed at the expense of the heiresses' powers. One must not be misled though. While gender-differentiated treatment and inequalities among men and women at equal position and birth rank prevailed, the women did enjoy greater power as heiresses or heirs' wives, than women of comparable status in other parts of France or Europe.[20]

All non-migrating women however did not enjoy the same rights and status. Those who did not inherit or marry an heir had an unfavourable position and status in the rural environment. That is why many women from propertied families tried a new life elsewhere. Those who remained in the village married down, with landless artisans or small farmers, others remained single all their life, either in the family house (the tradition in the Old Regime) or in the village.[21] The women who experienced downward social mobility were very few though. Rather than accepting these conditions in the village, they settled in cities, alone, or migrated to America where their brothers sometimes fared well. While during the Old Regime, celibacy at home was a perfectly acceptable condition for a woman who maintained her status in the community and was cared for through life, these conditions were no longer as acceptable for women in the nineteenth century. Other opportunities were available besides life-long service, obedience, and submission to a brother or sister in the family house. By contrast, their celibate brothers continued to accept life-long service in the house under the authority of the heir or heiress. This was linked to the male option of raising cattle privately and separately from the farm, through hard work. Men could save money and subsequently acquire a small property, something which celibate women could not, as succession data indicate.[22] These professional and financial conditions and gender inequalities explain why there were more celibate men in the village than celibate women (see tables 7.2 & 7.3).

Finally those who did not reside in the house as celibates, did not marry an heir, or did not inherit, lived a less comfortable life. These were women who married down, received a very small dowry, if any, and lost their family status within the community. Their conditions were poorer and perhaps shameful, especially if they had illegitimate children. These cases however were extremely rare. Families seemed to always make sure that all their children lived decent lives in the village or elsewhere. To avoid social degradation, some women could receive help from parents or siblings in order to supplement a dowry to marry into a local proper-tied family, or settle decently in a local town or regional city, or finance their fare to America where they were welcomed by a relative (a father, uncle, brother or cousin) already established there.[23] Rather than accept the conditions which the rural environment offered those who did not inherit or marry an heir, propertied families' daughters embraced urban migration or overseas emigration.

Female Destinies in Towns or Cities

As indicated earlier urban migration was more attractive to women than men. At least 15.5 per cent of the daughters of the propertied couples of the sample and 17.2 per cent of their granddaughters had settled in towns or cities (see table 7.1). The men by contrast were reluctant to settle in cities: 3.7 per cent of the sons and 4.1 per cent of the grandsons only. Why did more women settle in cities than men and in what conditions?

The women who settled in cities preferably settled in local district towns as Tardets, Saint-Jean-Pied-de-Port, Saint-Palais or coastal towns as Saint-Jean-de-Luz and Biarritz, and to a lesser extent in local cities as Bayonne or Pau, or regional cities as Bordeaux, Toulouse, and even Paris.[24] These local towns and regional cities had developed economic activities as major market centres for the sale of agricultural products, dairy products, and local manufactured goods, and for the sale of industrial products (mining, textile, and crafts). They natu-rally attracted a lot of people from the area and from other regions and served as economic magnets for the purchase, sale or exchange of goods. Finally they offered many skilled and unskilled jobs to rural qualified and unqualified labour.[25] Urban employment opportunities became more and more attractive in the course of the nineteenth century and the early twentieth century, yet they seemed to attract more women than men.

Because both propertied sons and daughters were trained as potential heirs or heiresses, all received an education which qualified them to assume the responsibilities, powers and authority which corresponded to the position. All were trained to manage the family farm professionally and financially in order to make the family business viable over time, and to transmit it successfully and intact to the next generation. While the women were often in charge of man-aging the family poultry and the sale of farm animals, vegetables and fruit in the local market, the men were in charge of the crops and their sale in the local

market. Besides farm work, the women weaved or sewed and the men maintained the farm, as carpenters, blacksmiths, or house builders. Consequently all
had multiple training (as managers, farmers and crafts men), a professional capital which opened the doors to wide-range employment opportunities in cities
and overseas. Both the men and the women used their family background, their
education, and their social status (the earlier-mentioned human, social and professional capital) to gain access to jobs which could secure them higher revenues
and therefore a decent life. As a consequence, when the sons and daughters of
these propertied families did not inherit or did not marry and heir or heiress,
they all aspired to a destiny that secured them equal well-being and status as their
parents', if not better. While the women seemed to find what they looked for in
towns and cities, the men did so in America.

Men and women in towns and cities had different professional, social and
marital strategies and destinies. While the men had access to skilled jobs as craftsmen, civil servants (working for the police, the army or customs), or as priests,
the women were only offered unskilled jobs as maids, weavers, seamstresses,
and shop attendants. The men consequently had a better life in cities than the
women. Actually the men generally experienced stable or upward social mobility
while the women experienced stable or downward social mobility. Indeed, some
of the women's destinies were poorer than the men's. Why did these women
accept such conditions knowing that some of their brothers or cousins, fared
well in America and would welcome them?

Family reconstitution data indicate that around half of the women who settled in towns and cities remained single in the course of the century. As stated
earlier, high celibacy in urban setting in the nineteenth century was linked
to the unbalanced sex ratio and marriage market which remained negative to
women. Yet this alone does not explain why so many of the women of the sample remained single and consequently accepted inferior destinies.[26] Indeed the
data indicate that 47.8 per cent of the daughters of the propertied couples of the
sample residing in towns or cities and 53.7 per cent of their granddaughters lived
as single women (see table 7.2). By contrast the men residing in towns or cities
had no problem getting married. Few remained single of the second generation,
only 25 per cent of the sons of the propertied couples of the sample in the mid-
nineteenth century. They were crafts men who managed to get skilled jobs and
married comfortably. Later the celibate men in cities grew in number, 80 per
cent of the grandsons of the sample residing in towns or cities remaining single
(as table 7.3 indicates). They did so not because they could not find wives but
because of their professions as military or custom officers. They moved around
the country a great deal and therefore could not settle long enough to envisage
marriage. Sometimes they remained single until retirement. They then returned
to their village of birth and occasionally married very late (if ever). The others

were priests, not entitled to marry according to the Catholic doctrine. Celibacy among the men established in towns or cities was therefore required as part of their employment. They experienced upward social mobility and chose status and perhaps freedom of movement at the expense of marriage.

It is hard to conceive that many of the women in towns and cities were forced to celibacy solely because of a negative sex ratio and an unfavourable marriage market. Instead I am inclined to believe that some women of our sample actually chose to remain permanent celibates. While some opted for celibacy by choice, as for example those who entered a convent and lived there as nuns all their life, it appears that others accepted celibacy because they were unable to make a good marriage. These women had qualifications (the above-mentioned capital) which turned them into attractive wives, managers and/or employees. They could contribute to the family income working outside the home as seamstresses, weavers or shop attendants or else, manage a family business as professionals and wives. After working in cities, many successfully collected decent savings in order to marry quite well. While some fared well by marrying propertied farmers, propertied artisans or civil servants, others did not. Instead they remained single, working as unskilled landless female labourers losing their social status (Tables 7.4 and 7.5). These women however did not live a poor life. They worked hard and were often offered decent jobs and salaries, enough to retire with sizable savings (several hundreds of francs sometimes, as succession records indicate). The size of their savings indicates that they could probably have married a propertied artisan or a civil servant, men who could have secured them a stable, decent, perhaps honorable life in towns or cities. Instead, these women chose differently, either because potential husbands had incompatible cultural backgrounds or marriage opportunities did not meet their standards. In any case, they remained single, refusing an exogamous marriage or a low status marriage.

It thus appears that more women in the sample preferred to settle in cities rather than depart to America where their siblings sometimes were doing well. When they settled in cities, they married propertied artisans or civil servants, men who secured them status, responsibilities in the house and in the family business. Status and power at home were two major priorities for these women. They had human, social professional capital which entitled them to such standards. When they could not marry decently, they preferred celibacy. They thus sacrificed status for autonomy. They had no difficulty finding decent jobs in towns and cities, employment opportunities that secured them revenues to support themselves and protect them from poverty. They might have lived a modest life but one which allowed them to make their own decisions and experience the freedom of movement and a decent retirement.

Urban migration and celibacy in towns and cities thus seemed to be a choice, probably not the preferred choice but a choice anyway, when inheritance and marriage with a propertied man or a civil servant was impossible. This was indeed a choice because otherwise they would have accepted their relatives' call to America. Why did so many remain deaf to their relatives' or compatriots' call from America?

Table 7.4: Professional destinies of the children from the 120 families (second generation), percentages.

Destination Profession/sex	Rural		Urban		Overseas	
	Male	Female	Male	Female	Male	Female
Farmers	70.5	48.4	27.3	16.7	36.35	57.1
Artisans	14.3	2.5	18.2	3.3	36.35	0
Self-employed	1.8	0	4.5	3.3	9.1	0
Civil Servants	2.7	0	36.4	0	0	0
Unskilled labourers	8	19.7	9.1	43.4	9.1	0
Religion	0	0	0	3.3	0	0
None	2.7	29.3	4.5	30	9.1	42.9
N° of cases	112	157	22	30	11	7

Sources: see Table 7.1.

Table 7.5: Professional destinies of the grandchildren from the 120 families (third generation), percentages.

Destination Profession/sex	Rural		Urban		Overseas	
	Male	Female	Male	Female	Male	Female
Farmers	62.1	39.4	34.2	2.7	60	20
Artisans	13.8	1.2	26.3	0	4	0
Self-employed	4.1	0	0	0	28	0
Civil Servants	4.1	0	26.3	0	00	0
Unskilled labourers	8.7	24.4	0	37	4	20
Religion	3.1	2.7	5.3	11	0	0
None	4.1	32.3	7.9	49.3	4	60
N° of cases	195	254	38	73	25	5

Sources: see Table 7.1.

Female Destinies in America

America offered quite decent living conditions to the daughters and grand-daughters of the propertied families of the sample because the men fared quite well there as propertied cattle raisers, farmers or artisans in Argentina, Uruguay, Chile, Mexico, and the United States in particular.[27] Yet the data indicate that women avoided emigration compared to men: 12.9 per cent of the daughters and 12.3 per cent of the granddaughters from the propertied families of the sample left, as opposed to 22.4 per cent for the sons and 30.6 per cent for the grandsons (see Table 7.1). When looking at family reconstitution, the patterns clearly emerge: several of the men within the same family migrating together to America while their sisters settled in different French towns or cities. One might expect that several migrating women from the same family envisaged settlement together in a town or city so that they could live nearby (or together) and help one another. Instead, family reconstitutions indicate that sisters settled in different towns or cities rather than together, each assuming all decisions alone and living without anyone's help. Why did women accept to face the difficult urban life alone, in view of a marriage market that was unfavourable to them? It appears that these were strong-minded women who were not afraid to face settlement alone and in distant, unknown places. Why did they not settle in America? This paper wants to highlight that, despite men's economic success in America, living conditions there were so harsh (more so than in cities) that women were reluctant to join their relatives established there.

It was probably difficult for men to have access to land in rural France and to decent jobs in French cities, hence their departure to America as a way to improve their conditions. Contrary to France, America offered them great land opportunities and therefore great material potential for land ownership and upward social mobility as cattle raisers, large propertied farmers, and propertied artisans. These opportunities expanded as the American population grew over time as well as people's material and food needs. Those who had settled in towns and cities in America had no difficulty attracting their sisters and female relatives but those who had settled in remote, isolated areas (as the Pampas in Argentina or the American West in the United States) had difficulty encouraging their sisters to join them. Words had quickly gone around about America's harsh living conditions. The men offered great material conditions because some became quite wealthy property owners. The women could use their social and professional capital as potential heiresses to become partners or co-owners of the sizable family business with their husbands. They could assume extensive responsibilities, taking care of the house and the children and managing the family business together with their husbands. These conditions supposedly resembled those they knew at home. Yet the extent of their responsibilities and the geographic and ecological conditions which America offered at the time discouraged the emigration of many women.[28]

Basque men in America could often offer their wives better material, financial and professional well-being. They had the financial means to acquire a comfortable home, secure their family with high revenues, and live well off their professional activities (as cattle raisers and farmers in particular). Consequently, through marriage, women had access to status, one which fit their personal and family standards. In addition, the marriage market in America was very favourable to Basque immigrant women, most of whom married within three months on arrival. Why did few women emigrate and marry in America?

Looking at Basque living conditions in America more closely, one may understand the female reluctance. The men's jobs as cattle raisers and farmers were difficult because it involved long distance travel across the American wide-open spaces in order to reach their locations. Men were therefore forced to long absences from home. As housewives, the women remained alone in the house in charge of the children and the daily responsibilities around the house. As business managers, these women were also in charge of running the family business during their husbands' absences. In addition, they had to adjust to isolation. Indeed, geographically, the family house was located in remote areas, as in the Pampas or the American West, a long way from the closest local towns and even further away from the regional city. As for the climate, it was much harsher than in the Pyrenees, with colder winters and hotter summers. Finally, they could rarely visit their family at home, fares across the Atlantic Ocean remaining costly, even for well-off immigrants.

The reasons for female reluctance to emigration were therefore various: hard working-conditions, hard living conditions, heavy family and professional responsibilities, isolation from the closest urban environment, isolation from their village of birth and from their family, and the harsh climate both in the winters and in the summers. Conditions in America were therefore far from being similar to those in the Pyrenees. One may argue that propertied families' daughters were willing to assume extensive professional and family responsibilities and obligations but not in the conditions which America offered. Interviews with aging French Basque migrant women in the American West show that a number of the women had the capital and capability to manage the family house and business and to adapt to American conditions, despite Basque businesses being larger and more complex than in the Pyrenees.[29] Yet some had so much difficulty adjusting to the isolation and the harsh climate, that they talked their husbands into selling the family business and move to American towns or return to France. Some women who refused to cope with their American lifestyle even threatened to divorce if the family did not move to more urban areas.

As long as recent modern communication and transportation means remained unavailable in the wild open spaces of the American West or the Pampas, life remained very harsh, hence women's preference for urban migration rather than overseas emigration. Their financial and social sacrifices could be great in French cities as they often remained single and lived a modest life or accepted exogamous marriages with civil servants or artisans. Yet these sacrifices were probably smaller compared to the ones imposed upon women in America. Overseas emigration did offer great opportunities for social, economic, professional, and material well-being. Basque women could preserve their lifestyle there, assume headship with their husbands as co-owners of the family business, and therefore maintain (or improve) their status and authority.

Yet the daily reality was perceived by many women as being a lot harsher than the men acknowledged, the latter probably proud of the high status that they had gained and the comfortable material life they could offer their family. Only women of strong character and of skillful business minds could resist and survive in America. In any case, the harsh conditions seemed to justify women's reluctance towards overseas emigration and their preference for migration to French cities where they indeed lived modestly but more independently and closer to their village of birth and their family.[30]

Conclusion

Similar to men, women originating from propertied families in the Basque Country, in the nineteenth and twentieth century, all wished to maintain their status, play a major role in the decisions around the house and the family business, and marry within their family, social, professional, and cultural environment. As propertied families' daughters entitled to inheritance, they had the necessary capital and capability (family culture, training, and education) to assume headship and become heirs of the house. They hoped to maintain the status and powers that corresponded to the position as heiresses or heir's wives. Many did maintain their parents' lifestyle and status in the village or nearby. Yet as family size increased in the nineteenth century, it soon became impossible for all of the children to establish themselves comfortably in the village or nearby. While during the Old Regime, the number of surviving adult children amounted to three on average, in the nineteenth century families could have four surviving children. Before the French revolution, one child inherited, another married an heir or heiress and the third remained single in the house, irrespective of the sex of the children, all receiving equal treatment at equal status and birth rank. In the nineteenth century, however, with the implementation of the Civil Code of 1804, not all children were equally treated: one child inherited, another married an heir or heiress and about two others were excluded from inheritance and had to settle elsewhere. While during the Old Regime, celibacy at home was imposed upon the third child, in the nineteenth century celibacy at home could no longer be imposed, in the name of gender equality and liberty. Migration was then used as a strategy to avoid partition and conceived as a solution to perpetuate inequalities between siblings (and especially women).

Migration, to America in particular, was an option soon adopted by the men when they did not inherit or marry an heiress. The women by contrast resisted overseas migration. As cities offered extensive female employment and sometimes good marriage opportunities, women chose not to emigrate. While an increasing number of them continued to settle in the rural environment in order to perpetuate family traditions and lifestyle as heiresses or heirs' wives, with the rights, obligations, and status that went with the positions, others preferred urban settlement rather than overseas migration. What cities then offered were lower or stable social destinies depending on whether the women chose celibacy or exogamous marriage. Though America generally secured upward social mobility, women shunned America as a result of the harsh professional, ecological, and climatic conditions they had to face there. All these propertied families' sons and daughters had capital and capabilities which enabled them to achieve a decent life and status in France or in America, yet status was not all that mattered for women. Some indeed refused to give up their decision-making powers, their status, and liberty. As a consequence we find gender-differentiated strategies and destinies, as well as prevailing gender inequalities.

8 WOMEN AND PROPERTY IN EIGHTEENTH-CENTURY AUSTRIA: SEPARATE PROPERTY, USUFRUCT AND OWNERSHIP IN DIFFERENT FAMILY CONFIGURATIONS

Margareth Lanzinger

When Peter Ochswieser died in 1797, he left behind a widow, Margareth Kühebacherin. The couple had no children. In their marriage contract of 1784, they had agreed that if the marriage produced no offspring, the spouse who survived would have a lifelong right of usufruct to the other's assets.[1] The right of usufruct meant that the widow, although not enjoying the status of owner, would be able to manage her deceased husband's property and use its profit for herself. She was not allowed to sell, mortgage or bequeath the house, but for her lifetime she could head the household and make all the decisions that arose in everyday life.

Within a regime of separate property, usufruct was an important balancing mechanism. When one of the spouses died, the wealth brought into the marriage by bride and bridegroom could otherwise be broken up into its original components. This was also true in the area studied in this paper, at least in terms of the formal legal situation. Certain women – women who held property as daughter-heirs, well-off widows or women who had themselves bought a house or a share in a house – remained in a comparatively secure position, but they were far fewer in number than women who had married into the property of their husband.[2] Furthermore, it was usual, especially in cases when a woman had inherited a substantial amount, for the husband to receive at least half of his wife's wealth upon marriage; the converse was almost never the case. Either way, widows' scope for action narrowed or expanded in line with the size of their own fortune. If they brought little with them into the marriage, the division of the property at the end of the marriage could put them in a precarious position.

This was because within the system of property separation, the assets of the deceased spouse were assigned to his or her heirs, primarily the children. If there were no children, the property fell to the deceased's own relatives, often a nephew or a niece; the surviving spouse had no claim upon it whatsoever. This applied in equal measure for the husband and the wife. However, if men were privileged in terms of inheritance law and/or inheritance practice, there was a gender-specific inequality of access to property through inheritance, which had a serious impact on the situation of women in widowhood. Things were very different under a community of property regime, the effect of which was, among other things, to even out the inequality of wealth between the bride and bridegroom right at the start of the marriage – to a greater or lesser extent, depending on whether the community of property was general or partial. When one of the spouses died, the widow or widower was entitled not only to her or his own property, but also to half of the joint property, irrespective of how much he or she had originally brought into the marriage.[3]

In questions of access to wealth, historical research on families and kinship has so far focused largely on inheritance law and practice, and on the different strategies deployed under the various models of impartable inheritance and division of land. Marital property law has tended to be neglected, even though it was equally capable of regulating access to resources – it could channel the flow of wealth to a substantial degree, and thus left as lasting a mark on the structure of marriage, family and kinship as did inheritance law.[4] For women especially, it made a considerable difference whether separation of property or community of property was the predominant matrimonial regime. The hardships associated with property separation arose primarily when a woman was widowed, and it therefore made sense to plan provision for this period of one's life as early as possible, preferably by means of a marriage contract.[5] Equally, the position of men who had married into property varied according to the matrimonial regime. My objective in this paper is to explore the implications of the separation of property in eighteenth-century Tyrol. At the same time, I will show the broad range of different arrangements for handling property and assets that were possible within a single model of property law.

Along with inheritance and property rights, marital property law is a crucial factor, especially in gender history. It helped determine the right to utilise wealth and the configuration, deployment and limits of individuals' agency; in this way, it played a part in shaping gender identities.[6] Marriage contracts reveal with particular clarity the interplay of power and negotiation within the intimate family environment,[7] and I have therefore taken them as the basis of the following discussion.

Especially in German-language historiography, there are still large gaps in the area of the history of civil law – of non-contentious jurisdiction in the sense of the social practice of law in everyday settings.[8] Research exists primarily on the aristocratic and royal milieu[9] and from a legal-history perspective.[10] We might also mention historical studies focusing on social and economic aspects,[11] and finally studies that include reference to gender-historical and legal contexts, most of which address the urban environment.[12] A broader range of studies have focused on the Mediterranean region,[13] although important research on other countries has also been published.[14]

Sources, Area Investigated and Legal Framework

The sources used in this paper will be 250 marriage contracts dating mainly from the second half of the eighteenth century, along with other, associated documents of civil law which also regulated property arrangements.[15] The area investigated covers two neighbouring court districts in the Habsburg crown land of Tyrol, located in today's South Tyrol in western Austria: the court of Innichen and that of Welsberg. In these districts it was not obligatory to keep a formal court record of marriage settlements. Verbal agreements, or records of such agreements in the form of private documents kept in the home, were customary. Only those bridal couples (or their families) concerned to safeguard the agreement in the fullest possible way made use of the option of a formal record in the court's protocol. Approximately the same number of marriage contracts, survive from both courts, with slightly more from Innichen. This point is interesting in that the Innichen court only covered Innichen itself, a market town with a population of around 1,000 during the period concerned. The Welsberg court district, in contrast, extended over several villages and valleys, and served a population of around 5,000. Civil jurisdiction was organized on a decentralized basis, so that a marriage contract could be written down by a local court representative, of whom there was one in every village, then sent to the seat of the court. As a result, the smaller number of marriage contracts institutionally recorded and deposited in the Welsberg court is not explained by greater geographical distance from the centre. Instead, we should assume that the two districts showed a different culture in the handling of legal instruments. The more frequent recourse to the court on non-contentious matters by people of Innichen may be regarded as part of the habitual distinction of the market burghers, largely active in crafts and commerce, in contrast to the neighbouring villagers with their more rural and agrarian structure. The high proportion of exogamous marriages in the market town of Innichen – the bride came from outside the town in 43.4 per cent of marriages in the second half of the eighteenth century – may provide a further explanation.[16] Exogamous patterns are also conspicuous in the marriage contracts of the Welsberg court, and indicate a greater desire for protection. The same is true of the comparatively large number of contracts relating to daughter-heirs and men marrying into their family and house.

The legal framework was set by Tyrol's law code, the *Tiroler Landesordnung*, in its 1573 form. This left the question of succession relatively open. Thus, in some Tyrolean regions inherited land was partitioned between the heirs, while in others impartible inheritance applied; likewise, preferential inheritance for the youngest or for the oldest son or daughter was practised.[17] What was, however, generally accepted by this time was the separation of property, which dominated early modern practices regarding marital property.[18] The law provided for community of property only in the case of poor couples,[19] but in the specific area investigated in this paper it was in fact difficult for unpropertied men and women to marry at all, due to a socially restrictive marriage policy.[20] The first centralized state codification of civil law, the Josephinisches Gesetzbuch of 1786, was issued during the period under investigation. Like the later Allgemeines Österreichisches Gesetzbuch, the Austrian Civil Code of 1811, the Josephinisches Gesetzbuch brought the region several changes of detail but no significant upheavals: both codes also set down the separation of property.

Variants of Marital Property Law

We might describe Tyrol's matrimonial property law as occupying a position between the Mediterranean dotal system, which gave daughters a dowry but excluded them from inheritance,[21] and the models applied in most of the Habsburg monarchy's other lands, which tended more towards community of property.[22] In the Outer Austrian lordship of Triberg, for example, Michaela Hohkamp shows that passing on property within the marriage was controversial, but that preference for the spouse's claims to the property predominated, gradually supplanting the claims of the respective natal families.[23] Studies of urban and rural societies in German territories, too, have shown that in the course of the early modern period, claims to property shifted in favour of the married couple as opposed to children and relatives. Thus, as early as the sixteenth century, inheritance law in Ravensburg regarded the surviving spouse in childless marriages as the sole heir – and thereby, argues Gesa Ingendahl, 'entirely abrogated the older framework of the ties of blood kinship'. This arrangement gave rise to numerous legal disputes with surviving relatives, throughout the seventeenth and even into the eighteenth century; Ingendahl infers that, in this case, the law drawn up in the urban setting almost completely contradicted the customs practised among the population.[24]

In the German juridical literature, from the seventeenth century onwards community of property was considered particularly beneficial for commerce and thus for the economy. In this sector, a community of accrued gain – *Errungenschaftsgemeinschaft* or *Zugewinngemeinschaft* – was widespread: the assets that were generated during the marriage became joint property, whereas those that had been brought into the marriage remained separate.[25] At the same time, the legal discourse considered community of property to be an essential part of the 'nature' of a marriage. The Bamberg *Landrecht* of 1769 argued as follows:

In the bishopric of Bamberg, a community of goods of this kind has existed since time immemorial and is based upon most reasonable grounds, appropriate to the married state, to such an extent that most of the subjects of Bamberg will always have believed themselves to be true and actual married people only if they united, just as their bodies and souls, also their fortunes.[26]

In contrast, the separation of property, which also forms the basis of the dotal system, strictly speaking means that the party marrying in remains a 'stranger' in the family, at least in terms of property law.

Usufruct as a Way of Balancing Interests

According to the Tiroler Landesordnung of 1573, a widow was to receive back her *Heiratsgut* – the specified sum she had contributed to the new family economy as a bride – and any other assets she had brought into the marriage, not unlike the arrangements for the dowry in the dotal system. If a *Morgengabe*, the gift presented by the husband to his wife the morning after the wedding, had been agreed, this too was generally supposed to go to the widow as provision for her widowhood. In addition, the widow was to receive one third of the couple's movable possessions. However, no increase in the sum of the *Heiratsgut* was required, unlike in other models. In the Italian dotal system, for example, the husband was entitled to manage the dowry for the duration of the marriage, but was also obliged to increase it by one third or one quarter in a system known as *terzo* or *quarto dotale* or *aumento* – the husband had to invest the dowry profitably.[27] Something similar also applied in the French regions with statutory law, where the widow could claim an *augment* at a level specified in the marriage contract. An increase of one third in the dowry was usual, or one half among the nobility.[28] Tyrol also lacked the principle of the *Widerlage*, which was very widespread in the German-speaking area as a whole. The *Widerlage* was a sum taken from the husband's assets, set down in the marriage contract as a proportion of the *Heiratsgut*, frequently the same as or half of the wife's contribution, and was intended to go to the widow for her usufruct. Another missing element in the Tyrolean Landesordnung was the widow's *Leibzuchtrecht* or *Leibgedingerecht*, a lifelong usufructuary right which normally consisted in a right to habitation and to food and clothing.[29] Maintenance at a level befitting a widow's social status was stipulated only for the first year of widowhood, an arrangement referred to as *Jarspeise*.[30] On the death of the wife, in contrast, her *Heiratsgut* and any additional assets were to pass immediately to her heirs – once again to her children or to relatives from her own family line.

It seems that this fragmentation of the property immediately on the death of husband or wife imposed an unduly harsh burden on household economies, because in practice alternative models were given preference, as is documented by the marriage contracts deposited with the Welsberg and Innichen courts in the eighteenth century.[31] In one such alternative, the wife's assets stayed with the property of the deceased husband and interest was paid on them. The widow – usually only for as long as she remained without a husband – was granted specific usufructuary rights, chiefly in the shape of a right to habitation and maintenance. That is, she was supposed to withdraw from the household and its economic management, into a form of lodging known as *Herberg*. This entitled her to a room in the house and the use of the common areas, especially the kitchen and living room along with the garden. As for widowers, the marriage settlement in many cases granted them lifelong usufruct of their wives' assets. Unlike for women, for men (with very rare exceptions)[32] the death of the spouse changed nothing in their position and status within the household, even if they had married into the household of a daughter-heir.

Towards the end of the eighteenth century, especially in the marriage contracts of the Innichen court, this model with its gendered inequality was more and more frequently superseded by lifelong usufruct of the deceased spouse's assets for both widow and widower – as in the settlement between Peter Ochswieser and Margareth Kühebacherin that I mentioned above. Usufruct may be regarded as an instrument to offset the hardships and potential conflicts associated with the separation of property.[33] It granted the surviving spouse the unrestricted utilization of the deceased partner's possessions and wealth. This left the widow to decide for herself when she would like to retire from managing the household, and in cases where the marriage was childless, it also saved her from having to come to terms with 'stranger' heirs immediately after her husband's death. Usufruct also worked as a way of balancing out competing interests and claims. Although the inheritance of the property by children or relatives of the deceased was blocked in practice, for as long as the widow or widower remained alive or actively involved in managing the household, the rights of the children or relatives were not curtailed in principle, since they were and remained the heirs and future owners.

Having said that, a certain potential for conflict did remain, given the long period of time that might elapse before the heirs came into their inheritance. This can be inferred from the agreements reached in the marriage contracts, in that unlimited mutual usufruct was usually to apply only in the case of childlessness. Couples often agreed on a time limit to the right of usufruct if children were to issue from the marriage. If Margareth Kühebacherin and Peter Ochswieser had had children, for example, their mutual right of usufruct would have lasted only until those children reached the age of twenty.[34] Up to that time, the children had to be provided with 'victuals and clothing'; they were to learn reading, writing and calculating, the boys a trade and the girls sewing.[35] In other marriage contracts the age limit was set at sixteen, eighteen or twenty-four years old.

Towards the end of the eighteenth century, there were however two principal situations where bridal couples promised lifelong use of each other's property and assets irrespective of the presence of offspring. Firstly, in the Welsberg court this variant was chosen in marriage contracts between daughter-heirs and men marrying in to their household, a constellation that occurs with particular frequency in my sample. As a rule, upon marriage the bridegroom was granted half the property that had already been inherited by the bride or which she expected to inherit. The reverse case, with the bride receiving *Kaufrechte* or the right to buy half the bridegroom's property upon marriage, occurred only in very rare individual cases, where the woman was very wealthy.[36] The greatest degree of equality in terms of property tended to apply in cases of daughter-heirs and married-in men who had acquired ownership rights. This may explain the unrestricted mutual usufruct that was often negotiated by such couples.

Where the bridal couple could not expect to inherit property, but instead acquired it together through work, savings, or small amounts of money inherited or obtained from other sources such as rents, and established their own household on that basis, a degree of equality between bride and bridegroom seems to have existed. It was almost impossible for relatives to put forward successful claims in cases of this kind. Maria Kühebacher, one of many siblings in a large farming family from the mountains, and Philipp Holzer, a day labourer, settled 'on each other upon the demise of one or the other party the lifelong usufruct of the entire estate left behind ... and this whether or not the marriage produces children.'[37] This mutual usufruct excluded some items of material nature that made up the classic components of a bride's trousseau, namely undergarments, table linen and bed linen.[38] There was usually no explicit mention of these in marriage contracts, and here we may interpret the note as indicating an economically weak household. The couple most probably no longer expected to have children of their own – Maria Kühebacher was forty-two years old at her marriage[39] – and it seems that at least these items from the woman's trousseau were to be secured for a relative of hers. It may be noted in general that less well-off bridal couples tended to reach more equitable agreements, since they had to take little account of claims by their relatives. The distinction between inherited property, on which the relatives had a certain claim, and property acquired by oneself, which could be more freely disposed of, was one of the guiding principles in dealing with property in this early modern society.

Competing Interests: The Relatives versus the Widow

Marriage contracts, did not only serve to document the property brought into the marriage, to set out how it would be administered during the marriage and to stipulate how it would be protected. They also offered the opportunity at a very early stage – before the wedding ceremony – to settle arrangements for the period after the marriage ended.[40] The agreements reached on this issue could be used to add detail to the legal provisions or amend them in line with the couple's own preferences, to safeguard the position and rights of particular people, to establish a particular minimum standard or to facilitate the enforcement of the negotiated arrangements in any future dispute.[41] Often, marriage contracts offered a range of variations alongside the fundamental principles they laid down. After all, the agreements made might not be put into practice until the distant future, and it was impossible to predict in detail the life situations for which the contract would then have to provide.

The role of the marriage contract was therefore to outline a spectrum of possibilities and bestow a certain guarantee, while the actual implementation of the postmarital arrangements had to be agreed at the moment of widowhood, in the context of the probate proceedings. Marriage contracts were often just one part of a whole web of documents – for example, the marriage contract might have been amended at a later date, the deceased might have written a will stipulating different arrangements, or by the time of the spouse's death an agreement to transfer ownership to future heirs might have been concluded. The various documents had to be presented at the probate proceedings, which were attended by the widow and the other people affected. The proceedings aimed to clear up any contradictions and to find as acceptable a resolution as possible for all those involved.

Occasionally, the actual arrangements for postmarital property turned out very differently from what the marriage contract's stipulations might have led the widow to expect. In both the contract itself and its practical implementation, key decisions were based on judgements about the relative merits of claims put forward by the spouse and by the deceased's own kin. The material analysed reveals, in a range of different contexts, a strong interest in the continuity of property within the natal family line. Here, it is important to note that the family of origin was not represented solely by the male line but also by daughters – primarily in their role as heiresses.

When Peter Ochswieser's three sisters, Maria, Kunigunde and Christina Ochswieserin, came to a compromise settlement with the widow Margareth Kühebacherin in 1797, the situation had changed radically compared to the provisions of the marriage contract. According to the 1784 contract, the widow would have been awarded the property and assets of her husband for her lifelong usufruct – as mentioned above, and indeed as was noted at the beginning of the probate proceedings. Because there were no children, Peter Ochswieser's three sisters were designated as his heirs, following the logic of the line that ran via his dead parents.[42] The marriage contract and Ochswieser's will, which was kept with that document, were read out. The will names a fixed sum for Holy Masses to be read. In addition, it lists sums of money that the testator owed his sisters or bequeathed to them; the list does not mention his wife. This is followed by an inventory of his entire immovable and movable property. The widow asserted her claim to the *Heiratsgut* she had brought into the marriage, the level of which was confirmed by a receipt held by her brother Joseph Kühebacher. Based on this, a compromise was reached: the widow agreed to claim usufruct only until St Candidus Day 1798, the name-day of the local convent's patron saint also being the market day and the customary date for payments. After that, interest of 3 per cent was to be paid on the 700 gulden that she had brought into the marriage, and she was to be paid this interest in lieu of lifelong usufruct. Up to St Candidus Day 1798, an interest rate of 3.5 per cent was to apply. The settlement included the option for either side to revoke it at any point before St Candidus Day 1799.[43] It is not easy to gauge what advantages or disadvantages this compromise involved for the widow compared with the marriage contract. The option of revocation hints at a certain imbalance in the situation: it looks very much as if the three sisters of the deceased had managed to force through their own interests, for they were now authorized to do as they pleased in the 'half dwelling in Oberdorf including a garden' and on some further plots. This was a role that, according to the marriage contract, would actually have been due to the widow.

The Continuity of the Line

It was also part of the logic of concern for the biological family and line of descent that children from a first marriage took priority over children of later marriages with respect to inheritance. This arose as a potential problem particularly when a widow with children remarried. If her property had belonged to her late husband, any children from her second marriage were only entitled to inherit if the new husband acquired it in consultation with the children's legal guardians and in return for appropriate financial compensation. This was most likely to be done when the second husband was a very good 'catch' in terms of his profession, social status and financial resources, or else when the widow found herself in a very difficult economic position. Marriage contracts from both the Innichen and the Welsberg courts include safeguards designed to prevent or at least impede manoeuvres of this kind as far as possible. The relevant passage in such contracts stipulated that the property must always go to the children of the soon-to-be-concluded marriage, often explicitly excluding children of any subsequent marriage. In a case like this, the second husband might be granted usufructuary or leasehold rights for a limited period of time – for example until one of the children of the earlier marriage had reached majority and/or was able to succeed to the title.[44] In a joint property regime, by contrast, the surviving spouse (whether husband or wife) could take on the rights of ownership from the deceased partner and, on this firmer financial ground, marry again – regardless of whether he or she had inherited the property or married into it. The new husband or new wife, in turn, received a right to ownership of the shared part. In extreme cases – such as in Belm, Triberg or Lower Austria –[45] this led to veritable chains of remarriages, in the course of which the younger generation was prevented from inheriting the property and was paid off with sums of money instead. Here, no account was taken of the continuity of a particular family owning one property.

Exceptions to the inheritance precedence of children from the first marriage were rare, but not unheard of, the few cases were found in the Welsberg contracts, from a peasant milieu. In cases where the first marriage was to produce, 'merely' daughters, or if the only son would die, a son from the second marriage could be accepted as the principal heir and succeed to the title. In one marriage settlement from Welsberg, the contract was constructed not to exclude the eldest daughter of the first marriage completely: if 'no male heirs were produced' in the first marriage, the estate was to go to any future son of the second marriage, but he would have to share equal inheritance rights with the eldest daughter of the first marriage.[46] A farmer from the Innichen market, Anton Bergmann, with two daughters from his first marriage, drew up a settlement that nullified the right of the daughters to preferential treatment after his death. If the planned second marriage was to produce a son, that son would become the heir and owner.[47] In the peasant setting, where continuity of ownership meant continuity of work, this aspect of the marriage contracts highlights the interest in a male successor. At the same time, arrangements of this kind could potentially improve position of the second wife if she became a widow.

While transfer of ownership from father to son, irrespective of birth order, could be seen as logical from a kinship point of view transfer of ownership via daughters posed another problem. Where continuity of property within the line was considered important, the critical factor in a marriage of a daughter-heir and a married-in son-in-law was childlessness. If there were children, the line passed from the father via the daughter-heir to these children, since – as mentioned above – families could be represented by daughters, not only by sons or other male relatives. In this case the precedence of children from the first marriage applied as well.[48] However, if the marriage with a daughter-heir produced no offspring, the situation changed entirely. Marriage contracts set down safeguards for such a case, if anything more rigorously if half the property had been transferred to the bridegroom upon the marriage. Infrequently, there was an option that any children resulting from the son-in-law's second marriage would be permitted to succeed to the property.[49] More common in the marriage settlements reached by such couples was an agreement that the future husband could remain in the house or on the farmstead for his lifetime, but that after his death the property would revert to the relatives of the bride. In the marriage contract concluded between the weaver Johann Mayr and Anna Gantschiederin from Niederdorf at the Welsberg court, for example, the bridegroom was granted ownership rights to half of the house and garden that had been inherited by the bride. If the couple had no children, the property would revert on the death of the husband, 'in natura' to the bride's kin, from whence (thus the contract) it originally came.[50] In cases like these, the assets that the bridegroom had brought into the marriage were to be repaid to his kin.[51]

This means that the rights of ownership received by the bridegroom in fact went no further than his own lifetime and his own person: as a rule, they did not extend to his descendants from a possible later marriage, and certainly not to his own relatives. This phenomenon ultimately raises the question of how such restrictions affect the status of an 'owner' in conceptual terms. Here, an individual's own kin and the preferential continuity of ownership along family lines takes precedence over gender. As other studies have shown, a continuity of ownership and family could be constructed through a virtual 'incorporation' of the son-in-law, either by his taking on the bride's family name or the name of the farm replacing the family name.[52] Such endeavours seem to have been more strongly rooted in peasant communities.[53] This is also suggested by the absence of any arrangements of this kind in the marriage contracts from Innichen, a market town oriented towards crafts and commerce. In contracts made in the town, for women with property or inheritance prospects, either there was no particular specification beyond the widower's lifelong usufruct or he was granted *Kaufrechte* after the death of his wife.[54]

Variations on Access to Property

If a favourable opportunity arose, women could convert money into property. In February 1790 Maria Hueberin, the childless widow of an Innichberg farmer, took a second husband after almost thirty years of marriage. He was Andrä Gatterer, servant of the Innichen manor's *Pfleger* (a local official acting as notary and judge). Maria Hueberin seems to have brought quite some money into the marriage: the exact amount is not named in the marriage contract, but the fact that she promised 199 gulden to her future husband as a *Morgengabe* suggests it was substantial[55] (although the codifications of the late eighteenth and the nineteenth century make no specific reference to a *Morgengabe* promised by a widow to an unmarried bridegroom,[56] it was no rarity in the early modern period). In addition, Maria Hueberin gave her bridegroom-to-be two options in the case of her dying before him. Either he could be awarded the usufruct of her entire fortune, or he could lay claim to a proportion of the fortune – 250 gulden – as his 'free property', even though this sum went beyond the amount she was entitled to bequeath freely. In the second case, the money would be defined as a gift. Finally, in the last point of her marriage contract, the bride also agreed to pay the costs of the wedding and the bridegroom's admittance into the town's citizenry.[57] As for the groom, the marriage contract included no obligations towards the widow or for the period after the marriage. His property consisted of a house with a garden and a share of a farm building.

Andrä Gatterer died soon after his marriage, and one year later, in March 1791, Maria Hueberin married for the third time. Her new husband was Jakob Flätscher, who like Gatterer was not a native of Innichen and who worked as a servant for the innkeeper Joseph Fuchs. By then, Maria Hueberin had bought her deceased second husband's quarter-share in the house, with all its fittings, from his heirs. The advantage of shares like this was that they could fluctuate more freely than entire houses. For people new to an area and men who had not inherited any property, as well as for widows, former servants and generally the less well-off, they were within easier reach – often acting as a kind of 'starting home' or a temporary solution.[58] Equally, heirs were more inclined to sell estate of this kind, especially if they were not resident in the area. Her purchase of the share made Maria Hueberin a proprietor, and she remained such throughout her third marriage. In the new marriage contract, she gave her bridegroom the right, if she died before him, to buy the property she had purchased. It was to cost him 200 gulden.[59] Otherwise, the contract laid down reciprocal usufruct, and once again the bride agreed to pay the costs of the wedding. Whereas the second husband's entitlement had needed to be protected by declaring it a gift, in her third marriage Maria Hueberin had a more comprehensive right to dispose over what was now property she had acquired herself. In view of her age, she no longer expected any children of her own, and the arrangements made in the marriage contract would not leave her relatives empty-handed; they were entitled to the purchase price that Jakob Flätscher would one day have to pay for the quarter house.

However, the situation of Maria Hueberin had been rather exceptional. In the majority of cases, the groom brought his house or his farm into the marriage and this property did not, upon his death, go to the widow, but to the eldest son or another child. If the children were minors the widow was entitled to govern the wealth of her deceased husband – but she did not become owner of the property. If no children were present, a close relative of the deceased husband would become the new owner, a nephew or niece, for example. Usually, only in their position as heiresses women were able to direct the allocation of property. A certain positive effect of the separation of marital property can be seen in the fact, that women could not be made liable with their assets for the debts of their husbands.

If a heiress married the property could remain in her hands, it could be ceded in part or in its entirety to the husband, but it could also be transferred directly from the parent generation to the son-in-law. It appears that property transfers from a heiress to the future husband took place primarily in professions requiring intensive use of production means: in crafts that required a larger workshop with elaborate equipment or separate auxiliary buildings (dyers, tanners, locksmiths), in agriculture in the case of larger farms. In response, women insured themselves accordingly in such cases – for the rest of their lives and for the children of the marriage – in contract provisions: in case of widowhood, childlessness or the husband's remarriage. The implications that these different constructions had for everyday life, for the interrelationship and the power hierarchy between the sexes cannot be determined from the material treated. It may be assumed that an heiress – even if she conceded her inheritance wholly or partially to her husband, or if it had been transferred directly to the son-in-law – in terms of decision making was still in a better position in comparison with a woman who married into a family.[60]

Interest on the Wife's Contribution

Even if women were not in a position to acquire ownership rights as Maria Hueberin did, their power to make decisions increased in line with the size of their fortune, and wealthier women could secure a certain degree of independence through the system of interest payment. This system formed the basis of a relationship between a widow and the heir to the property that in some ways resembled a credit relationship, and that was tied into an intricately structured power balance. Such arrangements were given detailed shape in property transfer agreements or in the specific widow's contracts[61] documented at the Innichen court. If marriage contracts, drawn up at the time of the wedding, dealt with future contingencies and options in the conditional form, these additional documents had the function of specifying more precisely what was to happen when the actual situation of withdrawal from active housekeeping arose, in old age or upon widowhood. Like property transfer agreements or contracts of purchase, widow's contracts also contained the points included in marriage contracts, but they were normally specified in more detail.

The contribution to the family assets by Maria Felizitas Klammerin, widow of the trader and innkeeper Franz Peintner, was stated as 3,000 gulden in her widow's contract. With an expected interest rate of 4 per cent, it amounted to 120 gulden in annual interest. In the widow's contract concluded in 1784 with Michael Peintner, her son and the new owner of the property, she agreed that these 120 gulden should remain with the joint assets for as long as she, his mother, found it suitable.[62] The remaining clauses, however, set out other provisions. For the first year of widowhood, it was agreed that Maria Felizitas Klammerin would have a claim to free board and clothing. In addition, she wished to receive 50 gulden of the above-mentioned 120 gulden interest, or paid out in kind - as grain, poppy seed, peas, salt, smoked meat, bacon, lard, cheese, candles, oil, flax, wine and daily fresh milk.[63] Uniquely in the sample of documents analysed, she withdraw from any obligation to participate in 'housework'. In other agreements of this type, widows or parents who transferred property were expected, as far as they were able, to contribute labour to the household, and this was quite a significant element of intergenerational reciprocity.

From the end of her first year of widowhood, Maria Felizitas Klammerin planned to live in another house belonging to the family, which was still in need of renovation, and also to use the garden there. In this case, her son was to pay out her annual 120 gulden of interest and, additionally, to provide her with eighteen pounds of flax every year and a particular quantity of milk every day, along with the necessary domestic and kitchen utensils. However, the widow also left herself the option of remaining in her son's house. In that case – without the family being permitted to ask any work of her, and for as long as both parties agreed – she was to be given food, drink, clothing and a daily breakfast of her own choosing, as well as a sum of 50 gulden from her interest every year. If, as a third possible scenario, she decided to leave Innichen, all the negotiated benefits in kind would lapse. Instead, her son would be obliged to pay out her 120 gulden of interest and add another twenty gulden per year to that sum.[64] Maria Felizitas Klammerin was the daughter of an innkeeper from 'Firholz', as was recorded on the occasion of her marriage in 1743.[65] This may have been the village of Fürholz in Lower Bavaria, which lay on an old trading route. Because innkeepers and merchants often chose to marry members of their own occupational sector and also had access to extensive contact networks, the marriage horizons for people in this sphere of work extended over comparatively large areas. We do not know which form of 'widow's residence' Maria Felizitas Klammerin ultimately chose. It seems, at least, that she did not move away from Innichen, because her death in 1793 is recorded in the local register. Her substantial contribution to the marriage and corresponding social status opened up options well beyond what was usual in the period, and allowed her particular freedoms such as a certain degree of mobility and relief from the burden of work.[66]

Conclusion

We have seen that the form of marital property regime had a considerable impact on, in particular, the position and future of widows, because access to property and the associated scope to make decisions – including decisions to remarry –

clearly differed according to whether community of property or separation of property applied. That was true independently of the practices of inheritance. In the court districts of Innichen and Welsberg, just as in Belm and in rural Lower Austria, impartible inheritance predominated. However, the question of who had a claim to property was not regulated solely by inheritance and succession between the generations; it was also dependent on the predominating matrimonial regime – and primarily on whether or not wives and husbands were able to lay claim to each other's property.

If not, as was standard in a separate property regime, then there were substantial consequences for the surviving spouse: the deceased's children and relatives were at an advantage over widows and widowers who had married into the property. In this situation, rights of usufruct which continued after the end of the marriage, were a key instrument for balancing the inequality of wealth between bride and bridegroom, and the competing interests of the designated heirs. Here, property rather than gender was the most important distinction-building category, and husbands marrying in were also affected by the precedence given to continuity of property within the family line. At the same time, however, it has become clear that a regime of separate property left room for many variants, allowing specific arrangements to be reached depending on how gender relations were positioned vis-a-vis family interests in any one case. Not having ownership rights did not mean being powerless. The various concessions and specifications of the spouses' options within the each marital property regime can be glimpsed through marriage contracts, which provide information on contemporary repertoires of action and on notions of what was appropriate, what required explicit regulation.

Marriage contracts also show how married couples positioned themselves – in relation to their children, their biological family and kin, and towards each other through mutual promises or withholding of goods. Knowing how this edifice was structured and balanced is important for our understanding of a society, because it shapes such fundamental social relationships and orders as marriage and kinship. The central position of the married couple was inscribed into the history of western modernization at the same time as the nuclear family,[67] but within western Europe there were significant divergences. That applies, for example, to 'stem families', three-generation households that were, in their classic form, subject to the authority and leadership of the father.[68] There were also different chronologies for the legal and sociocultural shift in favour of the married couple in terms of equality and reciprocity. The late eighteenth and early nineteenth century was a pivotal moment in this process,[69] which was reflected not only in the 'dethronement' of the father,[70] but also in new provisions for matrimonial property.

Translation: Ginger A. Diekmann

NOTES.

Introduction

1. L. Abrams, 'Introduction', in L. Abrams, E. Gordon, D. Simonton and E. J. Yeo (eds), *Gender in Scottish History since 1700* (Edinburgh: Edinburgh University Press 2006), pp. 3–4.
2. B. Todd, 'The Remarrying Widow Reconsidered', *Continuity and Change*, 9:3 (1994), pp. 421–450 on p. 423–430; M. Pelling, 'Who most needs to Marry? Ageing and Inequality among Women and Men in Early Modern Norwich', in L. Botellho and P. Thane (eds), *Women and Ageing in British Society since 1500* (London: Longman, 2001), pp. 31–42.
3. O. Hufton, 'Women without Men: Widows and Spinsters in Britain and France in the Eighteenth Century', *Journal of Family History*, 9:4 (1984), pp. 355–76.
4. J. Dupaquier, E. Helin, P. Laslett, M. Livi-Bacci and S. Sogner (eds), *Marriage and Remarriage in Populations of the Past* (London, New York: Academic Press, 1981), pp. 6–10; A. McCants, 'The Not-So-Merry Widows of Amsterdam 1740–1782', *Journal of Family History*, 24:4 (1999), pp. 441–67; K. Matthijs, 'Frequency Timing and Intensity of Remarriage in Nineteenth-century Flanders', *History of the Family*, 8:1 (2003), pp. 135–62.
5. Matthijs 'Frequency', p. 141.
6. P. Laslett and R. Wall, *Household and Family in Past Time* (Cambridge: Cambridge University Press 1972).
7. B. Reay, *Microhistories, Demography, Society and Culture in Rural England 1800–1930* (Cambridge: Cambridge University Press, 1996); C. Chinn, *They Worked All Their Lives, Women of the Urban Poor 1880–1939* (Lancaster: Carnegie Publishing, 2006), pp. 21–2, 27,32; M. Jordan, *Hulme Memories* (Manchester: Neil Richardson, 1989), pp. 5, 8, 22–3.
8. A. L. Bowley, and A. Burnett-Hurst, *Livelihood and Poverty, A Study of Economic Conditions of Working – Class Households in Northampton, Warrington, Stanley and Reading* (London: Routledge, 1915), p. 63.
9. K. Snell and J. Millar, 'Lone Parent Families and the Welfare State: Past and Present', *Continuity and Change*, 2:3 (1987), pp. 387–422 on pp. 389–90.
10. E. Gordon and G. 'Nair, Middle-Class Family Structure in Nineteenth Century Glasgow', *Journal of Family History* 24:4 (1999), pp. 468–77 on pp. 475–76; E. Gordon and G. Nair, 'The Myth of the Victorian Patriarchal Family', *The History of the Family* 7;1 (2002), pp. 125–38.

11. Gordon and Nair 'The Myth', pp. 126, 132–3; S. Hahn, 'Women in Older Ages – Old Women?', *History of the Family*, 7:1 (2002), pp. 33–58 on pp. 45, 50–2.

12. R. Fuchs, *Gender and Poverty in Nineteenth-Century Europe* (Cambridge: Cambridge University Press, 2005), pp. 235–36; I. Chabot, 'Lineage Strategies and the Control of Widows in Renaissance Florence', in S. Cavallo and L. Warner (eds), *Widowhood in Medieval and Early Modern Europe* (London: Longman, 1999); D. Simonton, 'Work, Trade and Commerce', in L. Abrams, E. Gordon, D. Simonton and E. J. Yeo (eds), *Gender in Scottish History since 1700* (Edinburgh: Edinburgh University Press, 2006), pp. 199–234 on pp. 208–209; B. Moring, 'Widows and Economy, Introduction', *History of the Family*, 15 (2010), pp. 217–18.

13. Hufton, 'Women without Men', pp. 365–6; D. Green and A. Owens, *Family Welfare: Gender Property and Inheritance since the Seventeenth Century* (London, Westport: Praeger, 2004); B. Moring, 'The Standard of Living of Widows: Inventories as Indicators of the Economic Situation of Widows', *History of the Family*, 12:4 (2007), pp. 233–49.

14. J. Humphries, 'Enclosures, Common Rights and Women', *Journal of Economic History*, 50 (1990), pp. 17–42; J. Humphries, 'From Work to Dependence? Women's Experience of Industrialization in Britain', *Refresh*, 21 (1995), pp. 5–8.

15. T. Sokoll, *Household and Family among the Poor, the Case of Two Essex Communities in the Late Eighteenth and Early Nineteenth Centuries* (Bochum: Universitetsverlag Brockmeyer, 1993); R. Wall, 'The Residence Patterns of Elderly English Women in Comparative Perspective', in L. Botelho and P. Thane (eds), *Women and Ageing in British Society since 1500* (London: Longman, 2001), pp. 139–65; R. Wall, 'Elderly Widows and Widowers and their Co-Residence in late Nineteenth and Early Twentieth-Century England and Wales', *History of the Family*, 7:2 (2002), pp. 139–55; S. Rose, 'The Varying Household Arrangements of the Elderly in Three English villages, Nottinghamshire 1851–1881', *Continuity and Change*, 3:1 (1988), pp. 115–16; P. Thane, 'Intergenerational Support in Families in Modern Britain', in T. Addabo, M. Arrizabalaga, C. Borderias and A. Owens (eds), *Gender Inequalities, Households and the Production of Well-Being in Modern Europe* (London: Ashgate, 2010), pp. 112–13; J. Robin, 'Family Care of the Elderly in a Nineteenth Century Devonshire Parish', *Ageing and Society*, 4 (1984), pp. 505–16.

16. E. Higgs, 'Women's Occupations and Work in the Nineteenth Century Censuses', *History Workshop Journal*, 23 (1987), pp. 59–82; N. Goose, 'Introduction' in N. Goose (ed), *Women's Work in Industrial England* (Hertfordshire: Local Population Studies 2007); D. Gittins, 'Marital Status, Work and Kinship 1850–1930', in J. Lewis (ed.), *Labour and Love, Women's Experience of Home and Family 1850–1940* (Oxford: Blackwell,1986), p. 252.

17. S. Horrell, and J .Humphries, 'Old Questions, New Data and Alternative Perspectives: the Standard of Living of Families in the Industrial Revolution', *Journal of Economic History*, 53:4 (1992), pp. 849–880; S. Pennington and B. Westover, *A Hidden Workforce, Home workers in England 1850–1985* (London: Macmillan 1989).

18. M. Anderson, 'The Social Position of Spinsters in Mid-Victorian Britain', *Journal of Family History*, 9:4 (1984), pp. 377–93 on p. 391.

19. Fuchs,'*Gender and Poverty*'; Wall, 'The Residence Patterns'; Robin, 'Family Care'; Rose, 'The Varying Household Arrangements'.

20. J. Goodman and K. Honeyman, *Gainful Pursuits, the Making of Industrial Europe 1600–1914* (Bath: Edward Arnold, 1988).

21. A. Levine, 'Poor Families, Removals and "Nurture" in Late Old Poor Law London', *Continuity and Change*, 25:2 (2010), pp. 244–46.

22. Sokoll, 'The Household'; Hufton'Women without men'; Hahn, S. 'Women in Older', pp. 33–58.

23. Chabot, 'Lineage strategies'.

24. Pelling, 'Who most needs', A. Froide, 'Old maids: the lifecycle of single women in early modern England', in L. Botellho and P. Thane (eds), *Women and Ageing in British Society since 1500* (London: Longman, 2001), pp. 89–110.

Wall, 'Widows, Family and Poor Relief in England from the Sixteenth to the Twentieth Century'

1. D. Davies, *The case of the labourers in husbandry stated and considered* (1795) (London, Fairfield: Augustus M. Kelley, 1977), pp. 148–9. All payments are expressed in the currency of the time: pence, shillings and pounds. Each shilling comprised 12 pence and each pound, 20 shillings or 240 pence.

2. Statistical Society of London, 'Report to the Council of the Statistical Society of London from a Committee of its Fellows appointed to make an investigation into the state of the poorer classes in St. George's in the East', *Quarterly Journal of the Statistical Society of London* (1848). Reprinted in R. Wall (ed.), *Slum conditions in London and Dublin* (Farnborough: Gregg International, 1974), pp. 193–249.

   R. Wall, 'Gender based economic inequalities and women's perceptions of well-being in historical populations', in B. Harris, L. Galvez-Munoz and H. Machado (eds), *Gender and wellbeing in Europe: historical and contemporary perspectives* (Farnham: Ashgate, 2009), pp. 23–42, on p. 28.

3. M.F., Davies, *Life in an English village – An economic and social history of Corsley in Wiltshire* (London: T Fisher Unwin, 1909), pp. 178, 218–20).

4. However, there is a suspicion that some purchases or gifts of food have been omitted from the budget as no vegetables are mentioned yet vegetables were part of some of the meals of the widow during the two weeks that a record was kept of what she was eating. Davies, *Life in*, pp. 140, 145.
   Davies, *Life in*, pp. 194–5.

5. There are 16 ounces (oz.) to the pound (lb.) and four ounces to the quarter. One ounce is 28.4 grams, a quarter 113.4 grams and a pound 0.45 kilograms).

6. Davies, *Life in*, pp. 193, 218–20, 229–33; B.S. Rowntree, *Poverty. A study of town life* (1901) (London: Thomas Nelson & Sons, 1914), pp. 319, 325.

7. Rowntree, *Poverty*, p. 325.

8. Davies, *The case of*; F.M., Eden, *The state of the poor. Or an history of the labouring classes in England* (1797) (Bristol: Thoemmes Press, 2001); M. F. Davies, *Life in*.

9. Out relief represents payments to the poor living in their own households or in lodgings as opposed to the support provided by moving the poor into an institution such as a workhouse. For examples of surveys of the poor see J.F. Pound J. F., *The Norwich census of the poor1570* (Norwich: Norfolk Record Society XL, 1971), P. Slack, *Poverty in early Tudor Salisbury* (Devizes: Wiltshire Record Society, 1975) and J. Webb, *Poor relief in Elizabethan Ipswich* (Ipswich: Suffolk Record Society IX, 1966).

10. For an illustration of this approach see R. Wall, 'The contribution of the Poor Law in England towards alleviating the economic inequality of the elderly at the end of the

eighteenth century', *Revista de Demografía Histórica* , XXIV: II (2006), pp. 136–54, on p. 141.

Table 1 based on analyses of information on wage and out relief payments for late eighteenth century England in Eden (1797), *State of the Poor*.

11. King studied four communities: Calverley (West Riding of Yorkshire), Charing (Kent), Cartmel (Lancashire and Westmorland) and Farthinghoe (Northamptonshire), S. King, *Poverty and Welfare in England – A Regional Perspective* (Manchester: Manchester University Press, 2000), p. 115, 137.

12. These percentages are estimates based on my interpretation of the bar charts in King, he states that the recipients of out relief constituted much less than 20 per cent of all persons who might be deemed poor, King, *Poverty and Welfare*, pp. 115–16.

13. For the Cardington census, see D. Baker, *The Inhabitants of Cardington in 1782* (Bedford: Bedfordshire Historical Record Society 52, 1973). The Corfe Castle census of 1790 was analysed from a photocopy in the Library of the Cambridge Group, Department of Geography, University of Cambridge.

14. Lynn Lees noted that in 1834 that the incidence of female pauperism in England and Wales was much lower than the rates of widowhood, L. Lees, *The Solidarities of Strangers, The English Poor Law and the People, 1700–1948* (Cambridge: Cambridge University Press, 1998), p. 196.

15. King, *Poverty and Welfare*, pp. 115–16.

16. Such estimates can be derived with varying margins of error from counts of families or households, the number of taxpayers or the numbers of baptisms, marriages and burials. There is a margin of error to all such estimates as family or household size may be larger or smaller than is assumed as may be the rates of fertility, nuptiality and mortality while the proportion of householders who were taxpayers is difficult to estimate unless those excused payment on the grounds of poverty are also listed as was the case with the hearth tax in England in the second half of the seventeenth century (cf. Chapter 3).

17. Sources and explanations of who has been considered poor are given in the note to Table 1.1.

18. D. Baker, *The Inhabitants of Cardington in 1782* (Bedford: Bedfordshire Historical Record Society 52, 1973); R. Wall, 'Leaving Home and the Process of Household formation in pre-industrial England', *Continuity and Change,* 3:1 (1987), pp. 77–101, on p. 93, notes that in Cardington more daughters than sons aged ten and over remained with their parents and particularly with a widowed mother than in many other populations.

19. The demographic micro-simulation programme, CAMSIM, was developed by Jim Oeppen when at the Cambridge Group. For other output from the simulation, see chapter 2.

20. This seems particularly likely in the case of Wolverhampton in 1796 where no widow under forty was listed on outdoor relief lists and only 5 per cent of widows assisted were aged forty to fifty-nine.

21. Older widows seem most likely to have been at risk of removal to an institution due to their reduced earning capacity and greater need of care. A younger widow, however, might have some of her children taken into a poorhouse or workhouse to safeguard the economic viability of her household.

22. Cardington, for example has a lower proportion of its population over sixty than in many other communities in England in the later eighteenth century. Compare Baker, *Inhabitants of Cardington*, p. 36, and P. Laslett, *Family Life and Illicit Love in Earlier Generations* (Cambridge: Cambridge University Press, 1977), p. 188.

23. Rowntree, *Poverty,* p. 155, for the definition of primary poverty see note to Table 1.3.

24. Lees, *The Solidarities*, p. 196.
25. Eden, *State of the Poor*, vols 2–3 passim. Thirty-four lists from fifteen different counties were analysed which detailed 1,362 recipients of out relief. Geographical coverage ranged from Wiltshire in the south to Cumberland in the north although it is evident that populations from southern England are under-represented. Dependants of recipients were not counted as many lists did not specify them consistently and sometimes not at all. Three lists were not analysed (Bury and Lancaster, Lancashire) and Epsom (Surrey) due to inadequate specification of the marital status of the women.
26. 'Smaller' was defined by the presence of fewer than twenty persons on the lists of recipients of out relief.
27. Widows constituted 35 per cent of all recipients in intermediate sized settlements (20–49 names on the out relief lists) and in some larger populations such as Wolverhampton in 1787, Kendal (Westmorland) and Bradford (Wiltshire) in 1792.
28. Information was available for six widows from Ipswich in 1597, nine from Salisbury and seven from Corfe Castle. Two estimates are given for the share of total income derived from the Poor Law in the case of widows from Corfe Castle as the actual amount provided by the Poor Law authorities is unknown. The lower of the two estimates assumes a contribution of 12 pence per widow and the second a contribution of 18 pence. Less assistance might have been provided than the average amount paid to recipients of out relief as these widows had no dependents. On the other hand advanced age (all but one of the widows in Corfe Castle was sixty-five or older) may have necessitated increased assistance from the Poor Law as their capacity to work declined. The estimate of 60 per cent of income contributed by the Poor Law is therefore probably more realistic. See also Davies, *The case of*, p. 173, who reports the payment of out-relief to childless widows for Marsham, Norfolk, in 1790 of 12 pence per week plus rent and fuel, with the allowance increasing to 24 pence per week if the widow was no longer able to earn anything.
29. No information was available as to the income of widows living alone in Ipswich in 1906.
30. Davies, *The Case of Labourers*; Eden, *State of the Poor*.
31. S. Horrell and J. Humphries, 'Old Questions, New Data and Alternative Perspectives on Families' Living Standards in the Industrial Revolution', *Journal of Economic History*, 52 (1992), pp. 849–80; S. Horrell, J. Humphries and J. Voth, 'Structure and Relative Deprivation: Fatherless Children in Early Industrial Britain', *Continuity and Change*, 13:1 (1998), pp. 73–115; J. Humphries, 'Female-Headed Households in Early Industrial Britain: the Vanguard of the Proletariat', *Labour History Review* (1998), pp. 31–65; S. Horrell and J. Humphries, 'Women's Labour Force Participation and the Transition to the Male Breadwinner Family, 1790–1865', *Economic History Review*, 48 (1995), pp. 89–117; S. Horrell and J. Humphries, 'The Origins and Expansion of the Male Breadwinner Family: The Case of Nineteenth-Century Britain', in A. Jansens (ed.), *The Rise and Decline of the Male Breadwinner Family?* (Cambridge: International Review of Social History Supplement 5, 1998), pp. 25–64.
32. For example in the East London working-class parish of St George in the East in 1845, the households of widows with children contained on average just 2.4 children, see Statistical Society of London (1848), p. 200.
33. These scales were first used in R. Wall, 'Some implications of the earnings and expenditure patterns of married women in populations in the past', in J. Henderson and R. Wall (eds), *Poor Women and Children in the European Past* (London: Routledge, 1994), pp. 312–35, and have since been used by Susannah Ottaway to evaluate the value of the Poor Law payment of out relief to elderly men and women in eighteenth-century Puddletown

(Dorset) and Terling (Essex), see S. Ottaway, *The Decline of Life: Old Age in Eighteenth-Century England* (Cambridge: Cambridge University Press, 2004), p. 230–1. Horrell, Humphries and Voth, *'Structure and Relative'*, p. 79, assumed equality of consumption between adults (= 1) except for married couples who were assessed at 1.75. Children regardless of age were assessed at 0.43 of a non married adult. Their estimates assume women, married and unmarried, consumed a greater proportion of household resources and children somewhat less than in the estimates here and in Wall, *'Some Implications'*, 1994.

34. Davies, *The Case of Labourers*, p. 142; other assumptions were built into some of the other budgets, for example that eldest sons of the deserted wife in Newent were resident with their mother and contributing to the household budget when it was not known whether they were present and their presence was in fact considered to be unlikely, see Davies, ibid., p. 161. Another assumption that was made was that the cost of clothing and the number of working days lost due to sickness and bad weather was the same in Newent as reported by Davies for Barkham, Berkshire.

35. The proportion of household earnings provided by widows and deserted wives is considerably less in these budgets than the 38 per cent calculated by Horrell and Humphries, *'The Origins and Expansion'*, p. 61 from their analysis of these and other budgets from the period 1787–1816.

36. Findings are based on the median percentages contributed by the female household head and by the Poor Law as set out in Table 1.6.

37. Earnings were lowest when the eldest child was twelve or under and largest when there was a son present aged sixteen or of working age.

38. The savings represented interest from the sale of farm stock following the death of her father.

39. There is, however, considerable variation in income from widow to widow. The same also applies in the case of the labourers and the deserted wives (see Table 1.7).

40. The median income of consumption units in similarly sized households of labourers (6–7 members) was one penny less than that in households of deserted wives and the median income of consumption units in households of 4–5 members just under two pence more than that of consumption units in the households of widows.

41. Horrell and Humphries, *'The Origins and Expansion'*, p. 60, analysed the same and other budgets (but calculating adult equivalent income in a different way) and concluded that female headed households were poorer than the households of males except perhaps those employed in low wage agriculture. It is this group of labourers that widows are compared in the present study.

42. Horrell and Humphries, *'The Origins and Expansion'*, p. 61.

43. Davies, *The Case of Labourers*, p. 150; Horrell and Humphries, *'The Origins and Expansion'*, p. 61 advance a number of other explanations for lower rates of self provisioning in female-headed households such as the urban bias of their data (not applicable to the budgets selected for the present study) and vigilant means testing by the poor law authorities (which seems inconsistent with their willingness to grant out relief to widows with resident wage-earning children and some contributions from children living elsewhere. More plausible is their third suggestion; that female-headed households needed to concentrate on cash generating activities. Differences in the way self provisioning has been recorded in different surveys make it difficult to determine whether disparities between female and male headed households in regard to the extent of self-provisioning have changed over time. For example, M. F. Davies in her study of the economy of poor fami-

lies in Corsley, Wiltshire, in 1906–7 simply assumed that on average any profit from the garden, including that consumed by the family, would be equivalent to the amount of rent and therefore excluded both rent and the value of garden produce when calculating the income and expenditure of the households, see Davies, *Life*, p. 141.

44. Census of Corfe Castle 1790, copy in Library of Cambridge Group.

45. Eden, *State of the Poor*, pp. 797–8.

46. The value of the food provided has been estimated using the information on the cost of these items when purchased by other families in Corsley. See M. F. Davies, *Life in*, but see also note 2 above.

47. Ibid., p. 190.

48. Royal Commission on the Poor Laws and Relief of Distress 1909, *Appendix volume XVII. Report by Miss Constance Williams and Mr Thomas Jones on the effect of outdoor relief on wages and conditions of employment*. British Parliamentary Papers volume XLIII Cd 4690. Interim Report 4: 217.

49. Ibid., Appendix to Interim Report 5, Appendix B 92) Govan p. 180.

50. Wall, 'Relationships', p. 81; calculated from Booth, *The Aged Poor*, p. 339–40. Wives supported by the earnings of their husbands were included by Booth among those with earnings. I have interpreted Booth's term 'own resources' as indicating income derived from property and savings.

51. Rowntree, *Poverty*; Davies, *Life in*, and the Royal Commission (1909), Appendix to Interim Report 5, Appendix B 92 Govan: 180 and Appendix E (13) Paisley, p. 195.

52. On the availability of kin see Wall, '*Gender Based*'.

53. Royal Commission on the Poor Laws (1909) Interim Report 3, pp. 182–3.

54. Davies, *The Case of Labourers*, p. 142, 161, no mention was made of the cost of the bread consumed by girls. However, lads between the ages of seven and sixteen were assumed to have consumed as much bread as a woman who was not breastfeeding.

55. See for instance the expenditure by widows and labourers with large households in Tanfield and in Monks Sherborne and Basing.

56. Davies, *The Case of Labourers*, p. 161.

57. 60 per cent in St Austell and 66 per cent in Newent, see above and cf. the estimates in Wall, '*Some Implications*'.

58. All percentages are medians and have been derived from the information in Table 1.8.

59. Twelve of the fourteen households were headed by labourers and were allocated by Rowntree to the lowest of his three classes in that their weekly earnings were less than 26 shillings per week. These were the only detailed budgets for this class that Rowntree published and no unpublished data appear to have survived.

60. Expenditure on food totalled from the information given by Rowntree, *Poverty*, pp. 310–37, divided by the number of consumption units (see last row of Table 1.9).

61. Nine of the households provided the information in 1901, five in 1900 and two in 1899 and usually at different times of the year although seven relate to a week in June. See Rowntree, *Poverty*, pp. 275, 277 and 310–37.

62. Details of the meals were usually provided by the wife but occasionally by a child or other family member and refer to weeks during January 1906 or 1907. See Davies, *Life*, p. 196–249.

63. The definition of primary poverty used by Davies for Corsley follows that of Rowntree, *Poverty*, p. 139–41; secondary poverty is defined, Davies, *Life*, p. 145–6.

64. The diets of those households that were above the poverty line according to Davies although more likely to contain fish or meat than those Rowntree placed in his class 1

(earnings less than 26 shillings per week) were, however, considerably poorer than those of households in York earning more than this. In York, 64 percent of the meals taken in four households in Rowntree's class 2 (earnings over 26 shillings per week) contained meat or fish as did 58 percent of the meals taken in six households that kept servants but who, according to Rowntree 'lived simply'. See Rowntree, *Poverty,* pp. 294, 297–9 and 339–49.

65. Rowntree made a similar observation for York: 'As usual with poor families, the husband comes off better as regards food than the rest of the family, for although Mrs. T and the children have no meat for breakfast, her husband, she explained, "must have a bit of bacon to take with him for his breakfast, or else all the others would talk so."' Rowntree, *Poverty,* p. 332.

2 Lamfus, 'Survival Strategies of Poor Women in Two Localities in Guipuzcoa (Northern Spain) in the Nineteenth and Twentieth Centuries'

1. J. V. Daubié, *La femme pauvre au 19e siècle* (Paris 1866) new edition: Paris 2007. The author concedes extraordinary relevance to the situation of inferiority of women in society which, in his opinion, is the cause of their salaries being below those of the men and which reduces them to a life of poverty. All this supports the insistent claim for 'an equal job for equal pay.

2. 'Today, as in centuries past, the vast majority of those whom we would identify as poor, are made up of children under 15, the elderly who usually live alone, and families whose head is a woman. Their condition of poverty is related to particular phases of especial vulnerability in their life or family cycles.' ... 'More surprising is the constant presence of widows, either with or without a family', S. Wolf, *Los Pobres en la Europa Moderna* (Barcelona 1989), p. 13. In the USA in 1968 'Half of all the family units are headed by women. Just over a quarter of these are black', J.K. Galbraith, *La Sociedad Opulenta* (Barcelona 1987), p. 253. Both these quotations come from the study of M. A. Martinez Martín: *Guipúzcoa en la vanguardia del reformismo social. Beneficencia, Ahorro y Previsión* (San Sebastián 1996), p. 67,no. 20.

3. Probably the most famous work of this minor genre of the romantic novel is *Jane Eyre* by the English author, Charlotte Brontë, published in London in 1847.

4. *⁴ Bases for the Compiling of Censuses of the Poor with a right to free medical and pharmaceutical assistance, 1898,* San Sebastian Municipal Archives, A–17 – 166–11.

5. R. Castel, 'La inserción y los nuevos retos de las intervenciones sociales' in F. Alvarez Uría (ed.), *Marginación e inserción (*Madrid: Ed. Endymión, 1992), pp. 25–36.

6. A. De Toqueville, *Memoria sobre el Pauperismo* – Preliminary Study, pp. 21–2, 'So, in the England of the industrial revolution, when its global wealth multiplied considerably, one sixth of the population were living on public charity ... Is inequality, then, the necessary driving force, and the contrast between extreme poverty and opulence the inevitable result of economic growth? Was it not believed that the history of modern society was a progressive and continuous movement towards the eradication of poverty in the world?'.

7. Among others, the work of C. Booth could be cited: *Life and Labour of the people in London* (London 1889–1991); S. Rowntree, *Poverty: A Study of Town Life* (London 1901), both written for England; for France, among others worthy of mention would be the very apt study by the legitimist Catholic viscount, A. de Villneuve-Bargemont: *Économie*

politique crétienne, ou recherches sur la nature et les causes du pauperisme en France et en Europe, et sur les moyens de le soulager et de le prévenir (Paris 1834).

8. It is commonly known and documented that, in some factories, the owner went down into the workshops in the afternoon to recite the rosary, in Basque, with the working men and women, while they continued with their tasks. This was a follow-on from the custom that existed in some homes of reciting the rosary with the servants; the master of the house and, later, the owner of the factory were responsible for the good conduct of the people in their charge.

9. J Gracia, 'Aspirando a sobrevivir. Hogares y familias pobres en Bilbao a finales del siglo 19', in L. Castells (ed.), *El rumor de lo cotidiano* (Bilbao: University of the Basque Country, 1999), pp. 117–58.

10. This activity, so common in all industrialized countries which exploited the weakest forms of manpower, women and children (saving on workshops, light, water, machinery etc.) had a strong generic component: the woman worked without leaving the house, giving up hours of sleep and rest; that is to say, after having fulfilled all her domestic duties, all she received for her piece-work was a very meagre salary. Sometimes, whole families of unemployed dedicated their time to these jobs, transforming the home into an unhealthy workshop but which, by its very nature and conditions (in the home, badly paid, no fixed hours and compatible with ordinary housework) was the lot of the women. Among the studies carried out on this subject, we could cite those of E. Boris, *Home to Work. Motherhood and the Politics of Industrial Homework in the United States* (Cambridge: Cambridge University Press, 1994); M. Nash, *"Identitat cultural de genere, discurs de la domesticitat I definicio de treball de les donnes a la Espanya del segle XIX"*, Documents dÁnàlisi Geográfica (1995), 26, pp. 135–46; M. Baylina, *Trabajadoras en casa: el trabajo a domicilio* (El Campo, 1995), pp. 107–125; N. Pellegrin, *'Las Costureras en la historia: Mujeres y trabajo en el Antiguo Régimen'* (Arenal 1994), vol. 1, pp. 25–38. Also several articles by M. D. Ramos (ed.), *El trabajo de las mujeres: pasado y presente* (Malaga: Diputacion Provincial, 1996), discuss the same issues.

11. Perez-Fuentes, P. *Vivir y morir en las minas. Estrategias familiares y relaciones de género en la primera industrialización vizcaina 1877–1913* (Bilbao: University of the Basque Country,1993).

12. M. A. Barcenilla, *La Pequeña Manchester. Origen y consolidación de un núcleo industrial guipuzcoano, Errenteria (1845–1905)* (San Sebastián: Diputación Foral de Guipúzcoa, 1999).

13. M. Arbaiza Villalonga, 'La 'cuestión social' como cuestión de género. Feminidad y trabajo en España (1860–1930)', *Historia Contemporánea*, 21 (2000), pp. 395–458.

14. J. Gracia Cárcamo, **Ibid.**, p. 145.

15. D. Kertzer and M. Barbagli, *Historia de la familia europea. La vida familiar desde la revolución Francesa hasta la Primera Guerra Mundial (1789–1913)* (Barcelona: Païdós, 2003), vol. 2, p. 131.

16. Ibíd., p. 132.

3 Moring, 'Women, Work and Survival Strategies in Urban Northern Europe before the First World War'

1. R. Fuchs, *Gender and Poverty in Nineteenth-Century Europe* (Cambridge: Cambridge University Press, 2005), pp. 235–6.

2. E. Higgs, 'Women's Occupations and Work in the Nineteenth-Century Censuses', *History Workshop Journal,* 23 (1987), pp. 59–82.
3. J. Humphries, 'Female-Headed Households in Early Industrial Britain: The Vanguard of the Proletariat?', *Labour History Review,* 69:1 (1998), pp. 31–65, on pp. 31–5.
4. R. Wall, 'Relationships Between generations in British Families Past and Present', in C. Marsh and S. Aber (eds), *Families and Households, Divisions and Change* (London: Macmillan, 1992), p. 81; R. Wall, 'The Residence Patterns of Elderly English Women in Comparative Perspective', *Women and Ageing in British Society* (London: Routledge, 2001).
5. B. Hill, *Women, Work and Sexual Politics in Eighteenth-Century England* (London: Mc Gill, 1989), p. 148.
6. Higgs, 'Women's Occupations', pp. 23–4, 60–2; L. Karlsson, 'Mothers as Breadwinners. Myth or Reality in Early Swedish Industry?', *Uppsala Papers in Economic History,* 39 (Uppsala: University of Uppsala, 1995), pp. 25–6.
7. P. Lindert and J. Williamson, 'English Workers' Living Standards during the Industrial Revolution; A New Look', *Economic History Review,* 36:1 (1983), pp. 1–25.
8. S. Horrell and J. Humphries, 'Old Questions, New Data and Alternative Perspectives: The Standard of Living of Families in the Industrial Revolution', *Journal of Economic History,* 53:4 (1992), pp. 849–80 on pp. 850–1; C. F. Feinstein, 'Pessimism Perpetuated: Real Wages and the Standard of Living in Britain', *Journal of Economic History,* 58:3 (1998), pp. 627–30.
9. J. Goodman and K. Honeyman, *Gainful Pursuits, The Making of Industrial Europe 1600–1914* (Bath: Edward Arnold, 1988), pp. 115–16; S. Pennington and B. Westover, *A Hidden Workforce, Homeworkers in England 1850–1985* (London: Macmillan, 1989), pp. 11–12.
10. J. Bourke, Housewifery in working-class England 1860–1914 in P. Sharpe (ed.), *Women's Work, the English Experience 1650–1914* (London: Arnold, 1998), pp. 339–41.
11. K. Gleadle, *British Women in the Nineteenth Century* (London: Palgrave 2001), pp. 96–97.
12. N. Goose, 'The Straw Plait and Hat Trades in Nineteenth-Century Hertfordshire', in N. Goose (ed.), *Women's Work in Industrial England* (Hertfordshire: Local Population Studies 2007), pp. 97–137, on p. 120–5; N. Goose, 'Introduction', in N. Goose (ed.), *Women's Work in Industrial England* (Hertfordshire: Local Population Studies 2007), pp. 1–28, on pp. 20–1.
13. E. Roberts, *A Woman's Place, An Oral History of Working Class women 1890–1940* (Oxford: Blackwell, 1984), pp. 136–7; P. Malcolmson, *English Laundresses, A Social History 1850–1930* (Chicago, IL: University of Illinois Press, 1986), p. 8.
14. J. Humphries, 'Enclosures, Common rights and Women', *Journal of Economic History,* 50:17(1990), pp. 17–42.
15. Pennington and Westover, *A Hidden,* pp. 16–17, 20.
16. H. Sandvik, 'Kjonnsperspektiv pa tidlig moderne tids okonomi', in K. Tonneson (ed.), *Fra kvinnehistorie til kjonnshistorie* (Oslo: Norsk lokalhistorisk institutt, 1994), pp. 101–102; G. Lext, *Mantalsskrivningens historia i Sverige fram till 1860* (Goteborg: Goteborgs Universitet, 1968); B. Moring, 'Nordic Family Patterns and the North West European Household System', *Continuity and Change,* 18:1 (2003), pp. 77–103.
17. M. Lahteenmaki, *Mahdollisuuksien aika* (Helsinki: Societas Historica Finlandiae, 1995), pp. 48–57; K.Vattula, 'Lahtoviivallako? Naisten ammatissatoimivuudesta, tilastoista ja kotitaloudesta', in Laine & Markkola (eds), *Tuntematon tyolaisnainen* (Tampere:

Vastapaino, 1989), pp. 28–9; K. Vattula, Kvinnors forvarvsarbete i Norden under 100 ar (1870–1970), *Studia Historica Jyvaskylaensia 27* (Jyvaskyla: University of Jyvaslyla, 1983), p. 48.

18. L. Harmaja, 'Onko kotitalous vahapatoisyys?', *Kansantaloudellinen Aikakauskirja* , 25:25 (1929), pp. 417–29; L. Harmaja, 'The Role of Household Production in National Economy', *Journal of Home Economics,* 23:9 (1931), pp. 822–7.

19. M. Manttari, 'Koyhyyden syyt 1800–luvun alun Helsingissa', in A. Hakkinen (ed.), *Vahavakisten Helsinkia* (Helsinki: Institute of Economic and Social History, 1989), pp. 41–52.

20. C. C. Bocker, A Survey of the Economic Activity in Finnish Rural Areas 1830s, manuscript, The National Archive, Helsinki; A. Nyberg, 'The Social Construction of Married Women's Labour Force Participation; the Case of Sweden in the 20th Century', *Continuity and Change,* 9:1 (1994), pp. 145–51.; B. Moring,, 'Rural Widows, Economy and Co-Residence in the Eighteenth and Nineteenth Centuries', *History of the Family,* 15 (2010), pp. 239–54, on p. 242; M. Peltonen, *Talolliset ja torpparit* (Helsinki: Suomen historiallinen Seura, 1992), pp. 216–17.

21. G. Fougstedt and A. Raivio, *Suomen vaeston saaty ja ammattiryhmitys 1751–1805* (Helsinki: Tilastotoimisto, 1953), pp. 44–7; B. Moring, 'Retirement Contracts and the Economics of Widowhood in the Nordic Countries', *Continuity and Change,* 21:3 (2006), pp. 383–418, on pp. 389–91; B. Moring, 'Widowhood Options and Strategies in Pre–industrial Northern Europe', *The History of the Family,* 7:1 (2002), pp. 79–99.

22. Moring 'Widowhood options', pp. 89–95; Moring 'Retirement Contracts'; Moring 'Rural Widows', pp. 248–50.

23. Lahteenmaki, *Mahdollisuuksien,* pp. 120–1, 132–3; B. Moring, 'Strategies and Networks: Family Earnings and Institutional Contributions to Women's Households in Urban Sweden and Finland 1890–1910', in T. Addabo, M. Arrizabalaga, C. Borderias and A. Owens (eds), *Gender Inequalities, Households and the Production of Well-Being in Modern Europe* (London: Ashgate 2010), pp. 77–94.

24. B. Moring, 'Widows, Children and Assistance from Society in Urban Northern Europe 1890–1910', *Family History* (2008:1), pp. 105–17, on pp. 108–9; J. Jaakkola, *Armeliaisuus, yhtesoapu sosiaaliturva* (Helsinki: Sosiaaliturvan keskusliito, 1994), pp. 129–31; Suomen Virallinen Tilasto SVT (Official Statistics of Finland) XXI A. *Koyhainhoitotilasto* (Helsinki: Office of Statistics, 1898); Suomen Virallinen Tilasto SVT XXI A. *Koyhainhoitotilasto* (Helsinki: Office of Statistics, 1901), Helsinki Poor relief records 1890–1893, The Municipal Archive of Helsinki.

25. M. Salmela-Jarvinen, *Kun se parasta on ollut* (Helsinki: Tammi, 1965), p. 95.

26. The Census of Helsinki 1900, Original sheets, the archive of the Bureau of Statistics, The National Archive, Helsinki; Salmela-Jarvinen, *Kun se parasta,* pp. 38–9.

27. V. Hjelt, *Undersokning av yrkesarbetarnes lefnadsvillkor I Finland 1908–1909* (Helsingfors: Industristyrelsen, 1911), pp. 132–3.

28. V. Voionmaa, *Suomen talousmaantieto* (Helsinki: Wsoy, 1922), p. 158–9.

29. Pennigton & Westover, *A Hidden,* pp. 6–8, 11–13.

30. H. Waris, *Tyolaisyhteiskunnan syntyminen Helsingin Pitkansillan pohjoispuolelle I* (Helsinki:Helsingin Yliopisto,1932), pp. 327–8.

31. Salmela Jarvinen, *Kun se parasta,* p. 63; Hjelt, *Undersokning,* pp. 8–11, 25–6.

32. Bidrag till Finlands Officiela Statistik (Official Statistics of Finland) VI, 35, *Folkrakninen i Helsingfors, Abo, Tammerfors och Viborg 1900* (Helsingfors: Statistiska Centralbyran, 1904), p. 11; Bidrag till Finlands Officiela Statistik (Official Statistics of Finland) VI,

1722048   *Notes to pages 49–57*

44:8, *Folkrakninen i Helsingfors, Abo, Tammerfors och Viborg 1910* (Helsingfors: Statistiska Centralbyran, 1914), p. 8.
33. Bidrag 44 (1914), pp. 192–3; *Statistisk arsbok for Helsingfors stad 1914* (Helsingfors: Helsingfors statistiska kontor 1916), included 57,043 women over the age of fifteen.
34. Bidrag 44 (1914), pp. 192–5.
35. Census 1900, original sheets Northern, Helsinki, Harju and III Linja (working class district) 242 female headed households.
36. Census 1900 Helsinki, original sheets, families of husbands and wives.
37. Goose, 'The Straw Plait', pp. 120–2.
38. S. E. Astrom, 'Stadssamhallets omdaning' in R. Rosen, E. Hornborg and H. Waris (eds), *Helsingfors Stads Historia IV*, 2 (Helsingfors: Helsingfors stad, 1956), pp. 7–328, on pp. 42–3, 49; *Statistisk arsbok for Helsingfors stad 1905* (Helsingfors: Helsingfors statistiska kontor, 1908), pp. 263, 77.
39. O. Grounstroem, *Helsingin tyovaen taloudellisita oloista. Esitelma kansantaloudellisessa yhdistyksessa* (Porvoo: Kansantaloudellinen yhdistys, 1897), pp. 107–8, 114–15.
40. K. Willgren, 'Arbetarklassens ekonomiska framatskridande i Finland under de senaste decennierna', *Ekonomiska Samfundet i Finland, Foredrag och forhandlingar 5* (Helsingfors: Ekonomiska Samfundet, 1909), pp. 93–5.
41. P. Haapala, *Tehtaan valossa* (Helsinki: Societas Historica Finlandiae, 1986), p. 232.
42. Hjelt, *Undersokning*, pp. 10–43.
43. Astrom 'Stadssamhallet', pp. 70–4.
44. 1905 was the year of general strike action, S. Heikkinen, *Labour and the Market* (Helsinki; Finnish Society of Science and Letters, 1997), pp. 119–21; *Statistisk arsbok for Helsingfors stad 1905*, pp. 246–7.
45. Heikkinen, *Labour*, pp. 119–22.
46. Hjelt, *Undersokning*, pp. 20–31, Table 3.7.
47. Haapala, *Tehtaan*, p. 232; G. Snellman, *Undersokning angaende tobaksindustrin* (Helsngfors: Industristyrelsen, 1903); G. Snellman, *Undersokning angaende textilindustrin* (Helsingfors: Industristyrelsen, 1904); G. Snellman, *Undersokning angaende pappersindustrin* (Helsingfors; Industristyrelsen, 1912); K. Key-Aberg, 'Inom textilindustrien in Norrkoping sysselsatta arbetares lonevillkor och bostadsforhallanden'. *Skrifter ugifna af Lorenska Stiftelsen, 12* (Stockholm: Lorenska Stiftelsen, 1896), pp. 38–41; J. Leffler, 'Zur Kenntniss von den Lebens und Lohnverhaltnissen Industrieller Arbeiterinnen in Stockholm', *Skrifter ugifna af Lorenska Stiftelsen, 15* (Stockholm: Lorenska Stiftelsen, 1897), pp. 80–4; Heikkinen, *Labour*, pp. 87, 94.
48. T. Hultin, *Yotyontekijattaret Suomen teollisuudessa*, SVT D II, IX (Helsinki: Tilastotoimisto, 1911), pp. 22–3, 60.
49. Vattula, *Studia Historica*, pp. 44–5.
50. Willgren 'Arbetarkassens', p. 99; V. Hjelt, *Undersokning* av nålarbeterskornas yrkesforhallanden (Helsingfors: Industristyrelsen, 1908), pp. 40–2, 76–8.
51. Tilastollisia tietoja Suomen kasityoliikkeista vuodelta (statistical information on craft and small trade in Finland) 1913:15:VI, XI, Tilastollinen paatoimisto (the Bureau of Statistics), The National Archive, Helsinki .
52. Hultin, *Yotyontekijattaret*, pp. 43–5.
53. Hjelt, *Undersokning*, pp. 128–30, 146.
54. Hjelt, *Undersokning*, pp. 28–31.
55. M. Hentila, *Keikkavaaka ja kousikka, kaupan tyo ja sen tekijat 1800–luvulta itsepalveluaikaan* (Helsinki: Edita, 1999), pp. 30–2.

56. K. Vainio-Korhonen, *Ruokaa, vaatteita, hoivaa* (Helsinki: SKS, 2002), pp. 66–7.
57. Hentila, *Keikkavaaka*, p. 34.
58. Salmela Jarvinen, *Kun se parasta,* p. 38–41; A. Astrom and M. Sundman (eds), *Hemma bast– Minnen fran barndomshem i Helsingfors* (Helsingfors: Svenska Litteratursallskapet i Finland, 1990), p. 35; J. Koskinen, *Kallion historia* (Helsinki: Kallio seura ry, 1990), p. 277.
59. Hentila, *Keikkavaaka*, p. 32; Hjelt, *Undersokning*, p. 125; Salmela Jarvinen, *Kun se parasta*, p. 50,63.
60. Koskinen, *Kallion*, pp. 278–9; Hentila, *Keikkavaaka*, p. 33; P. Markkola, *Tyolaiskodin synty* (Helsinki: Societas Historica Finlandiae, 1994), pp. 114–16; Tampere Municipality, Poor relief inspector's notes on recipients of out relief, November 1899–November 1900, manuscript, The Municipal Archive of Tampere.
61. Z. Topelius, *Lasning for Barn* (Stockholm: Albert Bonnier, 1904), p. 106; Z. Topelius, *Lasning for barn* (Stockhom: Albert Bonnier, 1907), pp. 61–71.
62. Hjelt, *Undersokning*, pp. 119–21, 144–5, 149.
63. *Kalender ofver kvinnoarbetet i Finland* (Helsingfors: Finsk Kvinnoforening, 1894), p. 115.
64. Vainio-Korhonen, *Ruokaa,* p. 65–8, 118; G. R. Snellman, *Undersökning av de mindre bemedlades bostadsförhållanden i Åbo stad samt angränsande delar af St Karins och St Marie socknar* (Abo: G & co, 1906), p. 53.
65. *Statistisk arsbok for Helsingfors stad 1905*, pp. 196, 199; V. Sucksdorff, *Arbetarebefolkningens i Helsingfors bostadsforhallanden, redogorelse for Arbetarebostadsundersokningen ar 1900* (Helsingfors: Halsovardsnamnden, 1904), p. 273.
66. Sucksdorff, *Arbetarebefolkningens*, pp. 246–7, 262–3; H. Waris *Tyolaisyhteiskunnan syntyminen Helsingin Pitkansillan pohjoispuolelle II*, pp. 243–4.
67. Hjelt, *Undersokning*, pp. 114, 124, 148–49; Astrom & Sundman, *Hemma*, pp. 178, 196–7.
68. Astrom & Sundman, *Hemma*, p. 33,38–39, 52, 79; Vainio-Korhonen, *Ruokaa*, p. 117; Koskinen *Kallio*, pp. 89–90; S. Laakkonen, 'Itameren tyttaren likaiset helmat' in S. Laakkonen, S. Laurila and M. Rahikainen (eds), *Nokea ja pilvenhattaroita* (Helsinki: Helsinkin Kaupunginmuseo, 1999), pp. 122–8.
69. Koskinen, *Kallion*, pp. 306–7.
70. *Kalender 1894*, p. 115; Koskinen, *Kallion*, p. 53.
71. Laakkonen, 'Itameren', pp. 122, 126–32 .
72. Tilastollisia tietoja 1913:15: ix; Hjelt, *Undersokning*, p. 114, 122, 125, 146–7.
73. Waris, *Tyolaisyhteiskunnan II*, p. 253–60; A. Gauffin, *Bostadsbehof och barnantal med afseende sarskildt a inneboendesystemet i arbetarfamiljerna i Helsingfors* (Helsingfors: Foreningen for framjande af allmannyttig byggnadsverksamhet, 1915), pp. 24–27; Astrom & Sundman 'Hemma', pp. 33, 89, 92, 135; 179.
74. Sucksdorff, *Arbetarebefolkningens*, pp. 242–6; Gauffin, *Bostadsbehof*, pp. 8–9.
75. Gauffin, *Bostadsbehof*, pp. 8–9, 28–9; Astrom & Sundman, *Hemma*, pp. 152, 177, 179; Salmela-Jarvinen , *Kun se parasta*, pp. 49, 73–4.
76. Census for Helsinki 1900.
77. Waris, *Tyolaisyhteiskunnan II*, pp. 253, 256–62; Salmela-Jarvinen, *Kun se parasta*, pp. 104, 110–13.
78. Sucksdorff , *Arbetarebefolkningens*, pp. 250–1.
79. Gauffin, *Bostadsbehof* ', pp. 24–9; Census 1900, see also table 'Rents'.
80. Moring , 'Strategies and Networks', p. 89.

81. Census for Helsinki 1900.
82. Waris, *Tyolaisyhteiskunnan* vol. 2, p. 28, Astrom & Sundman, *Hemma,* p. 179.
83. C. Booth, E. Avery and H. Higgs, *The Income and Expenses of Twenty-Eight British Households 1891–1894* (London: The Economic Club, 1896), pp. 31–7.
84. Census of Helsinki, 1900, Harju; Hjelt, *Undersokning,* pp. 131–2.
85. Hjelt, *Undersokning,* pp. 123–6, 142–55.
86. Koskinen, *Kallion,* p. 307; Moring 'Widows, children', Moring, 'Strategies and Networks', pp. 89–91; G. af Geijerstam, 'Anteckningar rorande fabriksarbetarnes stallning i Marks harad' *Skrifter ugifna af Lorenska Stiftelsen,* 10 (1894; Stockholm: Lorenska Stiftelsen 1894), pp. 55, 57, 63.
87. Suomen Virallinen Tilasto SVT (Official Statistics of Finland XXXII:II), *Asuntolaskenta 1919* (Helsinki: Office of Statistics 1921), pp. 478–79; Suomen Virallinen Tilasto SVT (Official Statistics of Finland XXXII: 5, 1925), *Elinkustannukset tilinpitokaudella 1920–1921* (Helsinki: Office of Statistics), p. 33.
88. Pennington and Westover, *A Hidden Workforce,* p. 7.
89. Heikkinen, *Labour,* pp. 119–22; Hjelt, *Undersokning,* pp. 30–1.
90. Sucksdorff, *Arbetarebefolkningens,* p. 33, 248.
91. Moring 'Strategies and Networks', p. 88.
92. Hjelt, *Undersokning,* ibid.
93. Moring 'Strategies and Networks', 89, 94; Salmela-Jarvinen, *Kun se parasta,* pp. 112, 129.
94. Census for Helsinki, female-headed households, Kallio, Harju.
95. Hjelt, *Undersokning,* pp. 127–8; Koskinen, *Kallion,* p. 307.
96. Salmela-Jarvinen, *Kun se parasta,* p. 154; Astrom & Sundman, *Hemma,* pp. 97, 184; Topelius ibid.
97. Salmela-Jarvinen, *Kun se parasta,* pp. 89–90, Koskinen, *Kallion,* pp. 51, 78; G. Snellman, *Tutkimus Helsingin, Turun, Tampereen ja Viipurin kansakoululasten tyoskentelysta koulun ulkopuolella.* (Helsinki: Teollisuushallitus, 1908), pp. 20–1.
98. Hjelt, *Undersokning,* pp. 24–9, 55, 59, 63; Salmela-Jarvinen, *Alas lyotiin,* p. 10.
99. Moring, 'Widows, Children', pp. 111–12; Moring 'Strategies and Networks', p. 87, Hultin, '*Yotyontekijattaret,*' pp. 36–7, Census of Helsinki 1900; Suomen Virallinen Tilasto SVT. Official Statistics of Finland XXXII, 1, *Yotyontekijattaret* (Helsinki: Office of Statistics 1935), pp. 112–15.
100. Hjelt, *Nalarbeterskorna,* pp. 100–1, 112–16; SVT, *Yotyontekijattaret* (1935), pp. 8, 10–11, 98–9.
101. P. Sveistrup, 'Kobenhavnske syerskers og smaakaarsfamiliers kostudgifter', *Nationalokonomisk Tidskrift,* 3:7 (1899), pp. 578–629, on p. 581; G. Meyerson, *Arbeterskornas varld – Studier och erfarenheter* (Stockholm: Hugo Geber, 1917), pp. 123–5; Plymoth 199, pp. 65–7; Geijerstam 'Anteckningar', pp. 55, 57, 63; Leffler 'Zur kenntniss', pp. 103, 110.
102. Salmela-Jarvinen, *Kun se parasta,* pp. 104–5; Salmela-Jarvinen, *Alas lyotiin,* p. 8; Astrom and Sundman, *Hemma,* p. 89.
103. Census for Helsinki 1900.
104. Salmela-Jarvinen *Kun se parasta,* pp. 104, 112; Sucksdorff, *Arbetarebefolkningens,* pp. 244–6 Hjelt , *Undersokning,* pp. 185–6.
105. Hjelt, *Undersokning,* pp. 44–86; Moring 'Widows, Children'; 'Strategies and Networks', pp. 85–8; Moring, 'Rural Widows'.
106. S. Horrell, and J. Humphries, 'Old questions, new data and alternative perspectives: the standard of living of families in the Industrial Revolution', *Journal of Economic History,* 53:4 (1992), pp. 849–80; K. McNay, J. Humphries and S. Klasen, 'Excess Female Mortal-

ity in Nineteenth Century England and Wales', *Social Science History,* 29:4 (2005), pp. 649–81.; S. Horrell, D. Meredith and D. Oxley, 'Measuring Misery: Body Mass, Ageing and Gender Inequality in Victorian London', *Explorations in Economic History,* 46:1 (2009), pp. 93–119; J. Humphries, *Childhood and Child Labour in the British Industrial Revolution* (Cambridge: Cambridge University Press, 2010).

107. Sveistrup 'Kobenhavnske', pp. 578–82; M. Pember Reves, *Round about a Pound a Week* (London, 1913), pp. 16–17; Astrom and Sundman, *Hemma,* p. 181.

108. E. Rathbone, *How the Casual Labourer Lives* (Liverpool, 1909), pp. 13–14, 73; Paton *et al., Study of the Diet of the Labouring Class in Edinburgh* (Edinburgh 1902), pp. 17, 22.

109. Y. Hirdman, *Magfragan: Stockholm 1870–1920* (Stockholm: Raben & Sjogren, 1983), p. 23.

110. Waris, *Tyolaisyhteiskunnan* II, pp. 62–4.

111. R. Kempf, *Das Leben der Jungen Fabriksmadchen* (Lepzig: Duncker & Humboldt, 1911), pp. 152–4.

112. Hjelt, *Undersokning,* pp. 44–5, 70, 78–80, 190–201.

113. Waris, *Tyolaisyhteiskunnan* II, pp. 57–9.

114. Hirdman, *Magfragan,* p. 81; Salmela-Jarvinen, *Kun se parasta,* p. 111; Waris, *Tyolaisyhteiskunnan* II , pp. 33, 38, 44.

115. Hjelt, *Undersokning,* pp. 46, 202–34, Salmela-Jarvinen, *Kun se parasta,* pp. 76–77.

116. Salmela-Jarvinen, *Kun se parasta,* pp. 68, 79–80.

117. Moring 'Widows, Children', pp. 108–9; Moring 'Strategies and Networks', pp. 79–80; Moring, 'Rural Widows', p. 117.

118. Lahteenmaki, *Mahdollisuuksien,* pp. 86, 202, 247–51, 238–9.

119. Snellman, *Undersokning angaende,* 1912 p. 19–21; Hultin, *Yotyontekijattare*t, pp. 44–7.

120. Lahteenmaki, *Mahdollisuuksien,* p. 80.

121. Moring, 'Widows, Children', pp. 112–13; Moring 'Strategies and Networks', pp. 88–9; Salmela-Jarvinen, *Kun se parasta.*

4 Ottaway, 'Women, Households and Independence under the Old English Poor Laws'

1. Queen Elizabeth's Speech to a Joint Delegation of Lords and Commons, 5 November 1566, version 2, in *Elizabeth I: Collected Works,* ed. L. S. Marcus, J. Mueller and M. B. Rose (Chicago, IL: University of Chicago Press, 2002), p. 97.

2. *An Account of Several Work-Houses for Employing and Maintaining the Poor* (London: Joseph Downing, 1725), p. 30. Eighteenth Century Collections Online (hereafter ECCO), Gale. Carleton College. 31 January 2011.

3. K. Wrightson, *Earthly Necessities: Economic Lives in Early Modern England* (New Haven, CT: Yale University Press, 2002).

4. L. Fontaine and J. Schlumbohm, 'Household Strategies for Survival: An Introduction,' *International Review of Social History,* 45: Supplement S8 (2000), pp. 1–17.

5. N. Tadmor, *Family and Friends in Eighteenth-Century England: Household, Kinship and Patronage* (Cambridge: Cambridge University Press, 2001).

6. S. Hindle, 'Without the Cry of any Neighbours: A Cumbrian Family and the Poor Law Authorities, *c.* 1690–1730,' in H. Berry and E. Foyster (eds), *The Family in Early Modern England* (Cambridge: Cambridge University Press, 2007), p. 133.

7. But see P. Crawford, *Poor Parents and Their Children in Early Modern England* (Oxford: Oxford University Press, 2009); J. Henderson and R. Wall (eds), *Poor Women and Children in the European Past* (London: Routledge, 1994); J. Bailey, 'Reassessing Parenting in the Eighteenth Century', in Berry and Foyster, *The Family in Early Modern England.*

8. O. Hufton, *The Poor of Eighteenth-Century France* (Oxford: Oxford University Press, 1974); S. King and A. Tompkins (eds), *The Poor in England: An Economy of Makeshifts* (Manchester: Manchester University Press, 2003).

9. O. Hufton, 'Women Without Men: Widows and Spinsters in Britain and France in the Eighteenth Century', *Journal of Family History*, 9:4 (1984), pp. 355–76.

10. S. Hindle, *On the Parish? The Micro-Politics of Poor Relief in England, c. 1550–1750* (Cambridge: Cambridge University Press, 2004).

11. T. Hitchcock, *Down and Out in Eighteenth-Century London* (Hambledon: Continuum, 2004); D. Green, *Pauper Capital: London and the Poor Law, 1790–1870* (Farnham: Ashgate, 2010).

12. Tom Sokoll, for instance, has shown that pauper women were more likely to live in extended families than were the well-to-do. T. Sokoll, *Household and Family among the Poor The Case of Two Essex Communities in the Late Eighteenth and Early Nineteenth Centuries* (Bochum: Universitatsverlag Dr. N Brockmeyer, 1993), 167–71; P. Laslett and R. Wall (eds), *Household and Family in Past Time* (Cambridge: Cambridge University Press, 1972); R. Wall, 'Elderly Persons and Members of Their Households in England and Wales from Preindustrial Times to the Present', in D. Kertzer and P. Laslett (eds), *Aging in the Past: Demography, Society and Old Age* (Berkeley, CA: University of California Press, 1995).

13. William Moreton Pitt, MP, *An Address to the Landed Interest, on the Deficiency of Habitations and Fuel, for the Use of the Poor* (London: Elmsley and Bremner, 1797). ECCO. Gale. Carleton College. 31 Jan. 2011. <http://find.galegroup. com.ezproxy.carleton. edu/ecco/infomark.do?&contentSet=ECCOArticles&type=multipage&tabID=T00 1&prodId=ECCO&docId=CW105303646&source=gale&userGroupName=mnalm gl&version=1.0&docLevel=FASCIMILE>.

14. There was an endowed almshouse for six aged paupers in Corfe. 'Corfe-Castle – Corstone', *A Topographical Dictionary of England* (1848), pp. 685–93. URL: http://www. british-history.ac.uk/report.aspx?compid=50896 Date accessed: 25 January 2011.

15. S. Ottaway, *The Decline of Life: Old Age in Eighteenth-Century England* (Cambridge: Cambridge University Press, 2004). The Dawnay census is Dorset History Centre (DHC) PE/PUD OV1/4 and C. L. S. Williams, *Puddletown House Street and Family* (Dorchester: Dorset Record Society, 1988). Overseers' accounts are DHC PE/PUD OV1/1–4. Settlement examinations, removal orders and certificates can be found in DHC PE/PUD OV3/1/1–18, DHC PE/PUD OV3/2/1–112, DHC PE/PUD OV3/3/1–53, DHC PE/PUD OV3/4/1–24 and DHC PE/PUD OV3/5/1–5. Vouchers are in DHC PE/PUD OV1/8–41. A few other overseers' notes are in DHC PE/PUD OV1/63, DHC PE/PUD OV8/1–4. The charity records are scattered through the overseers' accounts and in DHC PE/PUD RE1/5 and 4/1; registers are DHC PE/PUD: RE 1/1–5, 3/1–3, 4/1–2.

16. Jane Flambert's husband, 'Old Flambert' had received relief before his death in 1720. Mary Daw received more charity than almost any other Puddletown resident, but the only 'Dawes' on the overseers' accounts were Grace and some children in the 1680s.

17. T. Sokoll, *Household and Family*, pp. 169–71; R. Wall, 'Introduction' to Wall, Peter Laslett and Jean Robin (eds), *Family Forms in Historic Europe* (Cambridge: Cambridge University Press, 1983); R. Wall, 'Elderly Persons and Members of Their Households.

18. J. Boulton, 'It is Extreme Necessity That Makes Me Do This: Some 'Survival Strategies of Pauper Households in London's West End during the Early Eighteenth Century', *International Review of Social History*, 45 (Supplement) (2000), pp. 47–69.

19. T. Sokoll, *Essex Pauper Letters 1731–1837*, Records of Social and Economic History New Series 30, Published for the British Academy (Oxford: Oxford University Press, Oxford, 2001), p. 292.

20. Sokoll, *Essex Pauper Letters*, p. 626. Another example is Mary Pavett, in Rainham, 1748, p. 560.

21. T. V. Hitchcock, 'The English Workhouse: A Study in Institutional Poor Relief in Selected Counties, 1696–1750' (D. Phil. Thesis, Oxford University, 1985); P. Slack, *The English Poor Law 1531–1782* (London: Macmillan, 1990).

22. S. Webb, *The Parish and the County* (London: Longmans, 1906); J. S. Taylor, 'The Unreformed Workhouse 1776–1834,' in E. W. Martin (ed.), *Comparative Development in Social Welfare* (London: George Allen and Unwin Ltd., 1972); A. Digby, *Pauper Palaces* (London: Routledge and Kegan Paul, 1978), p. 46; M. Barker-Read, 'The Treatment of the Aged Poor in Five Selected West Kent Parishes from Settlement to Speenhamland (1662–1797)' (Open University Ph.D. thesis 1988).

23. Essex Record Office D/P 299/12/3 and 8/2. She never did enter the workhouse, and perhaps as a response to this, she ceased to receive her pension from December 1796 until April 1797.

24. F. M. Eden, *The State of the Poor*, 3 vols (London: J. Davis, 1797), vol. 3, pp. 808–9. The parochial report for Inkborough is dated January 1796; Anna Clark, 'Wild Workhouse Girls and the Liberal Imperial State in Mid-Nineteenth Century Ireland,' *Journal of Social History*, 39:2 (2005), pp. 389–409.

25. Eden, *The State of the Poor*, vol. II, p. 435–6.

26. Ibid., vol. 2, p. 329.

27. Pitt believed the 'industrious labourer' had 'just pretensions to the care and protection of the legislature' and that a 'suitable habitation' was a 'comfort' to which a poor man 'had a claim'. Pitt, 'An Address', pp. 17–20.

28. E. Gillingwater, *An Essay on Parish Work-Houses: Containing Observations on the Present State of English Work-Houses with Some Regulations Proposed for their Improvement* (Bury St Edmunds: J. Rackham, 1786); J. Vancouver, *An Enquiry Into the Causes and Production of Poverty, and The State of the Poor: Together With the Proposed Means for their Effectual Relief* (London: R. Edwards, 1796).

29. Other mentions of women included those workhouses that specifically employed women in different occupations from men, most often in spinning, nursing or general housekeeping. (9, 64, 69) Newcastle upon Tyne is one of the very few that actually specified the number of men and women in the house in its observations. Great Britain. Parliament. House of Commons, *Report from the Committee Appointed to Make Enquiries Relating to the Employment, Relief, and Maintenance, of the Poor* ([London], 1776), esp. pp. 9, 64, 69. ECCO. Gale. Carleton College, 31 January 2011.<http://find.galegroup.com.ezproxy.carleton.edu/ecco/infomark.do?&contentSet=ECCOArticles&type=multipage&tabID=T001&prodId=ECCO&docId=CW104710756&source=gale&userGroupName=mnalmgl&version=1.0&docLevel=FASCIMILE>.

30. *An Account of the Work-Houses in Great Britain, in the Year M,DCC,XXXII. Shewing their Original, Number, and the Particular Management of them at* …, 3rd (London, 1786), p. 76 has one of the rare instances of men and women listed separately; the other ones occur on 87, 103, 131, 154, 159, 166; so seven out of dozens of listings separate men and women in their accounts, though many do note the different forms of employment between the sexes.

31. Eden, *The State of the Poor* (London, 1797), passim.

32. Ottaway, *The Decline of Life*, ch. 7.

33. T. Hitchcock, 'Unlawfully Begoten on Her Body': Illegitimacy and the Parish Poor in St Luke's Chelsea,' in Hitchcock, P. King and P. Sharpe (eds), *Chronicling Poverty* (NY: St Martins Press, 1997); Hitchcock, 'Paupers and Preachers: The SPCK and the Parochial Workhouse Movement', in L. Davison, *et al.* (eds), *Stilling the Grumbling Hive: The Response to Social and Economic Problems in England, 1689–1750* (New York: St Martin's, 1992), p. 148. See also E. W. Martin, who has called workhouses the 'Mecca of the Poor Law Reformer'. 'From Parish to Union', p. 32.

34. A. Levene, *The Childhood of the Poor: Welfare in Eighteenth-Century London* (Basingstoke: Palgrave Macmillan, forthcoming 2012).

35. Calderdale District Archives, HAS:214.

36. Crawford, *Parents of Poor*, p. 74.

5 Head-König, 'The Economic Strategies of Widows in Switzerland from the Mid-Ninetenth to the Mid-Twentieth Century'

1. Recensements fédéraux de la population du 10 décembre 1860 et du 1er décembre 1941.

2. A.-L. Head-König, 'Veuvage et remariage féminins en Suisse: le poids des facteurs culturels, démographiques, économiques et institutionnels (XVIIe–XIXe siècles)', in A.-L.Head-König & L. Mottu-Weber (eds), *Les femmes dans la société européenne/Die Frauen in der europäischen Gesellschaft. 8e Congrès des Historiennes suisses* (Genève: Soc. d'Histoire et d'Archéologie de Genève, 2000), pp. 317–36.

3. Statistique des ménages 1920, *Bulletin de statistique suisse*, 8, 1926, fasc. 1.

4. As was the case, for instance, for the *Allgemeine Armenpflege Basel.*

5. Two examples among others: in Geneva, for instance, those Swiss who did not possess local citizenship and foreigners, too, were assisted by the *Bureau central de Bienfaisance* created in 1868, whilst public welfare (*assistance publique*) for the Genevese citizens was centralized at the *Hospice général*. In Basle, those who did not belong to the commune and thus were not local citizens were assisted by the *Allgemeine Armenpflege Basel*, and the citizens of the town itself were assisted by the *Bürgerliches Fürsorgeamt der Stadt Basel.*

6. A. Ryter, *Als Weibsbild bevogtet. Zum Alltag von Frauen im 19. Jahrhundert. Geschlechtsvormundschaft und Ehebeschränkungen im Kanton Basel-Landschaft* (Liestal: Verlag des Kantons Basel-Landschaft, 1994), p. 224.

7. A.-L. Head-König, 'Populations âgées dans l'espace urbain suisse entre ségrégation et intégration: aspects démographiques, sociaux et résidentiels (milieu XIX- milieu XX s.)', in L. Lorenzetti (ed.), *Gli anziani e la città. (In)compatibilità, regolazioni sociali e ambiente costruito (secolo XVI–XXI)* (Roma: Caroci editore, 2010), pp. 23–42, on p. 38.

8. B. Keller, *Von Speziererinnen, Wegglibuben und Metzgern, Lebensmittelhandwerk und – handel in Basel 1850–1914* (Zürich: Chronos, 2001), p. 142.

9. K. Biske, 'Statistik der Frauenarbeit. Entwicklung in der Stadt Zürich und in der Schweiz', *Statistik der Stadt Zürich*, pp. 66, 1962.

10. Ibid., p. 89.

11. K. Biske, *Zürcher Mutterbefragung 1957/58. Tausend unselbständig erwerbende Mütter zu den Hintergründen und Auswirkungen ihrer Erwerbsarbeit* (Zürich: Statistisches Amt der Stadt Zürich, 1962), p. 69.

12. L. Trevisan, 'Das Wohnungselend der Basler Arbeiterbevölkerung in der zweiten Hälfte des 19. Jahrhunderts', *Neujahrsblatt, Gesellschaft für das Gute und Gemeinnützige*, 168 (1981), p. 91.

13. B. Koller, 'Gesundes Wohnen'. Ein Konstrukt zur Vermittlung bürgerlicher Werte und Verhaltensnormen und seine praktische Umsetzung in der Deutschschweiz, 1800–1940 (Zürich: Chronos Verlag, 1995), p. 273.

14. C. Hagmayer, *Bis dass der Tod euch scheidet. Witwen in der Schweiz um 1900* (Zürich: Chronos, 1994), pp. 102–3.

15. A.-L. Head-König, 'Les formes de garde des enfants placés en Suisse: politiques ambiguës, résistances et objectifs contradictoires (1850–1950)', *Paedagogica Historica*, 46, 2010, 6, pp. 763–773, on p. 770.

16. *Recensement fédéral de la population* (1930), vol. 21, p. 84.

17. The commune is the smallest administrative territorial division to which a Swiss needed to belong to - which means she or he had to posess its citizenship – in order to be assisted.

18. Ryter, *Als Weibsbild bevogtet.*

19. Die Armenpflege der Stadt Bern und die von ihr benutzten wohlthätigen Anstalten des Kantons (Bern: W. Büchler, 1889), p. 13.

20. N. Ramsauer, 'Verwahrlost'. Kindswegnahmen und die Entstehung der Jugendfürsorge im schweizerischen Sozialstaat, 1900–45 (Zürich: Chronos, 2000).

21. E. Steiger, 'Die unvollständige und die zerrüttete Familie als soziologisches, pädagogisches und fürsorgerisches Problem. Bericht über schweizerische Verhältnisse und Auffassungen', *Zeitschrift für schweizerische Statistik und Volkswirtschaft*, 68 (1932), pp. 284–303, on p. 289.

22. A.-L. Head-König, 'Farm Transfer, Marriage, Household and Parental Power in Rural Switzerland, 1860–1960', in A.-L. Head-König and P. Pozsgai (eds), *Inheritance Practices, Marriage Strategies and Household Formation in European Rural Societies*, Turnhout, Brepols, 2012 (Rural History in Europe, 7) (forthcoming).

23. Biske, *Zürcher Mutterbefragung 1957/8*, p. 69.

24. A.-L. Head-König, 'Populations âgées dans l'espace urbain suisse entre ségrégation et intégration: aspects démographiques, sociaux et résidentiels (milieu XIX- milieu XX s.)', in L. Lorenzetti (ed.), *Gli anziani e la città. (In)compatibilità, regolazioni sociali e ambiente costruito (secolo XVI–XXI)* (Roma: Caroci editore, 2010), pp. 23–42, on p. 36.

25. R. Wydler, Untersuchungen über das Armenwesen im Kanton Glarus : unter besonderer Berücksichtigung des Zeitraumes von 1840 bis 1930 (Glarus: Tschudy & Co., 1939), p. 62; Heer, G., Das Armenwesen des Kantons Glarus [...] (Schwanden: Aebly und Tschudy, 1913), pp. 25–6.

26. Tribunal fédéral. Arrêt de la IIe section civile du 13 mars 1913.

27. A.-L. Head-König, 'Citizens but not Belonging: Migrants' Difficulties in Obtaining Entitlement to Relief in Switzerland from the 1550s to the Early Twentieth Century', in S. King and A. Winter (eds), *Migration, Settlement and Belonging in Europe, 1500–2000: Comparative Perspectives* (New York: Berghahn, 2012) (forthcoming).

28. For Fribourg, see A. Hehli, *Le paupérisme rural en Gruyère 1880–1930: hospices et assistance au quotidien: le cas de la commune d'Avry-devant-Pont*. (Unpublished Master thesis, University of Fribourg/Suisse, 2003); for the town of Zurich, see the yearly *Geschäftsberichte des Stadtrates von Zürich*, or for the canton Berne, the yearly *Berichte über die Staatsverwaltung des Kantons Bern*.

29. *Pro Senectute*, 2 (1924), p. 74.

30. Ammann-Lang, S., *Armenrechtliche Heimschaffungen im Kanton Baselstadt in den dreissiger Jahren* (Unpublished Master thesis, University of Basle, 1988), vol. 1, p. 90.
    A.-K. Schmid, *Die verwaltete Armut: allgemeine Armenpflege in Basel 1898 bis 1911*(Unpublished Master Thesis, University of Basle, 1984), vol. 1, p. 86.

31. *Procès-verbal de la Conférence des Directeurs cantonaux de l'assistance publique les 28 et 29 juin à Genève, 1946* (Genève, 1946), p. 78.

32. Schmid, *Die verwaltete Armut*, vol. 1, p. 86.

33. G. Sutter, *Berufstätige Mütter: subtiler Wandel der Geschlechterordnung der Schweiz, 1945–1970* (Zürich: Chronos, 2005), pp. 327–8.

34. Even in the second half of the last century, the conception of part-time work varied all the time and those working only a few hours a week were not included at all in the official statistics until very late in the century. According to the 1960 census where more data are available, the proportion of working widows up to the age of sixty-five amounted to nearly 50 per cent (48.4) including those in full- and in part-time occupations. K. Biske, 'Frauen in Beruf und Haushalt. Entwicklung in der Schweiz und in der Stadt Zürich nach den Volks- und Betriebszählungen', *Statistik der Stadt Zürich*, 68 (1969), p. 7.

35. In 1930, the proportion of these widows who had to be assisted by the cantons on behalf of the Swiss Federal Government was 10.9 per cent and 15.5 per cent in 1940. Data calculated on the basis of the *recensements fédéraux de la population* and the *Feuille fédérale*, éditée par la Chancellerie fédérale, Berne, 91, 1939, vol. 1, 30 May 1939, p. 827 and 96, 1944, vol. 1, 26.20.1944, p. 935. But, in reality, the proportions were much higher: those assisted by local Assistance Boards were not included, and no data is available for the whole of Switzerland.

36. The only sporadic details we have relate to a specific type of assistance, which is that given to old people living in mountainous regions and who were not assisted by local authorities. In 1934 and 1935 34.8 per cent were widows, and of these 54 per cent lived alone and 46 per cent with kin. (*Pro Senectute*, 12, 1934 and 13, 1935).

37. *Feuille fédérale*, 81, 1929, vol. 2, p. 276. (henceforth FF).

38. FF, 96, 1944, vol. 1, 26.10.1944, p. 936.

39. FF, 98, 1946, vol. 2, 20.6.1946, p. 416.

40. C. Baumgartner, *AHV–Handbuch* [...] (Affoltern am Albis: J. Weiss, 1948), pp. 7–58.

41. FF, 98, 1946, vol. 2, 20.6.1946, pp 399–98.

42. F. Keller, *Die Ergebnisse der Statistischen Erhebungen der Allgemeinen Armenpflege Basel-Stadt im Jahre 1905* (Basel: Franz Wittmer, 1906), pp. 18–19.

43. The comparison of the help received by the citizens of Basle and the non-citizens shows the higher level of help received by the citizens. In 1930, when all cases of assistance were taken together, the non-citizens received on average Sfr 553 per case, and in 1940 the citizens Sfr 792 per case.

44. Bürgerliches Fürsorgeamt der Stadt Basel. Rechnung und Bericht und Statistik, 1941 (Basel: Verwaltungsbericht des Bürgerrates, 1941), pp. 21–2.

45. *Geschäftsberichte der Allgemeinen Armenpflege Basel,* 1905 and 1922 reports.

46. Biske, 'Statistik der Frauenarbeit', p. 71.

47. Ibid., p. 92.
48. Biske, Zürcher Mutterbefragung, p. 68.
49. Bulletin de statistique suisse, 8 (1926), fasc.1.
50. Biske, *Zürcher Mutterbefragung*, pp. 68–9.

6 Reyes and Ana Patricia Sosa Ferreira, 'Mexico: Women and Poverty (1994–2004): Progresa-Oportunidade Conditional Cash Transfer Programme'

Researchers from the Instituto de Investigaciones Económicas, UNAM. The authors are grateful to Bernardo Ramirez Pablo for his valuable assistance and technical support in preparing this paper. They would also like to thank Hilda Caballero and Susana Merino for their valuable opinions.

1. See World Bank, *Poverty Reduction and Growth: Virtuous and Vicious Circles* (Washington, 2006), particularly ch. 1: 'From Vicious to Virtuous Circles', and Chapter 9: 'Breaking the Cycle of Underinvestment in Human Capital in Latin America'.
2. In 1994, 38.2 per cent of women heading households were from forty to fifty-nine years of age, while in 2006 the percentage increased to 41.7 per cent. Special mention should be made of households headed by women sixty years of age and older: 34.9 per cent (1994) and 31.9 per cent (2006). In contrast, the percentage of male-headed households in 1994 was 17.1 per cent and for 2006 was 19.9 per cent Presumably these percentages can be attributed to the death of a spouse or abandonment. In any event, at the stage of life when it is most difficult to find employment, many women have to maintain their families. *Encuesta Nacional de Ingresos y Gastos de los Hogares 1994, 2002 y 2006* (México: INEGI).
3. See Estadísticas para la equidad de género, Table 6.9 of the statistical appendix.
4. Measuring informal employment both in Mexico and abroad presents difficulties due to conceptual and methodological changes over the past three decades.
5. The figures for formal employment in Mexico are based on enrollments in the Mexican Social Security Institute (IMSS). See *Las metas del Milenio y la igualdad de género. El caso de México* (Santiago de Chile: ECLAC-Inmujeres, 2005), pp. 31–2.
6. Ibid.; I. Arriagada (coord.), *Familias y políticas públicas en América Latina: una historia de desencuentros* (Santiago de Chile: ECLAC, 2007), p. 173.
7. A comparison of these percentages to those of other countries in Latin America, however, reveals Mexico's to be quite low; i.e., in 2004, Argentina, Chile and Brazil stood at 48 per cent, 42 per cent and 53 per cent, respectively.
8. A. Palacios Escobar, 'La participación actual de las mujeres en el mercado laboral mexicano' (Mexico: 2005), at www.cimacnoticias.com/numeralia/laparticpacion actualdemujeresenmercadolaboralmexicano.pdf.
9. S. Montaño, 'El sueño de las mujeres: democracia en familia', in *Cambio de las familias en el marco de las transformaciones globales: necesidad de políticas públicas eficaces*, Arriagada, I., and V. Aranda (comps.) (Santiago de Chile: CEPAL, 2004), Serie Seminarios y Conferencias 42.
10. A. Pazmiño, *Las mujeres indígenas de Latinoamérica en la agenda del desarrollo, Reshaping the Development Agenda: Worldviews and Notions of Development* (Conference Endogenous Development and Bio–Cultural Diversity: Geneva, 3–5 October).

11. OIT/ILO) International Labour Organization, 'Seguridad Social: Un nuevo consenso. Capítulo IV igualdad de género', *Informe de la Comisión de la Seguridad Social* (International Labour Conference, 2001), 89th Meeting.

12. S. Gammage and M. Orozco, *El trabajo productivo no remunerado dentro del hogar: desafíos empíricos y metodológicos* (México: ECLAC, 2008), unpublished material.

13. I. Arriagada, *Realidades y mitos del trabajo femenino urbano en América Latina* (Santiago de Chile: ECLAC, 1998), Serie Mujer y Desarrollo 21.

14. R. Deutch, *et al.*, *Working within Confines: Occupational Segregation by Gender in Three Latin American Countries* (Washington, DC: Inter-American Development Bank, 2002).

15. See *Uso del tiempo y aportaciones en los hogares mexicanos,* INEGI, p. 47.

16. Ibid., p. 51.

17. We used a week comprised of seven days, twenty-four hours per day for a total of 168 hours per week.

18. Since low productivity sectors include businesses that employ up to five people, almost 50 per cent of women employed in urban areas work in low productivity sectors, while for rural areas the figure is 80.1 per cent. For men, these figures stand at 41.3 per cent and 70.4 per cent, respectively, for urban and rural areas, reflecting less disadvantages *vs* employed women (ECLAC: 2005).

19. ECLAC-UNIFEM, *Estadísticas para la equidad de género. Magnitudes y tendencias en América Latina* (Santiago de Chile: 2007), Cuadernos de la CEPAL 92, prepared by Milosavljevic, V.

20. Indicators for tracking the condition of women in Mexico (INEGI: Mexico), 2009, electronic data base. The formula used is (IHMA/IHHA-PEMA/PEHA)/(IHMA/IHHA) where IHHA = Average hourly income of salaried men; IHMA = Average hourly income of salaried women; PEHA = Average educational level of salaried men; PEMA = Average educational level of salaried women.

21. For 2002, in slightly more than a quarter of the households, women were the primary breadwinners: 26.7 per cent in urban households and 27.4 per cent in rural households. 70 per cent of these are single-parent households most certainly headed by women. Women are also the main breadwinner in 12.9 per cent of the two-parent urban nuclear families and 15.8 per cent of the two-parent rural nuclear families (ECLAC: 2005, p. 34).

22. The programme consists of support in cash and kind; food, nutritional supplements for babies and economic support for families, enhanced by health and illnesses prevention counselling/education in health care centres and grants to encourage school attendance.

23. See Progresa, *Más oportunidades para las familias pobres. Evaluación de resultados del Programa de Educación, Salud y Alimentación,* Social Development Ministry (Sedesol): Mexico, 1999.

24. M. Molyneaux, 'Mothers at the Service of the New Poverty Agenda: Progresa/Oportunidades, Mexico's Conditional Transfer Programme', *Social Policy & Administration*, 40:4 (August 2006), pp. 425–49.

25. Aguado also points out that he or she is poor due to lack of education and he or she has little education due to the fact that he or she is poor. It is not enough to educate people to overcome poverty if a favourable macroeconomic environment is not guaranteed, specifically in terms of employment. L. A. Aguado, L. E. Girón and F. Salazar, 'Pobreza y educación urbanas en el valle del Cauca, Colombia', in *Revista Comercio Exterior*, 57:6 (Mexico: June 2007), p. 449, specifically the debate in the section on the theory of human capital.

7 Arrizabalaga, 'Gender and Migration in the Pyrenees in the Nineteenth Century: Gender-Differentiated Patterns and Destinies'

1. The historiography on Pyrenean emigration to America is too long to list here. Some examples are: A. Blazquez (ed.), *L'émigration basco-béarnaise aux Amériques au XIXe siècle* (Orthez: Gascogne, 2005); G. Callon, 'Le mouvement de la population dans le département des Basses-Pyrénées au cours de la période 1821–1920 et depuis la fin de cette période', *Bulletin de la société des sciences, lettres et arts de Pau*, 53 (1930), pp. 81–113; H. d'Arthuys de Charnisay, *L'Emigration basco-béarnaise en Amérique*, Seconde Edition (Biarritz: J & D Editions, 1996); A. Bruneton-Governatori, P. Heiniger, B. Moreux, M. Papy et J. Soust, *Lettres et correspondances d'émigrés du Sud-Ouest (1800–1950)* (Pau: Rapport présenté à la mission du patrimoine ethnologique, 1997); L. Etcheverry, 'L'émigration dans les Basses-Pyrénées pendant soixante ans', *Revue des Pyrénées* (1893), pp. 509–20; A. Gachitéguy, *Les Basques dans l'Ouest américain* (Urt: Éditions Ezkila, 1955); P. Hourmat, 'De l'émigration basco-béarnaise du XVIIIe siècle à nos jours', *Société des sciences, lettres et arts de Bayonne*, 132 (1976), pp. 227–54; C. Mehats, *Organization et aspects de l'émigration des basques de France en Amérique: 1832–1976* (Vitoria-Gasteiz: Gobierno Vasco, 2005); J. Saint-Macary, *La Désertion de la terre en Béarn et dans le Pays Basque* (Pau: Lescher-Moutone, 1939); M.-P. Arrizabalaga, 'L'émigration des pyrénéennes en Amérique du Nord aux XIX–XXe siècles', *Histoire sociale – Social History. Les femmes et l'émigration en Amérique du Nord / Women and Emigration to North America*, 40:80 (November 2007), pp. 269–95 and 'Les Basques dans l'Ouest américain, 1900–1910', *Lapurdum*, 5 (2000), pp. 335–50; J.-E. Braana, *Les Archives de Charles Iriart, agent de l'émigration basque aux Etats-Unis* (Saint-Jean-de-Luz: Ikuska, 1995); A. Etchelecou, *Transition démographique et système coutumier dans les Pyrénées occidentales* (Paris: PUF, 1991); P. O'Quin, *Du décroissement de la population dans le département des Basses-Pyrénées* (Pau: Vignancour, 1856) etc.

2. A number of studies have been completed on French emigration to America. Here are some references: N. Fouché, *Emigration alsacienne aux Etats-Unis, 1815–1870* (Paris: Publications de la Sorbonne, 1992); A. Foucrier, *Le Rêve californien. Migrants français sur la côte pacifique (XVIIIe – XXe siècles)* (Paris: Belin, 1999); A.-M. Granet-Abisset, *La Route réinventée. Les migrations des Queyrassins aux XIXe et XXe siècles* (Grenoble: Presses Universitaires de Grenoble, 1994); P. Lhande, *La France rayonnante: Argentine, Chili, Uruguay* (Paris: Gabriel Beauchesne, 1931) & *L'Émigration basque* (Paris: Elkar, 1910); H. Otero, 'L'immigration française en Argentine: une histoire ouverte', in A. Blazquez (ed.), *L'émigration basco-béarnaise aux Amériques au XIXe siècle* (Orthez: Gascogne, 2005), pp. 117–47; etc.

3. For a general overview on European immigration into the United States, see R. Daniels, *Coming to America: A History of Immigration and Ethnicity in American Life* (New York: Perennial, 2002).

4. Prior to the French Revolution, single inheritance was a common legal practice in France and in the Pyrenees in particular. With the Civil Code propertied families were forced to partition their assets equally between their children, male and female. In order to avoid partition, families compensated excluded children and encouraged them to leave, especially to French cities or overseas. For further information on the issues, see M.-P. Arrizabalaga, 'Les héritières de la maison au Pays Basque au XIXe

siècle', *Lapurdum*, 7 (2002), pp. 35–55 & 'Succession Strategies in the Pyrenees in the Nineteenth Century. The Basque Case', *History of the Family: an International Quarterly* (USA), 10:3 (2005), pp. 271–92; L. Assier-Andrieu, *Le Peuple et la loi. Anthropologie historique des droits paysans en Catalogne français* (Paris: Librairie de droit et de jurisprudence, 1987); G. Beaur, C. Dessureault and J. Goy (eds), *Familles, terre, marchés. Logiques économiques et stratégies dans les milieux ruraux (XVIIe–XXe siècles)* (Rennes: Presses Universitaires de Rennes, 2004); G. Bouchard, J. A. Dickinson and J. Goy (eds), *Les Exclus de la terre en France et au Québec, XVIIe – XXe siècles. La reproduction familiale dans la différence* (Sillery (Québec): Septentrion, 1998); A. Fauve-Chamoux and M.-P. Arrizabalaga (eds), *Family Transmission in Eurasian Perspective : The History of the Family, an International Quarterly*, 10:3 (2005), pp. 183–344; C. Lacanette-Pommel, *La Famille dans les Pyrénées, de la coutume au Code Napoléon* (Estadens: Pyréraph, 2003), etc.

5. On this particular methodology, see E. Wallerstein, *The Modern World-System*, 3 vols (Berkeley, CA: University of California Press, 2011).

6. Women usually lost their maiden names upon marriage and were therefore no longer identified with their maiden names. Women also lost their nationality of birth upon marriage with a man of another nationality until the 1920s. Finally, in some cases women could not inherit property until the twentieth century. These legal realities led to the preconceived idea that women followed men and therefore had the same patterns, strategies and behaviours as men.

7. D. Gabaccia and F. Iacovetta (eds), *Women, Gender, and Transnational Lives. Italian Workers of the World* (Toronto: University of Toronto Press, 2002), pp. 3–41; D. Gabaccia (ed.), *Seeking Common Ground. Multidisciplinary Studies of Immigrant Women in the United States* (London: Praeger, 1992); P. Hondagneu-Sotelo, *Gender and U.S. Immigration. Contemporary Trends* (Berkeley, CA: University of California Press, 2003). See also R. Ueda, *A Companion to American Immigration* (Oxford: Blackwell Publishing, 2006).

8. For a discussion on this approach, see T. Addabo, M.-P. Arrizabalaga, C. Borderias & A. Owens, 'Introduction: Households, Gender and the Production of Well-Being', in, T. Addabo, M.-P. Arrizabalaga, C. Borderias and A. Owens (eds), *Gender Inequalities, Households and the Production of Well-Being in Modern Europe* (London: Ashgate Publishing, 2010), pp. 17–24; M.-P. Arrizabalaga, D. Burgos-Vigna and M. Yusta, 'Introduction: Eléments de méthodologie générale pour une approche transnationale du Genre', in M.-P. Arrizabalaga, D. Burgos-Vigna and M. Yusta (eds), *Femmes sans frontières: stratégies féminines transnationales face à la mondialisation (XVIIIe–XXIe siècles)* (Bern, Peter Lang, 2011), pp. 1–30.

9. *Cadastre. Matrice des propriétés foncières*, serie 3P3, Archives Départementales des Pyrénées-Atlantiques. *Cadastre. Matrice des propriétés baties*, serie 3P2, Archives Départementales des Pyrénées-Atlantiques.

10. Let's indicate that about half of the families of the sample were propertied families and the other half were landless. Because individuals originating from landless families were sometimes hard to locate, did not own property and therefore did not show up in the succession records, and finally were difficult to trace in cities and overseas, I therefore collected a limited amount of information on them. For this reason, in this particular analysis I chose to set them aside in order to only consider propertied families whose

life-cycle events I traced in detail in the Basque Country, towns and cities in France and overseas.

11. *Enregistrement. Mutation après décès.* Records from seven cantonal seats: Labastide-Clairence, Hasparren, Saint-Jean-de-Luz, Ustaritz, Saint-Etienne-de-Baïgorry, Saint-Jean-Pied-de-Port, Saint-Palais, Mauléon-Licharre. Série Q, Archives Départementales des Pyrénées-Atlantiques, 269 volumes.

12. One must highlight that it was impossible to locate and determine the destinies of 12.7 per cent of the sons and 10.3 per cent of the daughters, as well as 19.4 per cent of the grand-sons and 13.5 per cent of the granddaughters. Among them, it is possible that some disappeared from the documentation because they emigrated to distant locations, as Paris or America for example. It is therefore possible that more of the men than indicated above settled in America (especially the grandsons of the sample) and more of the women indicated above settled in cities (especially among the granddaughters, many more of whom probably settled in Bordeaux or Paris) (see data in Table 7.1 above).

13. For further information on the evolution of Basque emigration patterns to America, see W. A. Douglass and J. Bilbao, *Amerikanuak, Basques in the New World* (Reno (USA): University of Nevada Press, 1975); Blazquez (ed.), *L'émigration basco-béarnaise* and A. Sarramone, *Les Basques en Amérique* (Anglet: Atlantica, 2004), among others.

14. Male or female primogeniture (*aînesse intégrale* or first-born inheritance no matter the sex of the first child) existed in these Pyrenean regions of the Basque Country, Lavedan and Bareges and became codified laws in the fifteenth or sixteenth century. These practices prevailed through the Old Regime, from the Middle Ages until the French Revolution when all local laws were abolished in order to impose a single, common French law, the Civil Code. The laws sustaining *Aînesse intégrale* were so much part of the local culture that in the Basque Country the system prevailed after the French Revolution, until recently. See M.-P. Arrizabalaga, 'Stratégies de l'indivision et rapport à la terre après le Code civil: le cas basque au XIXe siècle', in G. Béaur, C. Dessureault et J. Goy (eds), *Familles, terre, marchés. Logiques économiques et stratégies dans les milieux ruraux (XVIIe–XXe siècles)* (Rennes: Presses Universitaires de Rennes, 2004), pp. 171–83 & 'Female primogeniture in the French Basque Country', in E. Ochiai (ed.), *The Logic of Female Succession: Rethinking Patriarchy and Patrilineality in Global and Historical Perspective* (Kyoto: International Research Center of Japanese Studies, 2002), pp. 31–52.

15. The Pyrenean stem family imposed the cohabitation of two married couples, the parents and the heir or heiress, and their unmarried children in the same house. The Pyrenean house system necessitated their cohabitation, properties being too small to house more than two couples, one at each generation.

16. E. Cordier, *Le Droit de famille aux Pyrénées: Barège, Lavedan, Béarn et Pays Basque* (Paris: Auguste Durand, 1859); Assier-Andrieu, *Le Peuple et la loi*; J. Poumarède, *Les Successions dans le Sud-Ouest de la France au Moyen Age* (Paris: Presses Universitaires de France, 1972); M. Lafourcade, *Mariages en Labourd sous l'Ancien Régime. Les contrats de mariage du pays de Labourd sous le règne de Louis XVI (Etude juridique et sociologique)* (Bilbao: Universidad del País Vasco, 1989).

17. M. Durães, A. Fauve-Chamoux, L. Ferrer and J. Kok (eds), *The Transmission of Well-being. Gendered Marriage Strategies and Inheritance Systems in Europe (Seventeenth–Twentieth Centuries)* (Bern: Peter Lang, 2009).

18. C. Lacanette-Pommel, *La Famille dans les Pyrénées, de la coutume au Code Napoléon* (Estadens: Pyréraph, 2003); M.-P. Arrizabalaga, 'Droits, pouvoirs et devoirs dans la mai-

son basque: la place des hommes et des femmes au sein des familles basques depuis le XIXe siècle', *Vasconia. Cuadernos de Historia-Geografía*, 35 (2006), pp. 155–83.

19. M.-P. Arrizabalaga, 'Comment le marché de l'emploi national et international a-t-il influencé les destins individuels au sein de familles basques et les modalités de transmission du patrimoine au XIX siècle?', in C. Dussereault, J. Dickinson and J. Goy, *Famille et marché (XVIe – XXe siècles)* (Sillery (Québec): Septentrion, 2003), pp. 183–98 & 'Migrations féminines – migrations masculines: des comportements différenciés au sein des familles basques au XIXe siècle', in L. Lorenzetti, A.-L. Head-König, and J. Goy (eds), *Marchés, migrations et logiques familiales dans les espaces français, canadien et suisse, 18ᵉ–20ᵉ siècles* (Bern: Peter Lang, 2005), pp. 183–95.

20. For a comparison on this issue, see E. Ochiai (ed.), *The Logic of Female Succession: Rethinking Patriarchy and Patrilineality in Global and Historical Perspective* (Kyoto: International Research Center of Japanese Studies, 2002).

21. P. Bourdieu, *Le Bal des célibataires. Crise de la société paysanne en Béarn* (Paris: Seuil, 2002).

22. According to succession records, celibate men at home or in the village could accumulate savings and property of their own through their life. These could be sizable ones, sometimes reaching several hundred francs of taxable assets. While many of these celibate men had some wealth acquired alone during their life, celibate women residing at home did not. They lived and died with no wealth besides the share of the family assets they were entitled to but which they never claimed, as a compensation for lifelong care and well-being in the family house. Celibate women therefore died as destitute women (*indigente*) but rarely did men.

23. M.-P. Arrizabalaga, 'Basque Migration and Inheritance in the Nineteenth Century', in A. Steidl, J. Ehmer, S. Nadel and H. Zeitlhofer (eds), *European Mobility: Internal, International, and Transatlantic Moves in the 19ᵗʰ and early 20ᵗʰ Centuries* (Göttingen (Germany): V&R Unipress, 2009), pp. 135–50.

24. More women probably settled in cities as Bordeaux and Paris yet it was materially impossible to search through all the registers from these large cities in order to locate the unknown female cases of the sample.

25. M.-P. Arrizabalaga, 'Basque women and migration in the nineteenth century', *The History of the Family. An International Quarterly*, 10:2 (2005), pp. 99–117 and Destins de femmes dans les Pyrénées au XIXe siècle: le cas basque', *Itinéraires féminins. Annales de Démographie Historique*, 2 (2006), pp. 135–70.

26. A. Fauve-Chamoux (ed.), *Domestic Service and the Formation of European Identity. Understanding the Globalization of Domestic Work, 16ᵗʰ–21ˢᵗ Centuries* (Bern: Peter Lang, 2005).

27. Douglas and Bilbao, *Amerikanuak*.

28. M.-P. Arrizabalaga, 'Las mujeres pirenaicas y la emigración en el siglo XIX', *Mujer y emigración: una perspectiva plural*, Cátedra UNESCO 226 sobre migracións (Santiago de Compostela, Spain: Universitade de Santiago de Compostela, 2008), pp. 107–31 and 'Les femmes pyrénéennes et l'émigration transatlantique aux XIXe et XXe siècles: une réalité mal connue', in N. Lillo and P. Rygiel, *Rapports sociaux de sexe et migrations* (Paris: Publibook, 2006), pp. 59–70 and 'Cent ans d'émigration basque française en Amérique du Nord: Synthèse et nouvelles perspectives (1860–1960)', in A. Blazquez (ed.), *Emigration de masse et émigration d'élite cers les Amériques au XIXe siècle. Le cas des Pyrénées basco-béarnaises* (Orthez: Editions Gascogne, 2010), pp. 113–55.

29. In the 1980s I completed a score of interviews with older women (in their eighties or nineties) who grew up in the early twentieth century and who could speak for their mothers or grandmothers who had lived in the West in the nineteenth century. Some of these women were hotel owners and their testimonies on themselves and on the Basque male and female immigrants who settled in the West in the period enriched the data set with information which sometimes cannot be traced in archives.

30. This situation changed in the twentieth century. More women were drawn to America as life became easier and as communication and transportation improved.

8 Lanzinger, Women and Property in Eighteenth-Century Austria: Separate Property, Usufruct and Ownership in Different Family Configurations

1. Tiroler Landesarchiv (hereafter TLA), Innsbruck, Verfachbuch Innichen (hereafter VBI) 1784, fol. 706–709, point 4.

2. An analysis of 205 changes of ownership on twenty-seven Innichberg farms between the early eighteenth and the early twentieth century showed that daughters and nieces inherited in 15 per cent of cases overall. See M. Lanzinger, "'aus khainer Gerechtigkeit ..', sondern aus Gnaden". Erbinnen – Handlungsoptionen und Geschwisterkonstellationen', *Frühneuzeit-Info*, 15:1/2 (2004), pp. 20–8, on p. 21.

3. G. Langer-Ostrawsky, 'Vom Verheiraten der Güter. Bäuerliche und kleinbäuerliche Heiratsverträge im Erzherzogtum Österreich unter der Enns', in M. Lanzinger, G. Barth-Scalmani, E. Forster and G. Langer-Ostrawsky, *Aushandeln von Ehe. Heiratsverträge der Neuzeit im europäischen Vergleich* (Wien, Köln and Weimar: Böhlau, 2010), pp. 27–76.

4. See S. Rouette, 'Erbrecht und Besitzweitergabe: Praktiken in der ländlichen Gesellschaft Deutschlands, Diskurse in Politik und Wissenschaft', in R. Prass, J. Schlumbohm, G. Béaur and C. Duhamelle (eds), *Ländliche Gesellschaften in Deutschland und Frankreich, 18.–19. Jahrhundert* (Göttingen: Vandenhoeck & Ruprecht, 2003), pp. 145–66.

5. On this, see especially L. Botelho, '"The Old Woman's Wish": Widows by the Family Fire? Widows' Old Age Provision in Rural England, 1500–1700', *History of the Family*, 7:1 (2002), pp. 59–78; A. Fauve-Chamoux, 'Widows and their Living Arrangements in Preindustrial France', *The History of the Family*, 7:1 (2002), pp. 101–16.

6. See, for example, A. Arru, M. Stella and L. di Michele (eds), *Proprietarie. Avere, non avere, ereditare, industriarsi* (Naples: Liguori Editore, 2001); G. Calvi and I. Chabot (eds), *Le ricchezze delle donne. Diritti patrimoniali e poteri familiari in Italia (XIII–XIX)* (Turin: Rosenberg & Sellier, 1998); K. Gottschalk, *Eigentum, Geschlecht, Gerechtigkeit. Haushalten und Erben im frühneuzeitlichen Leipzig* (Frankfurt/Main and New York: Campus, 2003); *Clio. Histoire, Femmes et Sociétés*, 7, Special Issue : Femmes, dots et patrimoines (1998). Increased attention to the economic aspects of marriage is called for by A. L. Erickson, 'The Marital Economy in Comparative Perspective', in M. Ågren and A. L. Erickson (eds), *The Marital Economy in Scandinavia and Britain, 1400–1900* (Aldershot: Ashgate, 2005), pp. 3–20, on p. 3.

7. See N. Z. Davis, 'Cosa c'è di universale nella storia?', *Quaderni Storici*, 41:123 (2006), pp. 737–43, on p. 739.

8. This is observed by, for example: N. Grochowina, 'Geschlecht und Eigentumskultur in der Frühen Neuzeit', *Comparativ*, 15:4 (2005), pp. 7–20, on p. 8; G. Ingendahl, *Witwen in der Frühen Neuzeit. Eine kulturhistorische Studie* (Frankfurt/Main and New York:

Campus, 2006), p. 71, note 72; H. Siegrist and D. Sugarman, 'Geschichte als historisch-vergleichende Eigentumswissenschaft. Rechts-, kultur- und gesellschaftsgeschichtliche Perspektiven', in H. Siegrist and D. Sugarman (eds), *Eigentum im internationalen Vergleich (18.–20. Jahrhundert)* (Göttingen: Vandenhoeck & Ruprecht, 1999), pp. 9–30, on p. 18; H. Wunder, 'Herrschaft und öffentliches Handeln von Frauen in der Gesellschaft der Frühen Neuzeit', in U. Gerhard (ed.), *Frauen in der Geschichte des Rechts. Von der Frühen Neuzeit bis zur Gegenwart* (München: C. H. Beck, 1997), pp. 27–54; U. Gerhard, 'Einleitung', in Gerhard, *Frauen in der Geschichte*, pp. 11–22, on p. 15.

9.   See, especially, A. Hufschmidt, *Adlige Frauen im Weserraum zwischen 1570 und 1700. Status - Rollen - Lebenspraxis* (Münster: Aschendorff, 2001); K.-H. Spieß, *Familie und Verwandtschaft im deutschen Hochadel des Spätmittelalters, 13. bis Anfang des 16. Jahrhunderts* (Stuttgart: Steiner, 1993).

10. See W. Brauneder, 'Normenautorität und grundherrschaftliche Vertragspraxis', in W. Brauneder, *Studien II: Entwicklung des Privatrechts* (Frankfurt/Main: Lang, 1994), pp. 109–20; H. Demelius, *Eheliches Güterrecht im spätmittelalterlichen Wien* (Wien: Böhlau, 1970); K.-O. Giesa, *Eheverträge im Großherzogtum Baden in der 2. Hälfte des 19. Jahrhunderts* (Hamburg: Kovač, 2008).

11. See G. Bamberger, *Ehe- und Übergabeverträge in Hessen. Ein Überblick über Geschichte, Aufbau und Funktion* (Marburg: Jonas, 1998); H. Beißner, *Altersversorgung und Kindesabfindung auf dem Lande. Leibzucht- und Eheverschreibungen in der zweiten Hälfte des 18. Jahrhunderts unter besonderer Berücksichtigung der Schaumburger und Osnabrücker sowie benachbarter Gebiete* (Bielefeld: published by the author, 1995); H. Feigl, 'Heiratsbriefe und Verlassenschaftsabhandlungen als Quellen zur Alltagsgeschichte', in O. Pickl and H. Feigl (eds), *Methoden und Probleme der Alltagsforschung im Zeitalter des Barock* (Wien: Verlag der Österreichischen Akademie der Wissenschaften, 1992), pp. 83–99; D. Sauermann, 'Bäuerliche Brautschatzverschreibungen in Westfalen (17.–20. Jh.)', *Rheinisch-westfälische Zeitschrift für Volkskunde*, 18/19 (1972), pp. 103–53.

12. See H.-R. Hagemann and H. Wunder, 'Heiraten und Erben: Das Basler Ehegüterrecht und Ehegattenerbrecht', in H. Wunder (ed.), *Eine Stadt der Frauen. Studien und Quellen zur Geschichte der Baslerinnen im späten Mittelalter und zu Beginn der Neuzeit (13.–17. Jahrhundert)* (Basel and Frankfurt/Main: Helbing & Lichtenhahn, 1995), pp. 150–66; G. Signori, *Vorsorgen – Vererben – Erinnern. Kinder- und familienlose Erblasser in der städtischen Gesellschaft des Spätmittelalters* (Göttingen: Vandenhoeck & Ruprecht, 2001), pp. 63–144; Ingendahl, *Witwen in der Frühen Neuzeit*, pp. 47–9, 70–3.

13. To mention but a selection: Calvi and Chabot (eds), *Le ricchezze delle donne*; D. O. Hughes, 'From Brideprice to Dowry in Mediterranean Europe', *Journal of Family History*, 3:3 (1978), pp. 262–96; M. A. Kaplan (ed.), *The Marriage Bargain. Women and Dowries in European History* (New York: Harrington Park Press, 1985); A. E. Kasdagli, *Land and Marriage Settlements in the Aegean. A Case Study of Seventeenth–Century Naxos* (Venice: Hellenic Institute of Byzantine and Post-Byzantine Studies, 1999).

14. B. B. Diefendorf, 'Women and Property in *Ancien Régime* France. Theory and Practice in Dauphiné and Paris', in J. Brewer and S. Staves (eds), *Early Modern Conceptions of Property* (London and New York: Routledge, 1995), pp. 170–93; A. L. Erickson, 'Common Law Versus Common Practice: The Use of Marriage Settlements in Early Modern England', *Economic History Review*, 43:1 (1990), pp. 21–39; M. C. Howell, *The Marriage Exchange. Property, Social Place, and Gender in Cities of the Low Countries, 1300–1550* (Chicago, IL and London: University of Chicago Press, 1998).

15. The total sample includes around 250 marriage contracts and associated documents for the period between 1710 and 1850. The greatest concentration of material has survived from the 1780s and 1790s. See M. Lanzinger, 'Von der Macht der Linie zur Gegenseitigkeit. Heiratskontrakte in den Südtiroler Gerichten Welsberg und Innichen 1750–1850', in Lanzinger, Barth-Scalmani, Forster and Langer-Ostrawsky, *Aushandeln von Ehe*, pp. 205–326, on pp. 217–20; M. Lanzinger, 'Marriage Contracts in Various Contexts: Marital Property Rights, Sociocultural Aspects and Gender-specific Implications. Late-Eighteenth-Century Evidence from two Tirolean Court Districts', *Annales de démographie historique*, 121:1 (2011), pp. 69–97.

16. M. Lanzinger, *Das gesicherte Erbe. Heirat in lokalen und familialen Kontexten. Innichen 1700–1900* (Wien, Köln and Weimar: Böhlau, 2003), pp. 82–4.

17. See P. Rösch, 'Lebensläufe und Schicksale. Auswirkungen von zwei unterschiedlichen Erbsitten in Tirol', in P. Rösch (ed.), *Südtiroler Erbhöfe. Menschen und Geschichten* (Bozen: Folio, 1994), pp. 61–70; R. Palme, 'Die Entwicklung des Erbrechtes im ländlichen Bereich', in ibid., pp. 25–37.

18. For a general account, see H. von Voltelini, 'Zur Geschichte des ehelichen Güterrechts in Tirol. Eine rechtshistorische Skizze', in *Festgaben zu Ehren Max Büdinger's von seinen Freunden und Schülern* (Innsbruck: Wagner, 1898), pp. 333–64.

19. *New reformierte Landsordnung der fürstlichen Grafschaft Tirol* (Innsbruck [1573]) (hereafter *Tiroler Landesordnung*), 3. Buch, Tit. XX.

20. On the arrangements in the eighteenth and nineteenth century, see E. Mantl, '*Legal Restrictions on Marriage: Marriage and Inequality in the Austrian Tyrol during the Nineteenth Century*', History of the Family, 4:2 (1999), pp. 185–207; M. Lanzinger, 'La scelta del coniuge. Fra amore romantico e matrimoni proibiti', *Storicamente*, 6 (2010), at www.storicamente.org/07_dossier/famiglia/scelta_del_coniuge.htm [accessed 21 October 2010]. On the similar situation in Switzerland and in southern Germany, see A.-L. Head-König, '*Forced Marriages and Forbidden Marriages in Switzerland: State Control of the Formation of Marriages in Catholic and Protestant Cantons in the Eighteenth and Nineteenth Centuries*', Continuity and Change, 8 (1993), pp. 441–65; K.-J. Matz, *Pauperismus und Bevölkerung. Die gesetzlichen Ehebeschränkungen in den süddeutschen Staaten während des 19. Jahrhunderts* (Stuttgart: Klett-Cotta, 1980).

21. See, for example, Calvi and Chabot (eds), *Le ricchezze delle donne*; C. Klapisch-Zuber, *Women, Family, and Ritual in Renaissance Italy* (Chicago, IL: Chicago University Press, 1985); G. Bouchard, J. Goy and A.-L. Head-König (eds), *Mélanges de l'École Française de Rome. Italie et Méditerranée*, 110:1 (1998): *Nécessités économiques et pratiques juridiques: problèmes de la transmission des exploitations agricoles, XVIIIᵉ–XIXᵉ siècles*; J. G. Sperling and S. K. Wray (eds), *Across the Religious Divide. Women, Property, and Law in the Wider Mediterranean (c. 1300–1800)* (New York and London: Routledge, 2009).

22. Michael Pammer carried out sample surveys of inheritances for the period of the late nineteenth and early twentieth century, working on the area of today's Austria. His surveys revealed the consequences of the great regional diversity in practices respecting marital property: a clear east–west divide. In Lower Austria, located in the east, just under 83 per cent of independent peasants practised community of property; in Upper Austria the figure was just under 70 per cent; in Styria 56 per cent; in Salzburg (at the transition from east to west) nearly 31 per cent; in Vorarlberg 25 per cent (of which 5 per cent involved community of property between siblings). In Carinthia the sample showed no cases at all, and in North Tyrol they accounted for just 1.1 per cent. M. Pam-

mer, *Entwicklung und Ungleichheit. Österreich im 19. Jahrhundert* (Stuttgart: Steiner, 2002), p. 77.

23. M. Hohkamp, *Herrschaft in der Herrschaft. Die vorderösterreichische Obervogtei Triberg von 1737 bis 1780* (Göttingen: Vandenhoeck & Ruprecht, 1998), pp. 165–72.

24. Ingendahl, *Witwen in der Frühen Neuzeit*, pp. 174–90, quotation on p. 188 (my translation).

25. See, for example, the property arrangements made by Salzburg's merchants: G. Barth-Scalmani, 'Eighteenth-Century Marriage Contracts. Linking Legal and Gender History', in A. Jacobson Schutte, T. Kuehn and S. Seidel Menchi (eds), *Time, Space, and Women's Lives in Early Modern Europe* (Kirksville: Sixteenth Century Journal Publ., 2001), pp. 266–81; G. Barth-Scalmani, 'Ausgewogene Verhältnisse: Eheverträge in der Stadt Salzburg im 18. Jahrhundert', in Lanzinger, Barth-Scalmani, Forster and Langer-Ostrawsky, *Aushandeln von Ehe*, pp. 121–70; for the case of wholesale wine traders in the Netherlands: M. Sugiura, 'Heiratsmuster der *wijnkopers* in Amsterdam 1660–1710', in M. Häberlein and C. Jeggle (eds), *Praktiken des Handels. Geschäfte und soziale Beziehungen europäischer Kaufleute in Mittelalter und Früher Neuzeit* (Konstanz: UVK, 2010), pp. 407–47.

26. 'Des Kayserlichen Hochstifts, und Fürstenthums Bamberg verfaßtes Land-Recht. Desselben Erster Haupt-Theil von Civil- oder sogenannten Bürgerlichen Sachen handlend', 1769, cited in P. Landau, 'Bamberger Landrecht und eheliche Gütergemeinschaft', in H. Gehringer, H.-J. Hecker and R. Heydenreuter (eds), *Landesordnungen und Gute Policey in Bayern, Salzburg und Österreich* (Frankfurt/Main: Klostermann, 2008), pp. 1–18, on pp. 5–6.

27. On this, see S. Cavallo, 'Proprietà o possesso? Composizione e controllo dei beni delle donne a Torino (1650–1710)', in Calvi and Chabot (eds), *Le ricchezze delle donne*, pp. 187–207, on p. 197; Howell, *The Marriage Exchange*, pp. 197–8.

28. Diefendorf, 'Women and Property', p. 178.

29. Voltelini, 'Zur Geschichte', p. 359. Otherwise, throughout the Austrian region usufructuary rights applied, irrespective of gender, for the surviving spouse's lifetime to objects of the deceased's property. See W. Brauneder, 'Frau und Vermögen im spätmittelalterlichen Österreich', in Brauneder, *Studien II*, pp. 217–28, on p. 224.

30. *Tiroler Landesordnung*, 3. Buch, Tit. IX.

31. For the first half of the eighteenth century, the protocol books – *Verfachbücher* – of the courts investigated include only very few marriage contracts. It cannot be established whether this indicates that only such a small number of contracts were actually concluded at court, or whether they were not preserved or not bound in the protocol books.

32. See Lanzinger, 'Von der Macht der Linie', pp. 287–90. A clause on *Herberg* arrangements for the bridegroom appears just once in the Innichen court sample, twice in that of the Welsberg court. In two of these cases, the bridegroom married into the household of a widow who was managing the property of her first husband until such time as it could be taken over by one of her children from her first marriage. In the third case, it was not possible to determine the precise family configuration. See TLA Innsbruck, VBI 1791, fol. 41'; Südtiroler Landesarchiv (hereafter SLA) Bozen, Verfachbuch Welsberg (hereafter VBW) 1800, Teil 2, fol. 3–4; ibid., VBW 1800, Teil 2, fol. 21.

33. Dieneke Hempenius-van Dijk describes a similar situation for Holland. There, too, the possibility existed of using marriage contracts to soften the consequences of the separation of property for the surviving spouse. D. Hempenius-van Dijk, 'Widows and the Law. The Legal Position of Widows in the Dutch Republic during the Seventeenth and

Eighteenth Centuries', in J. Bremmer and L. van den Bosch (eds), *Between Poverty and the Pyre. Moments in the History of Widowhood* (London and New York: Routledge, 1995), pp. 89–102, on pp. 92–3.

34. TLA Innsbruck, VBI 1784, fol. 706–9, point 5.

35. Ibid.

36. At her second marriage, in 1770, the widow Maria Ranepacherin brought with her the considerable fortune of 1,900 gulden. The bridegroom's parents transferred half of their property to her in two versions of the marriage contract. TLA Innsbruck, VBI 1769, fol. 9'–14; ibid., VBI 1770, fol. 246–250'. This is an exceptional case.

37. TLA Innsbruck, VBI 1791, fol. 43. This was the only substantive clause of the contract, clause 1 containing just a standardized formula to state that the contract only came into force once the marriage was solemnized.

38. On the bequeathal of linen through the feminine line, see Gottschalk, *Eigentum, Geschlecht, Gerechtigkeit.*

39. Stiftsarchiv Innichen (hereafter STA), Familienbuch 1700–1900, families H 46 and K 41.

40. For example, in Basle postmarital property arrangements had been a customary part of prenuptial negotiations in prosperous families since the fourteenth century. See Hagemann and Wunder, 'Heiraten und Erben', p. 160.

41. E. F. Warnecke refers to this principle as a kind of 'life insurance'. E. F. Warnecke, 'Eheberedungen als Lebensversicherung im Hause von dem Bussche-Hünnefeld u. a.', *Osnabrücker Mitteilungen*, 102 (1997), pp. 187–94.

42. See TLA Innsbruck, VBI 1797, fol. 456–5'.

43. TLA Innsbruck, VBI 1797, fol. 464–5'.

44. See, for example, SLA Bozen, VBW 1780, fol. 41–2'.

45. See J. Schlumbohm, *Lebensläufe, Familien, Höfe. Die Bauern und Heuerleute des Osnabrückischen Kirchspiels Belm in proto-industrieller Zeit, 1650–1860* (Göttingen: Vandenhoeck & Ruprecht, 1994), pp. 475–80; Hohkamp, *Herrschaft in der Herrschaft*, pp. 168–72; Langer-Ostrawsky, 'Vom Verheiraten der Güter', pp. 27–30, p. 68, pp. 71–3.

46. See SLA Bozen, VBW 1790, fol. 33'. A marriage contract concluded in 1850 on the occasion of a second marriage includes a similar construct, but in this case without the equal claim for the eldest daughter. If the widow's only son from her first marriage died and there was a son from the second marriage, the latter would inherit; if the second marriage did not produce a son, then the property would fall to the surviving children (that is, the daughters) from the first marriage. See ibid., VBW 1850, Teil 1, fol. 71'.

47. TLA Innsbruck, VBI 1786, fol. 276'.

48. See, for example, SLA Bozen, VBW 1760, fol. 272–72'; fol. 533; ibid., VBW 1770, fol. 260'; ibid., VBW 1800, Teil 2, fol. 45'. In the last-mentioned of these contracts, there was an explicit note that the children of the first marriage could not be 'deprived' of the property, either by the surviving parent or by the children of any subsequent marriage.

49. SLA Bozen, VBW 1770, fol. 421; for similar cases, see ibid., VBW 1800, Teil 1, fol. 171; ibid., VBW 1810, fol. 40'.

50. SLA Bozen, VBW 1760, fol. 12; see also ibid., VBW 1770, fol. 459'. In this case, if there were no children the property was to go to the sister of the bride, who was the co-owner. Ibid., VBW 1810, fol. 300–300'. Here, children from the second marriage were explicitly excluded: if no children were produced in the planned marriage, the property would go to the heirs of the bride's father after the death of the husband, even if the husband had children from a different marriage.

51. SLA Bozen, VBW 1795, fol. 176. In the marriage contract between Melchior Grueber and Maria Stollin, this matter was set down in the fourth clause: if they had no children, the house and land was to go to the heirs of the bride, who would have to refund the bridegroom's assets in return.

52. In Belm a farm's owner and his family took on the name of the farm instead of the name inherited from his father, a fact that Jürgen Schlumbohm sees as indicating a focus on ensuring the continuity of the farm. See Schlumbohm, *Lebensläufe, Familien, Höfe*, p. 507.

53. On this, see also J. Rüffer, *Vererbungsstrategien im frühneuzeitlichen Westfalen. Bäuerliche Familien und Mentalitäten in den Anerbengebieten der Hellwegregion* (Stuttgart: Lucius & Lucius, 2008).

54. However, the Innichen court's marriage contracts also display a lineage-oriented thinking, namely in connection with a new regulation of intestate succession that was introduced in 1786. If a child died before majority without descendants, his or her share of the inheritance was to fall to both parents in equal parts – irrespective of the size of the mother's and father's respective inheritance. Because these parts generally differed in size, the arrangement meant that part of one family's wealth was transferred into the other family line. Subsequently, families made use of marriage contracts to prevent this case occurring. See Lanzinger, 'Von der Macht der Linie', pp. 304–5.

55. TLA Innsbruck, VBI 1790, fol. 680'.

56. The Allgemeines Bürgerliches Gesetzbuch of 1811 defines the *Morgengabe* as a 'gift that the husband promises to make to his wife on the first morning' (Art. 1232). There is no mention of the reverse case.

57. Andrä Gatterer came from a neighbouring village, and therefore had to be admitted as a burgher of the market town of Innichen. The fee set for this procedure at the time was approximately 50 gulden.

58. See Lanzinger, *Das gesicherte Erbe*, p. 197.

59. TLA Innsbruck, VBI 1791, fol. 8'–9.

60. Cf. also examples given by Maria Ågren, indicating these kinds of discrepancies between legal forms and perceptions as expressed in wills, for instance. M. Ågren, 'A Partnership between Unequals. The Changing Meaning of Marriage in Eighteenth–Century Sweden', in ch. Duhamelle and J. Schlumbohm (eds), *Eheschließung im Europa des 18. und 19. Jahrhunderts. Muster und Strategien* (Göttingen: Vandenhoeck & Ruprecht, 2003), pp. 267–90, pp. 282–5.

61. The fact that there was no corresponding 'widower's contract' underlines more precarious position of widows, due to the separation of goods and their unequal access to property through inheritance. In the Welsberg court material I examined there was no widow's contract, while my sample from the Innichen court includes fourteen such contracts.

62. TLA Innsbruck, VBI 1784, fol. 1021'–1022'. It may have been the desire to protect family interests that induced another widow, Eleonora Unterwegerin, to renounce her claim to the annual interest from her assets in favour of her son. See TLA Innsbruck, VBI 1776, fol. 252 and fol. 256.

63. The provisions promised to Maria Agatha Klettenhammerin, the widow of the innkeeper and merchant Josef Mayr, in a 1776 settlement were almost identical to this in their composition and quantity, although in her case it was specified that the wine must be good local wine. The foodstuffs guaranteed to a widow, it seems, were based on a supraindividual notion of what comprised a level of maintenance befitting to her rank. See TLA Innsbruck, VBI 1776, fol. 212.

64. TLA Innsbruck, VBI 1784, fol. 1022'–1023.

65. See STA Innichen, Familienbuch 1700–1900, P 66.

66. On social rank as an axis of differentiation in respect of both social and legal norms in the early modern period, see Wunder, 'Herrschaft und öffentliches Handeln', p. 30.

67. M. Mitterauer, *Warum Europa? Mittelalterliche Grundlagen eines Sonderwegs* (München: C.H. Beck, 2003), p. 78.

68. See A. Fauve-Chamoux and E. Ochiai (eds), *The Stem Family in Eurasian Perspective: Revisiting House Societies, Seventeenth–Twentieth Centuries* (Bern: Peter Lang, 2009); A. Fauve-Chamoux, 'Aging in a Never Empty Nest: The Elasticity of the Stem Familiy', in T. K. Hareven (ed.), *Aging and Generational Relations over the Life Course. A Historical and Cross-Cultural Perspective* (Berlin and New York: de Gruyter, 1996), pp. 75–99; M.-P. Arrizabalaga, 'The Stem Family in the French Basque Country: Sare in the Nineteenth Century', *Journal of Family History*, 22:1 (1997), pp. 50–69.

69. Other studies, though addressing different questions, also reveal similar results. In her comparison of household configurations between the end of the eighteenth and the middle of the nineteenth century, Antoinette Fauve-Chamoux observes that in the French Pyrenees the father's lifelong position of power was standard in the eighteenth century, whereas in the mid nineteenth century it became the dominant model for him to retreat from his position at a certain age; Fauve-Chamoux, 'Aging', p. 83. See also A. Collomp, 'From Stem Family to Nuclear Family: Changes in the Coresident Domestic Group in Haute Provence between the End of the Eighteenth and the Middle of the Nineteenth Centuries', *Continuity and Change*, 3:1 (1988), pp. 65–81.

70. C. H. Johnson, 'Das "Geschwister Archipel": Bruder-Schwester-Liebe und Klassenformation im Frankreich des 19. Jahrhunderts', *L'Homme. Z.F.G.*, 13:1 (2002), pp. 50–67, on pp. 50–51. He also refers to a 'family revolution'.

INDEX